touring

FLORIDA

Produced by AA Publishing

Written by Paul Murphy

Revised second edition published in this format 1998
First published 1992

Edited, designed and produced by AA Publishing.

Distributed in the United Kingdom by AA Publishing, Norfolk House, Priestley Road, Basingstoke, Hampshire, RG24 9NY.

A CIP catalogue record for this book is available from the British Library.

ISBN 0 7495 1655 0

The contents of this publication are believed correct at the time of printing. Nevertheless, the pub-lishers cannot accept responsibility for errors or omissions or for changes in details given in this guide or for the consequences of any reliance on the information provided by the same. Assessments of attractions and so forth are based upon the author's own experience and, therefore, descriptions given in this guide necessarily contain an element of subjective opinion which may not reflect the publisher's opinion or dictate a reader's own experience on another occasion. We have tried to ensure accuracy in this guide, but things do change and we would be grateful if readers would advise us of any inaccuracies they may encounter.

Published by AA Publishing, (a trading name of Automobile Association Developments Limited, whose registered office is Norfolk House, Priestley Road, Basingstoke, Hampshire, RG24 9NY. Registered number 1878835).

Colour separation: Daylight Colour Art, Singapore

Printed and bound by G. Canale & C. S.P.A., Torino, Italy

Front cover: *silhouette on the pier*
Inset: *art deco, Miami Beach*

Right: *lapping up the Sunshine State*

CONTENTS

ABOUT THIS BOOK

This book is not only a practical touring guide for the independent traveler, but is also invaluable for those who would like to know more about Florida.

It is divided into 7 regions, each with its own city and driving tours. The driving tours start and finish in those cities which we consider to be the most interesting centers for exploration.

There are special features on the Everglades, Walt Disney World™ and Kennedy Space Center.

Each tour has details of the most interesting places to visit en route. Boxes catering for special interests follow some of the main entries – for those whose interest is in history, or walking, or those who have children. There are also boxes which highlight scenic stretches of road and give details of special events, crafts and customs.

The simple route directions are accompanied by an easy-to-use map at the beginning of each tour along with a chart showing how far it is from one town to the next in miles and kilometers. This can help you to decide where to take a break and stop overnight. (All distances quoted are approximate.)

Before setting off it is advisable to check with the information center listed at the start of the tour for recommendations on where to break your journey and for additional information on what to see and do, and when best to visit.

For information on aspects of driving in Florida see page 162.

INFORMATION FOR NON-U.S. RESIDENTS

Consulates

There are two British consulates in Florida: Miami, Suite 2110, Brickell Bay Office Tower, 1001 S Bayshore Drive, tel: (305) 374–1522, or (404) 524–5856; Orlando, Suite 2110 Sunbank Tower, 200 S Orange Avenue, tel: (407) 426–7855.

Credit Cards

You can use credit cards almost anywhere. All the major credit cards are widely used and accepted throughout Florida.

Currency

The American monetary unit is the dollar ($) which is divided into 100 cents (¢). Coins are issued in cent denominations of 1 (penny), 5 (nickel), 10 (dime) and 25 (quarter). Notes (bills) are issued in denominations of one, five, 10, 20, 50 and 100 dollars. All bills, whatever their value, are exactly the same size and color. The value of the bill is clearly shown in all corners and each has its own US statesman pictured in the center. Not all banks offer money-changing facilities. Currency may be changed at some banks, bureaux de changes, airports and larger hotels, but it is best to take US dollar travelers' checks. Hotels, restaurants and shops in Florida will accept them as cash and give change where necessary.

Customs Regulations

Non–US residents aged 21 or over may bring in up to one liter of alcoholic beverages, 200 cigarettes (50 cigars or 4.4lb (2kg) of tobacco) plus up to $100 worth of gifts in addition to the tobacco allowance. There is no limit to the amount of currency (US or foreign) brought into America, but arriving and departing passengers must report to US customs all money in excess of $10,000. Not allowed: fresh meat, fruit, drugs (other than prescribed), and plants.

Electricity

The standard electricity supply in the US is 110–120 volts (60 cycles). You may have to bring an adaptor to convert. Sockets take plugs with two flat pins.

Emergency Telephone Numbers

Dial 911 (free call).

Entry Regulations

Visas are required by all visitors to the US, except for Canadian citizens, or nationals of Britain, France, Germany, Italy, Switzerland, the Netherlands, Sweden or Japan visiting the US for business or tourist purposes, for a stay not exceeding 90 days, and provided that a return, or onward, ticket is held. In these instances a passport only is required. It is best to check the requirements for specific holiday

plans before departure. The type and validity of US visas vary considerably, so seek advice from the nearest US Embassy or Consulate. American immigration officials are strict in these matters and passengers whose travel documents are not in order will not be accepted in the US under any circumstances.

Health Matters

It cannot be emphasized enough that arranging medical insurance before traveling is essential. Medical facilities are generally of an extremely high standard, but costs in the US are exorbitant so it is well worth taking out insurance cover beforehand. Insurance cover for an unlimited amount of medical costs is recommended. Treatment (unless for an emergency) will be refused without evidence of insurance or a deposit. If you need a doctor during your stay, ask at your hotel or look in the Yellow Pages under 'Physician'. No inoculations are required for a visit to Florida, but it is a rabies risk area. Tap water is generally safe to drink.

Post Offices

Post office hours vary both in central city branches and in small towns, so it is best to check. Stamps, however, may be purchased in hotels, motels, drugstores and transport terminals, usually by inserting correct change into a machine, though these do charge a 25 percent premium.

Telephones

Either a phonecard or exact change in 5, 10 or 25 cent coins is needed to place a call (minimum of 25 cents). For direct dialing international calls dial 011, plus country code, plus city code, plus telephone number. Country codes for international calls:

Australia 61
Canada 1
New Zealand 64
UK 44

Time

Most of Florida is on Eastern Standard Time (EST); for most of the year 5 hours behind Britain, 6 hours behind the rest of Western Europe and 15 hours behind Australia (Sydney). Part of the northwest, including Pensacola and Fort Walton Beach, is on Central Time, an hour behind the rest of Florida.

Tourist Offices

For information in the US on the whole of the state of Florida contact: the Office of Visitor Inquiry, Florida Division of Tourism, 126 West Van Buren Street, Tallahassee, FL 32399–2000. Tel: (904) 487–1462.The Florida Division of Tourism operates its visitor centers in major towns and resorts and at various roadside locations. For more specific information, there are also several local Chamber of Commerce offices.

THE SOUTHEAST

For adult visitors at least, the southeast corner of Florida, stretching from Miami Beach to Key West, is the most exciting part of the whole state. The place-names alone conjure up expectant magic, and even if the myth sometimes doesn't match the reality (neither the Everglades nor the streets of Miami are as wild as you might have thought), few vacationers leave disappointed. The contrasts are as vivid as the subtropical colors. Immigrants flock here from both hemispheres – senior citizens fleeing south from the cold northern states, refugees fleeing north from political turmoil in Cuba, Haiti and Nicaragua. Modern building developments, fueled by the tourist dollar, push ahead apace and, just a few miles separate sophisticated metropolitan suburbs from backwoods airboat shanties, glass-and-concrete canyons from deserted tropical islands, the Wall Street of the South from conch shell-blowing competitions. Southeast Florida works hard but also relaxes with some panache and all the vitality that its rich multiethnic mix has brought with it.

The man who put Miami and the Florida Keys on the map was Henry Morrison Flagler, railroad magnate and co-founder of the Standard Oil Company. In the 1890s he drove his railroad to the remote outposts of the mosquito-bitten south, inspired, so legend has it, by frost–free orange blossom sent to him from Miami. Flagler, envisaging trade with neighboring Cuba and the Caribbean, pushed on ever southwards, and the 'railroad that went to sea' finally made it to Key West in 1912.

The devastating hurricane of 1935 sent the railroad and over 400 unfortunate souls with it to a watery grave, but by then the die was cast. 'Flagler's Folly' was never reconstructed, but at least it provided a valuable base for the Overseas Highway that now links the Florida Keys.

Other tycoons followed Flagler, and rapid uncontrolled land development led to cycles of boom and bust that still occur today. Nevertheless, by the 1920s the sunniest part of the Sunshine State had become America's biggest vacation playground. Since then it has suffered the vagaries of economic depression, shifting fashions and all manner of other problems, including crime epidemics. In true Florida style, however, the wheel has come full circle, and once again the southeast is undoubtedly the place to be.

Getting that Caribbean feeling in the Florida Keys

Tour 1
The vibrant business and cultural hub of the region, the city has now largely shaken off the seamier side of its *Miami Vice* image while retaining its style and glamor. The monorail Metromover train makes skyscraper spotting easy and enjoyable, while Bayside Marketplace is a must for eating, drinking and shopping.

Tour 2
Art Deco hotels, washed in pastel shades, facing a golden beach, are the quintessential image of Miami Beach. At one time considered quite tasteless and so neglected as to become downright seedy during the 1970s, the Beach and its buildings have been extensively transformed over the last decade into one of the world's trendiest spots.

Tour 3
The tour of the southern suburbs emphasizes how multicultural and cosmopolitan Miami has become: Spanish architecture at Coral Gables, European sidewalk cafés and Bahamian lifestyles at Coconut Grove, Cuba transplanted at Calle Ocho. There is also a wealth of first-class tourist attractions for all tastes, including historic houses, wildlife parks, botanical gardens and beaches.

Tour 4
The northern suburbs will show you something of everyday Miami, including colorful ethnic neighborhoods, exclusive beach communities and tourist attractions unique to the state.

Tour 5
You can 'do' the Everglades in a day from Miami along the Tamiami Trail, but if you want to see more than a few alligators and an airboat, take the longer tour to Flamingo, stop off at the boardwalks en route and stay overnight. If you have any affinity for nature, you will find it well worthwhile.

Top: Hobie Cats at Key West
Above: delightful house in Key West's Eaton Street

Tour 6
The Keys tour is a must for water enthusiasts, but even at underwater havens such as the excellent John Pennekamp State Park, you don't need gills to enjoy the only living coral reef in the US. At the end of the line is Key West.

Tour 7
Key West is more Caribbean than North American. Its culture and atmosphere are very laid back and very bohemian. Nevertheless, there is plenty to see and do here, and just taking in the street architecture is a delight. The tour comes to a fitting climax at Mallory Square, watching street performers pay homage to the golden sunset.

Downtown Miami

The high-rise canyons of downtown Miami may be just a mere bridge away from South Beach, but they are a world removed from the tropical oceanfront culture. The easiest way to look around the city is aboard the Metromover, a fully automated shuttle train than runs on an elevated loop through the heart of the business district. Then relax and shop at Bayside Marketplace.

1 DAY

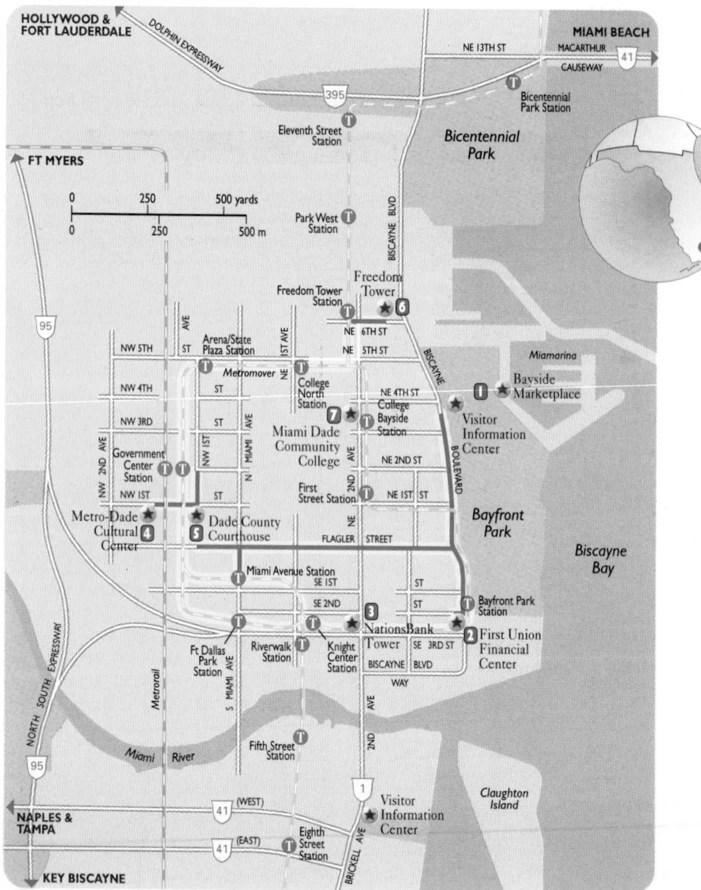

Visitor Center, Bayside Marketplace

Start the tour at Bayside Marketplace.

1 Bayside Marketplace

This ebullient waterfront complex of 150 shops, several restaurants (including a Hard Rock Café) and general entertainment, is downtown's favorite focal point. Whether you enjoy shopping or not, this is an ideal introduction to the colorful and vibrant multi-ethnic Miami scene. There is an excellent choice of eating places to suit all tastes and pockets, the shops offer a wide selection of high-quality arts, crafts and fashion clothing at reasonable prices, and the atmosphere is never less than lively thanks to the ever-present street entertainers and free nightly concerts. There is a whole fleet of modern yachts to see at the adjacent Miamarina, with over 200 berths, and you can cruise the bay and coast in any number of vessels. Both the *Paddlewheel Queen* and the *Island Queen* provide 90-minute excursions spotting the homes of the rich and famous, and other sights around the bay. Fully rigged tallships are also sometimes at berth here. At the adjacent Bayfront Park there is a waterfront amphitheater and a 100-foot (33m) laser tower that literally sheds a whole new light on downtown.

> **FOR CHILDREN**
>
> Although this tour is mostly spent appreciating art or architecture, children will enjoy the ride on the Metromover. Make a prolonged stay at Bayside Marketplace watching the clowns and street performers, then spend time at the hands-on exhibits in the Historical Museum of Southern Florida.

Cross the street and walk a few hundred yards left down Biscayne Boulevard.

2 First Union Financial Center

At 55 stories this is the tallest building in Florida. Walk below through its 1-acre (0.4-hectare) plaza and gaze up at the mini plantation of royal palms, which tower up toward a crisscrossed 'space canopy' of glass and steel.

Walk back towards Bayside and board the Metromover at Bayfront Park station. Alight at Knight Center station (or simply view from the Metromover).

Bayside Marketplace is the best excuse to stir from Miami Beach

3 NationsBank Tower
Another monument to Miami's financial status, the NationsBank Tower is smaller than the First Union Financial Center at 47 stories, but has a higher cultural rating as it boasts the J L Knight Concert Hall. Look for this landmark at night when it is brilliantly illuminated. Often red, white and blue, it changes seasonally (red and green at Christmas, purple and pink at Easter) – and when the tower turns orange, you know that the Miami Dolphins football team is at home.

▶ *At Knight Center Station take the Metromover and travel clockwise, getting off at Government Center Station. Walk south on NW 1st Avenue, and turn left onto NW 1st Street.*

4 Metro-Dade Cultural Center
An architectural mix of Modernism and Spanish Revivalism, this block holds the Miami Art Museum of Dade County, and the Historical Museum of Southern Florida. The former features touring exhibitions, plus a sculpture court. The latter is more accessible for all the family and takes an entertaining look at the settlement of Florida by means of large-scale re-creations (walk through a Spanish fort), restored exhibits (board a Miami trolley car), plus tableaux, audio-visuals and hands-on displays. If you would like to learn about southern Florida and the museum exhibits in greater depth, phone ahead to join the Museum Tour tel: (305) 375–1492. The outdoor plaza here is a good place for a cup of coffee, with a 360-degree view of some of Miami's tallest structures.

5 Dade County Courthouse
Located directly opposite the Metro-Dade Cultural Center, this Miami landmark, with its distinctive ziggurat roof, was the tallest building south of Washington DC when completed in 1928. It remained the tallest building in Miami until the 1970s. As dusk falls and its colony of roosting turkey vultures soars around its pyramidal peak, it takes on a rather sinister appearance. The public can sit in on court sessions.

Reach for the Sky – the 47-story NationsBank Tower

FOR HISTORY BUFFS

Some 10.000 years are compressed into the archives and artifacts of the Historical Museum of Southern Florida housed in the Metro-Dade Cultural Center.

▶ *Return to the Metromover. Travel clockwise and get off at Freedom Tower station (take the train heading for School Board station).*

6 Freedom Tower
This Spanish-Mediterranean-style tower was built in 1925 for the *Miami Daily News* as a replica of the Giralda Tower in Seville. It acquired its present name in 1962, when it was used as an emergency refugee-processing center during the period of flight from Castro's Cuba. (Not open to the public.)

▶ *Return to the Metromover. Travel south and get off at College Bayside station.*

7 Miami Dade Community College
There are two small avant–garde galleries here. Center Gallery (suite 1365) showcases experimental works and traveling exhibitions, while the Frances Wolfson Art Gallery (5th floor) displays works by students and Florida artists in a variety of media.

▶ *Either take the Metromover and travel clockwise to return to Bayfront Park station, or walk due east to Biscayne Boulevard.*

Miami Beach

2 DAYS

The Miami Beach area first became fashionable in the 1920s when its beachside core was built in stunning art deco style. Since then its fortunes have waxed and waned and it was not until quite recently that it was restored and acquired its present gleaming look. Today it is again one of the world's great resorts.

City at sea; a cruise ship at the Port of Miami

i Art Deco Welcome Center, 1001 Ocean Drive; Miami Beach Visitor Information Center, 1920 Meridian Avenue

RECOMMENDED WALKS

Join a guide from the Miami Design Preservation League at the Welcome Center at 10.30 on Saturday mornings and 6.30 Thursday evenings for a 90-minute walking tour of the Art Deco square mile. You will learn who built what, when, why, how much the buildings originally cost (and what they are worth today) and a whole host of trivia, including the hotels where you could have glimpsed many famous names. For a more relaxed stroll in an area devoid of buildings, head for the boardwalk, which stretches for 2 miles (3km) between 21st and 46th streets.

▶ *From downtown Miami cross the MacArthur Causeway (US 41). Turn right onto Alton Road.*

1 South Pointe Park

This is the start of South Miami Beach ('SoBe') – 3 miles (5km) of fine golden sands popular with stunt-kite flyers, swimmers, surfers and windsurfers. The southernmost tip is a favorite spot for fishing and also for watching the big boats entering and leaving the Port of Miami, the world's largest cruise ship port.

▶ *As you leave the park, turn right on Biscayne Street.*

2 Joe's Stone Crab Restaurant

The most famous restaurant in Miami, and possibly the state, Joe's is a fourth-generation family business, opened in 1913. The meal that has passed into Florida folklore here is stone crabs with mustard sauce, garlic spinach and hash browns. Always busy and often hectic. Reservations are not accepted, so arrive early to avoid a lengthy wait. The restaurant is closed from mid-May to mid-October, when stone crabs are out of season.

▶ *Take Ocean Drive to 6th Street.*

3 Art Deco District

The famous square mile runs from 6th to 23rd Street north–south and from Ocean Drive to Lenox Avenue east–west. Ocean Drive contains many of the best examples of Art Deco styling and, with the revival of the area, has established itself as one of Miami's trendiest strips. Everyone has his or her own favorite buildings, but look out for the classic lines of the Cardozo, the Park Central and the Cleveland hotels, and step into a lobby or two to admire the period fixtures and furnishings. To see most of the rest of the area, turn left onto Collins Avenue at 13th and head south back to 5th Street, then turn right onto Washington Avenue and head north again. The Spanish-themed, gas-lit Espanola Way (a favorite *Miami Vice* backdrop) and the lavishly refurbished ultra-trendy Lincoln Road Shopping District, both just off Washington, are also well worth exploring.

SPECIAL TO...

Visit the Art Deco district in mid-January during the Art Deco Weekend, a three-day festival during which the whole area goes into a pastel-tinged 1930s time warp. Vendors sell period clothing and antiques at a street fair, while vintage automobiles cruise the streets.

► *Continue north of Washington Avenue.*

4 Miami Beach Convention Center

This huge art deco-faced building is home to several major annual events. Next door to the center, on Convention Center Drive, is Miami Beach City Hall, built in 1927 and referred to as the doyen of Art Deco architecture. Adjacent on Washington Avenue is the Jackie Gleason Theater of the Performing Arts, which produces the best of Broadway and classical concerts.

BACK TO NATURE

Escape the hustle and bustle of the beach at the Miami Beach Garden and Conservatory, which adjoins the Convention Center. Here, exotic native earth and air plants flourish under a dome 32 feet (10m) high.

Miami Beach, where medieval art (above) – from the Bass Museum – meets arts deco (right)

► *Turn right onto Park Avenue.*

5 Bass Museum of Art

This cultural centerpiece of Miami Beach is housed in a handsome gray coral-rock, Art Deco-style building. Its splendid collection ranges from modern American masters, such as Roy Lichtenstein, back six centuries through ecclesiastic art, huge Flemish tapestries and a large body of works by European masters such as Rubens, Rembrandt and Toulouse-Lautrec. Changing exhibitions augment the permanent collection.

► *Turn right onto 22nd Street and left onto Collins Avenue.*

6 Fontainebleau Hilton Resort

Just before arriving at this Miami Beach landmark, you will see looming directly ahead a huge archway, beyond which is a great white sweeping building (the back of the Fontainebleau) set on a tropical lagoon. Don't be tempted to take a short cut, as the archway is a massive *trompe l'oeil.* This giant resort (known locally as 'the Big Blue') boasts over 1,200 rooms, a health spa, several restaurants, lounges and any number of sporting facilities. As with all American hotels, the general public is always welcome, so at the very least explore the lounges and lobbies which you will find either artful or kitschy depending on your taste. For an evening of lavish Las Vegas-style entertainment, try Club Tropigala, graced once by stars such as Frank Sinatra.

▶ *Head back down Collins Avenue and turn right onto Arthur Godfrey Road, which leads via the Julia Tuttle Causeway back to the mainland.*

FOR HISTORY BUFFS

While Florida's crops were wiped out in the winter of 1895, Miami's mild climate kept its produce frost-free. Legend has it that a sprig of Miami orange blossom sent to Henry Flagler convinced him to build his railroad this way.

TOUR
3

Greater Miami
South

South Miami contains Florida's premier zoo, the state's most stately home and more. Warm up on the beaches of Key Biscayne, explore the exclusive 'villages' of Coral Gables and earthy Little Havana, then chill out at trendy Coconut Grove, the quintessential Miami melting pot of chic European and laid-back Bahamian cultures.

1 DAY • 62 MILES • 100KM

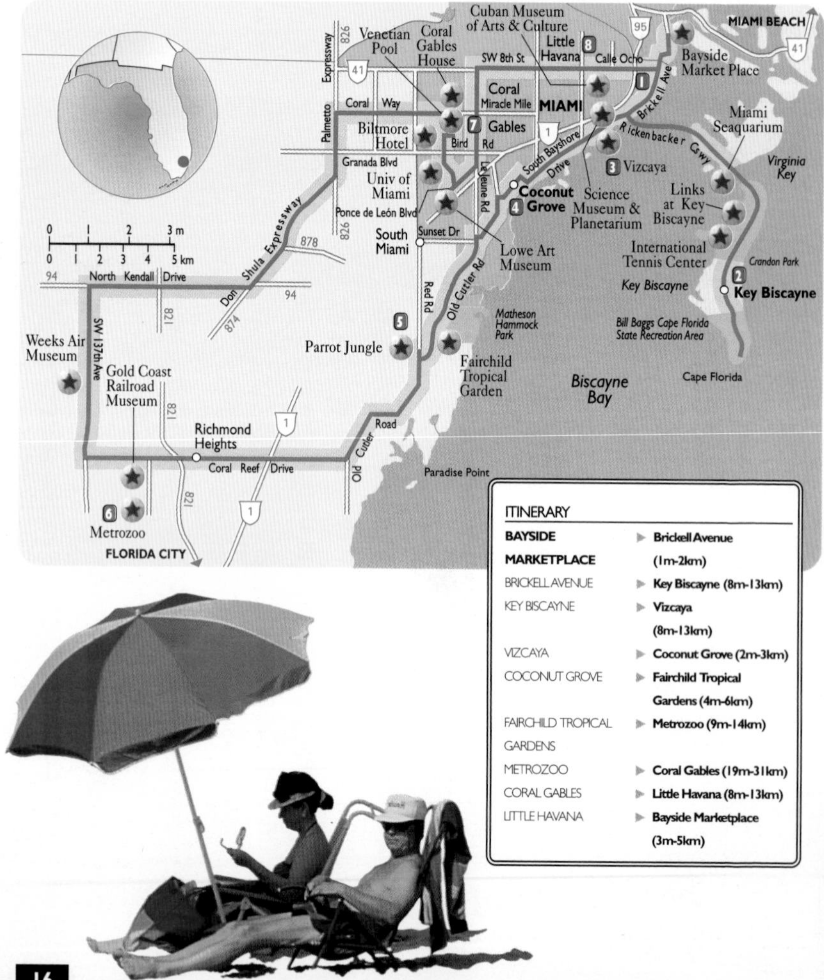

ITINERARY

BAYSIDE MARKETPLACE	▶ **Brickell Avenue (1m-2km)**
BRICKELL AVENUE	▶ **Key Biscayne (8m-13km)**
KEY BISCAYNE	▶ **Vizcaya (8m-13km)**
VIZCAYA	▶ **Coconut Grove (2m-3km)**
COCONUT GROVE	▶ **Fairchild Tropical Gardens (4m-6km)**
FAIRCHILD TROPICAL GARDENS	▶ **Metrozoo (9m-14km)**
METROZOO	▶ **Coral Gables (19m-31km)**
CORAL GABLES	▶ **Little Havana (8m-13km)**
LITTLE HAVANA	▶ **Bayside Marketplace (3m-5km)**

i m*Visitor Center, Bayside Marketplace*

▶ M*Starting at Bayside Marketplace take Brickell Avenue south.*

1 EBrickell Avenue

As you cross the Miami River, take a look below at the flotilla of business and pleasure craft that sails this busy waterway. Then look skywards to admire the mighty banking structures along Brickell. The soaring 33-story Barnett Tower is a domestic flagship, while the striking Banco de Venezuela, in stunning jet black, is a reminder of Miami's importance as a Latin American banking center. Serious business soon gives way to colorful residential condominiums; the two real eye-openers are the Villa Regina, where every balcony is painted a different pastel shade of the rainbow, and the fabulous 20-story Atlantis. The latter is unmistakable with its brilliant mirror surface, its completely rounded ends, and a massive red triangle on the roof: its trademark (familiar to millions of *Miami Vice* fans as the backdrop on the opening credits) is the 'hole-in-the-wall' between its 12th and 16th stories. Inside the hole stands a palm tree and a red circular staircase.

FOR HISTORY BUFFS

Key Biscayne was named by Ponce de León in 1513 on his first expedition to Florida. His sailors, unaware of the nearby sandbar and submerged reefs, would have much appreciated the Cape Florida Lighthouse erected in 1825. Hundreds of vessels have come to grief at this point. Tragedy of a different kind befell the lighthouse in 1836, when an attack by Seminole Indians left the lighthouse keeper's assistant dead. The lighthouse is the oldest surviving structure to be built in Greater Miami.

▶ M*Turn left onto the Rickenbacker Causeway for 8 miles (13km) to Key Biscayne.*

(3E)

2 EKey Biscayne

The peaceful pine groves and semitropical beaches on this beautiful island, so close to downtown, make a perfect retreat from the more fashionable sands, and bodies, of Miami Beach. Choose from either the rugged 2-mile (3km) sandy beach of Virginia Key, the 800 acres (325 hectares) of wooded parkland and 3 miles (5km) of beach at Crandon Park or the mile-long (1.5km) beach at Bill Baggs Cape Florida State Recreation Area. Key Biscayne is also a great spot for water thrills. The world's fastest boats compete here in the annual Offshore Grand Prix of Miami in early September. For everyday *Miami Vice*-style speedboat-spotting, try Sundays on the Bay at Crandon Boulevard, particularly around brunchtime. Miami Seaquarium is the largest and best of south Florida's marine parks, and features Lolita, the 10,000-pound (4,535kg) killer whale. A huge tropical aquarium, sea-lion and dolphin shows, manatees and turtles plus shark-feeding provide educational entertainment for the whole family. A little further on, the Links at Key Biscayne golf course is one of the country's finest public courses. Close by is the Tennis Center at Crandon Park, where

Climb the 95 feet (29m) to the top of Cape Florida Lighthouse

many international tournaments are staged, including the prestigious ladies' Lipton Championship (courts open to the public). Drive to the tip of the key to the Bill Baggs Cape Florida State Recreation Area, where you can climb inside historical Cape Florida Lighthouse and enjoy a picnic or a barbecue (grills provided) on Key Biscayne's prettiest beach.

BACK TO NATURE

On Key Biscayne, visit Bill Baggs Park and Bill Baggs Cape Florida State Recreation Area at the southern tip of the island. Look for brown pelicans, laughing gulls, terns, egrets and waders. During migration times – March to May and September to November – look out for migrant birds.

Return across the Rickenbacker Causeway and turn left onto South Miami Avenue/South Bayshore Drive for Vizcaya, 8 miles (13km).

SCENIC ROUTES

The views from the Rickenbacker Causeway as you drive back to the mainland are spectacular. The Miami skyline is framed to the right by jet skiers and to the left by windsurfers and anglers. Make the journey by night for an unforgettable view of the city and look out for the 'Miami Line', a 3,600-foot (1,100m) strip of colored lighting strung along the Metrorail bridge next to the NationsBank Tower. Once you get back to the mainland, head north on the elevated section of I–95 for even better views.

3 Vizcaya

Built in 1916 as a winter home for millionaire industrialist James Deering, this magnificent Italianate villa is one of the finest private houses in the US. Its name is Basque, meaning 'elevated ground'. A 50-minute guided tour of the downstairs area will show you opulent European furnishings and decorative arts dating back to the 16th century. You are then free to explore the rest of the villa's 34 public rooms at will. A bed that once belonged to Admiral Nelson's mistress, Lady Hamilton, a complete ceiling from a Venetian ducal palace, and tapestries which were once owned by the English poet Robert Browning are just a few of the eclectic treasures gathered from all over Europe. The splendid gardens, which open out onto the bay, comprise both formal areas and a natural subtropical jungle. President

Reagan and Pope John Paul II met in the house and gardens in 1987. Opposite Vizcaya is the Miami Science Museum and Planetarium.

▶ *Continue along South Bayshore Drive for 2 miles (3km).*

FOR CHILDREN

When the palatial splendor of Vizcaya starts to overwhelm the children, just cross the road to the Museum of Science and Planetarium. This educational discovery center is great fun for both children and adults and features over 140 hands-on exhibits plus a wildlife center. The planetarium stages astronomy and laser shows, and stargazers can visit its observatory free of charge on weekend evenings.

Left: old world-style at Vizcaya
Above: new world-style at Coconut Grove

4 Coconut Grove

Dinner Key Marina heralds the start of 'the Grove' and was the former home of Pan Am's romantic flying boats. Boats and romance still set the tone with fine restaurants and any number of companies renting out sailboats at what is now Greater Miami's largest marina. The lovely leafy suburb of Coconut Grove is the oldest part of Miami, and there are many reminders of its 19th-century origins. Start your tour on Main Highway at the Barnacle, built in 1886 and named after the shape of its steep, hipped roof. This was the home of Commodore Ralph Munroe, founder of the Grove, and is open to the public. The Spanish Colonial-style Plymouth Congregational Church on Devon Road is one of the most picturesque in Florida. The building's stones were all cut and set by hand in 1916. The fine door, over 300 years old, comes from a monastery in the Pyrenees. Near by, in a lovely garden setting, is a one-room wooden schoolhouse dating from 1895.

The center of Coconut Grove is buzzing, alive with street entertainers, European-style sidewalk restaurants and cafés, street markets, corner grocery shops, theaters (most notably the excellent Playhouse), and ultra-fashionable night spots. To see and be seen visit CocoWalk. For more serious shopping pay a visit to the streets of Mayfair Mall with its fine sculptures, gleaming exotic tiles and cascading fountains. In a city famous for its festivals, the Grove is a flag bearer. The big one is the three-day Arts Festival in February, which attracts over a million people. The other major festivals are the Bahamian-influenced King Mango Strut (late December) and the Goombay Festival (June). The best way to discover Coconut Grove is on foot or by bicycle. A novel way of seeing it by two wheels is to hire a rickshaw and let a strapping young college type provide the power. If you wish to learn about its history, however, join the free two-hour walking tour, conducted by The Villagers, on the last Saturday of each month.

i *Miami Visitor Center at CocoWalk, 3015 Grand Avenue*

▶ *Continue through Coconut Grove and pick up Old Cutler Road.*

5 Fairchild Tropical Garden, Parrot Jungle

Subtropical Matheson Hammock Park is 100 acres (40 hectares) of wilderness and mangrove swamp with a delightful man-made beach where the tide washes a salt-water atoll-style pool through gates. At its southern edge is the Fairchild Tropical Garden, the largest tropical botanical garden in the US. The collection of palms here is one of the finest in the world. Other features include a rare-plant house, a tropical rain forest, sunken gardens and a hibiscus garden. A guided tram tour gives an overview of the garden's 83 acres (34 hectares).

Continue a little way and turn right on Red Road (SW 57th Avenue) to Parrot Jungle. Established in 1936, this is one of Miami's oldest and best-loved attractions, and even if the bird shows are now looking decidedly dated, you can't help but be impressed by the free-flying birds in this magnificent subtropical jungle. Flamingos, giant banyan trees and delicate orchids complete the visit. Note: Parrot Jungle is due to move to Watson Island (between downtown Miami and Miami Beach) late 1998.

The wild side of Miami – an endangered white Bengal tiger finds a safe haven at Metrozoo

▶ *Turn around and head south back down Old Cutler Road and turn right onto Coral Reef Drive (SW 152nd Street) to the Metrozoo (13 miles (21km).*

6 Metrozoo

Hailed as the finest zoo in Florida, Metrozoo provides its residents with a 'near-natural', largely cage-free environment, where the only thing separating the public from most of the animals is a few feet of space. The star attractions of the zoo are its splendid rare white Bengal tigers, its lovable koalas (the only ones on permament display in the US outside California), 'Paws', a children's petting zoo and Asian River Life, featuring Komodo dragons. Take the overhead monorail to get a bird's-eye view and give your feet a rest. With over 900 animals and a variety of entertaining shows, the zoo makes a great family day out. The Gold Coast Railroad Museum (which shares the same site) is more likely to appeal to rail buffs and is a shambling but atmospheric collection of old steam locos recalling the early pioneering days. At the weekend trains are steamed for rides.

Turn left as you leave the site and right (north) onto SW 137th Avenue. Weeks Air Museum at the Tamiami Airport is dedicated to some 30 to 35 aircraft, most dating from the days of World War II.

▶ *Continue north on SW 137th Avenue, turn right at North Kendall Drive (SW 88th Street), cross Florida's Turnpike and turn left (north) onto* ***SR 874*** *(Don Shula Expressway) until it joins* ***SR 826*** *(Palmetto Expressway). Head north and turn off right at Coral Way (SW 22nd Street), 19 miles (31km).*

7 Coral Gables

Coral Gables is the most exclusive of Miami's many suburbs and, over 70 years after its creation by George Merrick, it still retains its old-world Spanish-Mediterranean ambience. Merrick's house, Coral Gables House on Coral Way, is open to the public.

Turn right immediately opposite the house, down Toledo Boulevard, to see the most beautiful public swimming pool in Florida. The Venetian Pool was carved from coral rock in 1924 and boasts rock caves, stone bridges and a small sandy beach, all in a setting worthy of a doge. Turn

The Venetian Pool at Coral Gables, possibly the country's most elegant 'swimming hole'

right onto Anastasia Avenue. Ahead of you is the architectural *tour de force* of the Gables, the magnificent Biltmore Hotel. Just like the downtown Miami Freedom Tower, its central 26-story tower is a 1925 copy of the Giralda in Seville. Turn left before you reach the hotel down Granada Boulevard. You are now heading through the campus of the University of Miami.

Turn right at Ponce de León Boulevard, and the excellent Lowe Art Museum is on the right, featuring pre-Columbian and Native American art, plus exhibits from Asia, Africa and Europe. Make your way back to Ponce de León Boulevard, follow it around to the left, crossing Bird Road and the Miracle Mile, until you reach SW 8th Street. Just before this street you will see the 40-foot (12m) archway known as the Douglas Entrance, erected in 1924 as the main gateway to Coral Gables.

▶ *Continue along SW 8th Street.*

8 Little Havana

The area which centers around SW 8th Street (or, in the vernacular, Calle Ocho) is Miami's Latin Quarter. There is little in the way of organized tourist attractions here, but for most visitors the rich tableau of Calle Ocho street life is reward enough. Don't miss the colorful open-air markets with their exotic fruits and vegetables, Havana cigars at Havana prices, old men in their bright *guayaberas* (blousons), Cuban cafés, and above all, Cuban food – either at a *tablao* (restaurant-nightclub with tableside flamenco) or from a simple sidewalk counter. The classic dish is *arroz con pollo* – chicken cooked in wine and spices and served with yellow rice. Order it with plantains and black beans.

▶ *Follow SW 8th Street back to Brickell Avenue and turn left to Bayside Marketplace, 3 miles (5km).*

RECOMMENDED WALKS

Within the area bounded by Red Road, the Tamiami Trail (SW 8th Street) and Douglas Road are a number of highly desirable luxury 'villages' boasting distinctive national architectural styles, including French (provincial and city), Dutch South African and Chinese. Stop on the Miracle Mile to window-shop and also to admire Coral Gables City Hall, an elegant Spanish Renaissance-style building dating from 1927. There is a charming old Congregational church from the same period on Columbus Boulevard, and close by in the northwest corner of the Gables is a series of reflection pools. This walk covers quite a large area, so a less tiring alternative may be to go native by cycling (the nearest rentals are at Coconut Grove) or, if you want to look super-cool, try rollerblades.

Colorful mural in Little Havana

Greater Miami North

1 DAY • 78 MILES • 125KM

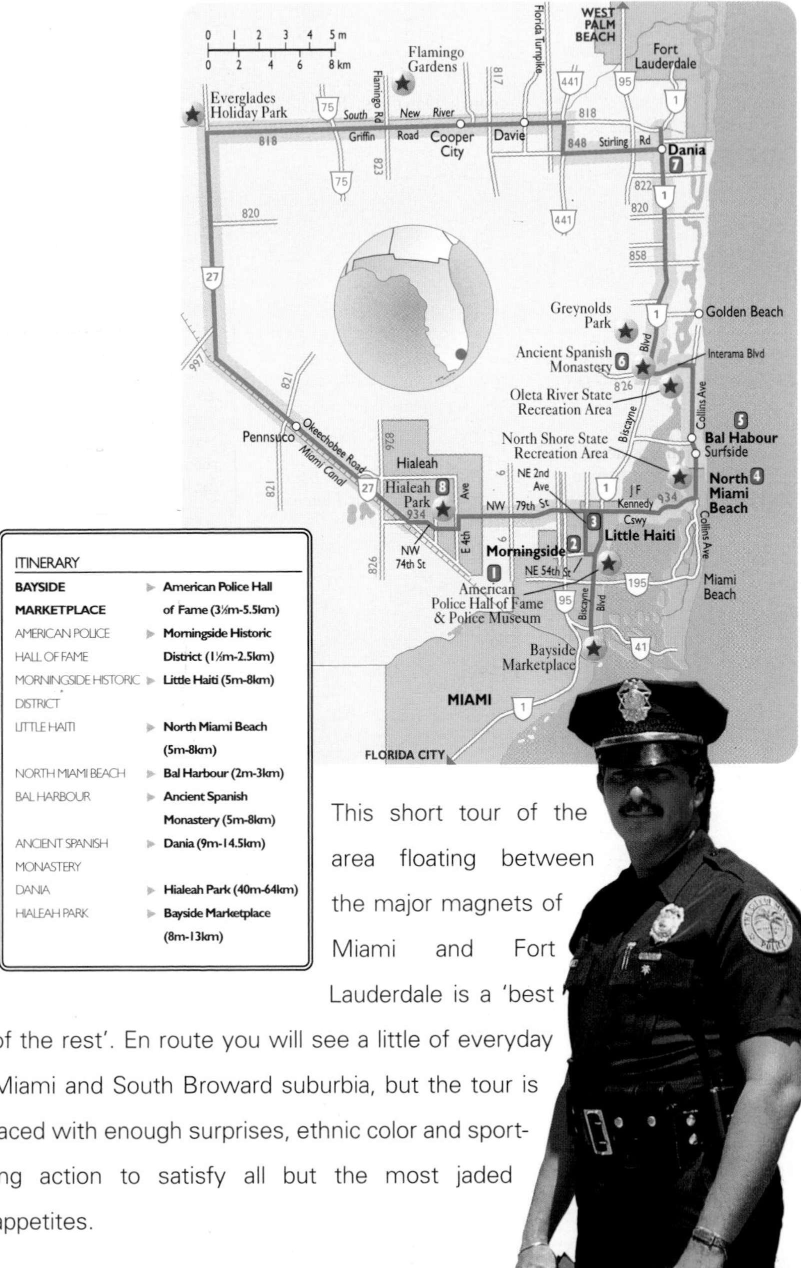

ITINERARY	
BAYSIDE MARKETPLACE	▶ **American Police Hall of Fame (3¼m-5.5km)**
AMERICAN POLICE HALL OF FAME	▶ **Morningside Historic District (1½m-2.5km)**
MORNINGSIDE HISTORIC DISTRICT	▶ **Little Haiti (5m-8km)**
LITTLE HAITI	▶ **North Miami Beach (5m-8km)**
NORTH MIAMI BEACH	▶ **Bal Harbour (2m-3km)**
BAL HARBOUR	▶ **Ancient Spanish Monastery (5m-8km)**
ANCIENT SPANISH MONASTERY	▶ **Dania (9m-14.5km)**
DANIA	▶ **Hialeah Park (40m-64km)**
HIALEAH PARK	▶ **Bayside Marketplace (8m-13km)**

This short tour of the area floating between the major magnets of Miami and Fort Lauderdale is a 'best of the rest'. En route you will see a little of everyday Miami and South Broward suburbia, but the tour is laced with enough surprises, ethnic color and sporting action to satisfy all but the most jaded appetites.

The colorful Caribbean Marketplace, based on the Iron Market in the Haitan capital, Port au Prince

[i] *Miami North – Visitor Information Center, Bayside Marketplace*

▶ *Start at Bayside Marketplace and head north on Biscayne Boulevard for 3½ miles (5.5km).*

1 American Police Hall of Fame and Police Museum

This unique and fascinating exhibit is a reminder of the seamier side of the city and the national crime problem. Over 10,000 artifacts are displayed, including a mock-up crime scene where you are challenged to 'solve the murder'. The massive marble memorial, which commemorates over 5,000 American police officers slain in the course of duty, is a sobering sight.

▶ *Continue north for 1 mile (1.5km). Turn left (west) onto NE 54th Street, then right (north) onto NE 2nd Avenue.*

2 Morningside Historic District

This collection of fine Art Deco and Mediterranean Revival homes was built as an early city suburb around 1925. It continues north for five blocks, and some of the larger estates can be seen on the bay front.

▶ *Continue north on NE 2nd Avenue for 1 mile (1.5km).*

3 Little Haiti

A 60,000-strong Haitian community clusters around NE 2nd Avenue. The best place to see their exotic fresh produce and colorful art and crafts (regarded as the best in the

Caribbean) is at the Caribbean Marketplace at the junction of NE 62nd Street. This ethnic enclave continues as far north as the suburb of El Portal, across the Little River (past NE 87th Street).

▶ *Turn right (east) onto NW 79th Street, which becomes the John F Kennedy Causeway. Turn left at the beach onto Collins Avenue, 5 miles (8km).*

4 North Miami Beach

These shores are much quieter, less stylish and much less sophisticated than those to the south, although the beach around 85th Street is popular with the high school crowd. After the soulless beachside condominiums, the 40-acre (16-hectare) North Shore State Recreation Area, which stretches from 79th to 87th Street, is a welcome oasis of lush tropical vegetation.

▶ *Continue north on Collins Avenue for 2 miles (3km).*

5 Bal Harbour

'A square mile of elegance' is how Bal Harbour likes to portray itself, and there is certainly no shortage of well-heeled style here. Costly condominiums and a lushly landscaped beach announce Bal Harbour, and the centerpiece is its striking shopping mall, where doyens of international style such as Gucci, Cartier, Chanel and Nina Ricci rub shoulders with top American fashion names including Neiman Marcus and the largest Saks Fifth Avenue in the state of Florida. The interior setting is a luxuriant tropical garden.

▶ *Continue on Collins Avenue, turn left onto Interama Boulevard (**SR 826**/NE 163rd Street), then right (north) onto **US 1**.*

RECOMMENDED WALKS

Lovely Oleta River State Recreation Area stands on the banks of the scenic Oleta River and the Intracoastal Waterway, just off Interama Boulevard (NE 163rd Street). Just a short distance away from the monotonous condominums and tawdry motels of the northern shores, you can walk, cycle a 1½-mile (2.5km) bike trail or take a canoe to explore the mangrove forest and surrounding aquatic areas. You will see a good variety of birdlife and small animals and the park is frequently visited by porpoises and the endangered Florida manatee. You can also do some saltwater fishing or relax on the sandy beach.

Another lazy day on the state's most famous beach

6 Ancient Spanish Monastery

The Ancient Monastery of St Bernard was originally built in Segovia, Spain, in 1141 and is now said to be the oldest reconstructed building in the western hemisphere. This beautiful structure was shipped piecemeal to America by the legendary millionaire William Randolph Hearst in 1925, destined for his San Simeon estate in California. After over 20 years in storage, however, it was sold and reassembled here and is now a fitting home to a fine museum of medieval art treasures.

In the pink at Hialeah Park

► *Continue north on **US 1** (West Dixie Highway) for 9 miles (14.5km).*

7 Dania

Entering Dania, you will start to see many of its antique shops along US 1. This is part of a four–block area of around 150 shops and stalls which sell (and buy) almost anything which is old and has value – furniture, lighting, silverware, china, glass, jewelry, and so on. It is also known for its *jai-alai* (pronounced high-a-lie) *fronton* (stadium) on Dania Beach Boulevard. This is the world's fastest-moving ball game, played by two (or four) players on a squash-style court. Using a basket-like glove strapped to the wrist, they catch and hurl a ball at speeds up to 188mph (303km/h). Although the game itself is an exciting spectacle, betting is a priority for most spectators.

► *Head west on Stirling Road, then north on **US 441**, and turn west through South Broward along Griffin Road (**SR 818**) to see Flamingo Gardens and the Everglades Holiday Park, then return south to Miami on **US 27**. Turn off left (east) onto **US 934** (NW 74th Street) and head east for 2 miles (3km). Turn left (north) onto East 4th Avenue*

SPECIAL TO...

The Friday night Five Star Rodeo at Davie draws professional cowboys (and cowgirls) from all over the country to compete in the thrilling and bruising events such as bronco and bull riding, steer wrestling and calf roping. Daring clowns risk life and limb for laughs, and everyone has a really good time. Don a stetson and go on down to the corner of Davie Road and Orange Drive. There's a smaller rodeo held here on Wednesday nights.

8 Hialeah Park

This luxuriant 228-acre (92-hectare) park is home to probably the world's most beautiful race track, and certainly to the world's largest flock of some 800 American flamingos. There's also an elegant French-Mediterranean-style clubhouse. The Hialeah racing season usually runs from March to May, but the park is open daily for tours.

► *Take East 25th Street west. This runs into NW 79th Street and after 5½ miles (9km) joins **US 1**. Turn right to head the 4 miles (6km) south back to the Bayside Marketplace.*

Sea of Grass & the Tamiami Trail

3 DAYS • 270 MILES • 434KM A short drive along the Tamiami Trail leads past several airboat operators into the heart of the vast Everglades wilderness. An airboat tour is great fun but to capture the unspoiled natural serenity of the 'glades, travel on to the Shark Valley, or take the road to Flamingo.

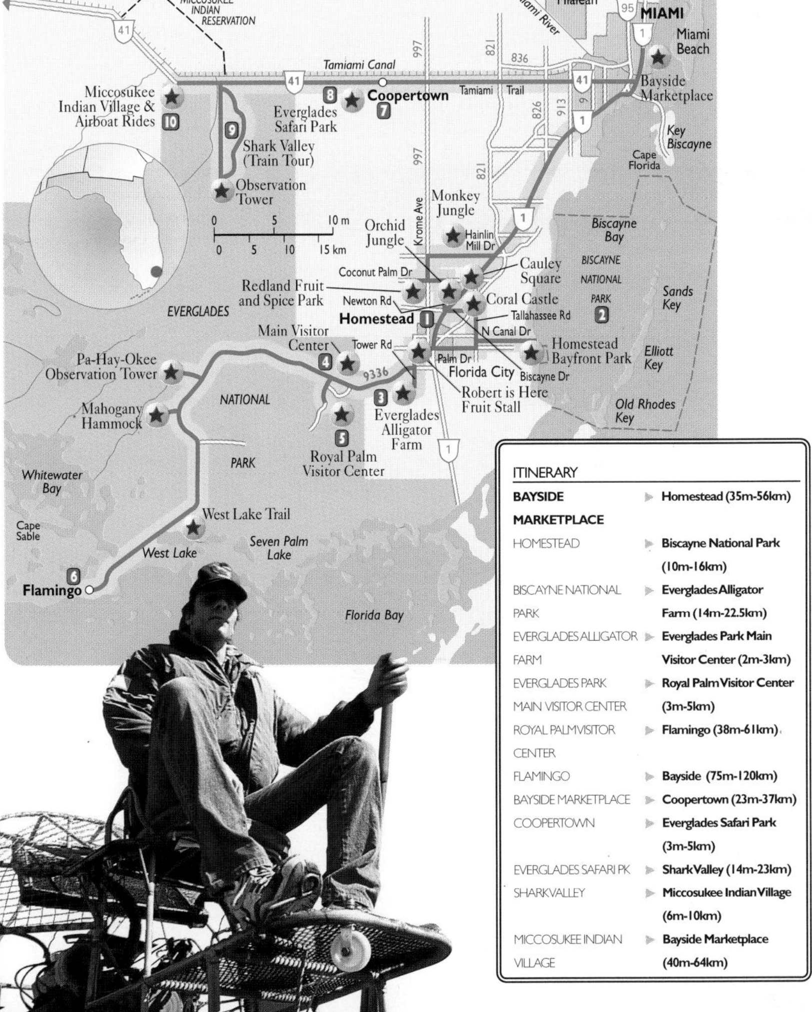

ITINERARY

BAYSIDE MARKETPLACE	**Homestead (35m-56km)**
HOMESTEAD	**Biscayne National Park (10m-16km)**
BISCAYNE NATIONAL PARK	**Everglades Alligator Farm (14m-22.5km)**
EVERGLADES ALLIGATOR FARM	**Everglades Park Main Visitor Center (2m-3km)**
EVERGLADES PARK MAIN VISITOR CENTER	**Royal Palm Visitor Center (3m-5km)**
ROYAL PALM VISITOR CENTER	**Flamingo (38m-61km)**
FLAMINGO	**Bayside (75m-120km)**
BAYSIDE MARKETPLACE	**Coopertown (23m-37km)**
COOPERTOWN	**Everglades Safari Park (3m-5km)**
EVERGLADES SAFARI PK	**Shark Valley (14m-23km)**
SHARK VALLEY	**Miccosukee Indian Village (6m-10km)**
MICCOSUKEE INDIAN VILLAGE	**Bayside Marketplace (40m-64km)**

▶ *From Bayside take the **I–95/ US 1** south for 22 miles (35km) and turn right (west) onto Hainlin Mill Drive (SW 216th Street).*

SCENIC ROUTES

The whole 36-mile (58km) drive from the main entrance of the national park to Flamingo is recommended. Drive slowly to take it in and try to spot the changing ecosystems. You will start in sawgrass prairie, pass through pinelands, then cypress forest, hardwood hammocks, mangrove and coastal prairie before reaching the Florida Bay estuary at Flamingo.

1 Homestead

At Monkey Jungle 25 species of chattering primates run free around 30 acres (12 hectares) of dense jungle, while the humans are caged within protective walkways. The shows here are excellent and star King, the mighty gorilla. Continue west, turn left on Krome Avenue (SW 177th Avenue), then right (west) onto Coconut Palm Drive (SW 248th Street). The Redland Fruit and Spice Park is a unique botanical garden growing over 500 kinds of fruit, vegetables, herbs, spices and nuts. Take a 'fruit safari', then make a selection from the bountiful gourmet and fruit store. Return east and turn right onto Newton Road (SW 157th Avenue). Orchid Jungle is the world's largest outdoor orchid garden, with over 9,000 varieties.

Continue south to the South Dixie Highway (US 1) and turn left (east) onto Biscayne Drive (SW 288th Street), where you will see Coral Castle. This unique achievement of coral sculptures and buildings was created singlehandedly by Edward Leedskalnin between 1920 and 1940. Its 1,000 US tons (907 metric tons) of coral carving includes a 9-US-ton (8-metric-ton) gate pivoted so that a child can open it, a 28-US-ton (25-metric-ton) obelisk and huge coral rocking chairs. How did he create such sculptures and move such huge weights without machinery, and what was his motivation? Head north on US 1 and turn off at Cauley Square, a renovated 1904 railway village which now houses themed restaurants and shops.

The Everglades isn't all sawgrass, airboats and alligators

FOR CHILDREN

Although children will undoubtedly enjoy Monkey Jungle at Homestead, the shorter and livelier Tamiami Trail is the better of the two Everglades tours for young families. Older children are bound to enjoy a canoe adventure, either at one of the boardwalk trails or with Backcountry Cruises in Flamingo. Because of the mosquito problem (and the heat), do not take young children to the Everglades in the summer, and carry insect repellent even in winter.

▶ *Return south to Coral Castle, go east (left) on Biscayne Drive, turn right (south) onto Tallahassee Road, then left (east) onto North Canal Drive (SW 328th Street).*

2 Biscayne National Park

As 96 percent of this park is submerged, the only way to see it is by boat. Excursions vary seasonally, but ranger-guided walks and canoe trips are usually available. The glass-bottom boat voyage to the offshore coral reef is a must. Hire a snorkel and mask to view the teeming sea life.

i *Convoy Point Information Station and Park Headquarters*

▶ *Return west on North Canal Drive, turn left (south) on Tallahassee Road (SW 137th Avenue) and right onto Palm Drive (SW 344th Street). Continue for 1½ miles (2.5km) to the intersection with Tower Road/Old 27 (SW 192nd Avenue), where the colorful 'Robert is Here' fruit stall stands. Turn down Tower Road and continue straight on past the junction with SW 376th Street.*

3 Everglades Alligator Farm

Although the alligator farm here is of interest, the main attraction is an airboat ride. There are more sophisticated and much quieter airboat rides available, but for a real backwoods setting and atmosphere this is one of the best. If you have a choice, opt for the 10-seat 'aircat', with a propeller driven by a powerful auto or aircraft engine, which rips across the sawgrass at up to 60mph (95km/h). With passengers sitting just inches above the water, the speed sensation is a real thrill. Earplugs (supplied) dull the roar of the engine, but when the boat stops, peace returns and your knowledgeable captain will point out the prevailing wildlife.

▶ *Return north on Tower Road and turn left onto **SR 9336**, 9 miles (14.5km).*

4 Everglades National Park Main Visitor Center

Stop at the Main Visitor Center for an introductory film and to see what ranger-conducted activities are scheduled for that day (look also in the visitor's guide you get at the park entrance). This will include informal introductory talks, walks along nearby trails and a campfire get-together.

▶ *A short distance away is the Royal Palm Visitor Center.*

5 Royal Palm Visitor Center

Another well-stocked visitor center, plus two of the park's most popular trails, are located here. On the ½-mile (800m) Anhinga Trail, alligators, turtles, and several species of fish and birds reside below the boardwalks that cross the slough (water hole). The Gumbo-Limbo Trail, also ½-mile (800m), will introduce you to a hardwood hammock.

▶ *From here the road continues for 38 miles (61km) to Flamingo with turn-offs only to more boardwalks and points of sightseeing interest (see Recommended Walks).*

6 Flamingo

This small settlement is basically a staging post for Everglades explorers, with a visitor information center and a small museum relating to the 'glades. Aside from camping, the only place to stay in the national park is the Flamingo Lodge, so booking is essential; tel: (305) 253–2241. You can board the Wilderness Tram (November to April) during the day, then catch one of the two sunset delights here. The first is a walk around Eco Pond, where hundreds of roosting wading birds can be seen flying in at dusk. The second is a romantic bay cruise. There are several charters from the marina, and trips out to Whitewater Bay and Cape Sable are recommended.

▶ *Return to Homestead, then take **US 1** back to Bayside, Miami, 75 miles (120km).*

RECOMMENDED WALKS

All the walks off the road to Flamingo have something special to show visitors, and most are quite short. The Anhinga Trail is the best of all for a general overview. The Pa-Hay-Okee features an elevated observation tower; at Mahogany Hammock you can see the largest living mahogany tree in the US; and at West Lake is a fine example of a mangrove forest.

This following section is a day's trip from Miami to the Everglades (see map on page 27), departing and returning along the Tamiami Trail (no recommended accommodation along the route). Look in the ditches beside the road for herons, egrets and limpkins. Snail kites are sometimes seen quartering the wetlands below.

▶ *From Miami Bayside head south on Brickell Avenue, then west on the Tamiami Trail (also known as Calle Ocho, SW 8th Street or **US 41**).*

7 Coopertown

Coopertown Airboat Rides (on SW 8th Street) is not only the closest operator to Miami, but the oldest in the Everglades, established in 1945. Tours last around 30 minutes.

▶ *Continue west along **US 41**.*

8 Everglades Safari Park

This relatively new, well-run attraction offers a good-value Everglades package of airboat tour, alligator wrestling and tropical jungle trail. The Miccosukee Indian Village, a little further on, has more authentic color.

▶ *Continue west along **US 41**, then turn south.*

9 Shark Valley

Pick up on what's happening daily at the information center before going on the 15-mile (24km) loop to see one of the best concentrations of wildlife in the whole of the Everglades National Park. Tram tours lasting two hours cover the area; bike rental is another option (no cars allowed). In winter it is best to book ahead for the tram tour; tel: (305) 221–8455. At the tour's southernmost point there is a 50-foot (15m) high observation tower from which to view the vast area of wetlands.

▶ *Return to **US 41** and turn left to Miccosukee Indian Village, 6 miles (10km).*

FOR HISTORY BUFFS

The local Miccosukee Indian tribe are descendants of the Creeks who migrated to Florida in the 18th and 19th centuries and became known as Seminoles – meaning 'wild runaways'. Clashes with settlers and the US army led, in 1818, to the first of the Seminole Wars. Determined to resist the white man's land-grabbing and deportation orders, the Seminoles carried out a bitter guerilla war lead by Chief Osceola. After Osceola's capture and death, Billy Bowlegs (who actually had no such deformity) led the surviving band of around 150 Seminoles deep into the Everglades. To this day they have never acceded to the government's treaties.

10 Miccosukee Indian Village and Airboat Rides

The Miccosukee tribe, hunters and farmers by tradition, has turned part of this village into a tourist attraction featuring craft and cookery demonstrations, alligator wrestling and a small museum. A 40-minute airboat ride will show you an old Indian camp.

▶ *Return to Bayside, Miami, east of **US 41**.*

The excitement of seeing the Everglades from an airboat

SPECIAL TO...

The best time to visit the Miccosukee Indian Village is between Christmas and New Year's Day, when some 40 tribes gather to dance, sing and exhibit at the Florida annual Indian Arts Festival. At the Miccosukee Restaurant you will get a rare chance to try American Indian food, including frog's legs, catfish, fry bread and pumpkin bread.

THE EVERGLADES

The Everglades stretch over 100 miles (160km) south from Lake Okeechobee in the north to Whitewater Bay in the southwest and some 50 miles (80km) east to the start of the Florida Keys. Technically this is a huge river but its flow is imperceptibly slow, and with an average depth of just 6 inches (15cm) it is like no other river in the world. In effect, it is a vast water prairie, or a sea of grass. There are no dramatic contrasts here, no bubbling muddy swamps beloved of TV adventures, and few tourist attractions. Aside from the thrill of an airboat ride, all is peaceful and calm – the charms of the region are purely natural.

Do not confuse the Everglades with the Everglades National Park. The latter is a legally protected, 2,000-square-mile (5,180sq km) area within the former. Its ecosystem is carefully preserved (airboats are prohibited in the national park) and interpreted for visitors by helpful and knowledgeable park rangers.

PRACTICAL CONSIDERATIONS

Never feed the animals. You risk at best a huge fine, at worst your life. Once an alligator is given food, it loses its fear of man and will subsequently equate all people with food. Alligator attacks are rare, but never approach them too closely as they are deceptively fast and enormously strong. For this reason never swim or wander off on your own in the Everglades. Snakes, too, can be dangerous, though very few are deadly. Don't put your hand or foot under a shady place, such as a rock, without checking first, and be aware of water snakes if you are fishing or canoeing. Finally, before making any independent excursions take advice from a park ranger.

Wildlife

The Everglades and the American alligator are virtually synonymous. In recent years legal protection has allowed the 'gator to increase its numbers, so that it is now a common sight throughout the area. So, too, is its prey of terrapins and frogs. Crocodiles, recognizable by their tapered snouts, are rare, as is the Florida panther, now reduced to a mere 30 or so, concentrated in the western 'glades and Big Cypress Swamp. However, you may see a 30- to 40-pound (14 to 18kg) bobcat in the pinelands of the national park or around the Flamingo area in the south. Nocturnal raccoons and opossums are common sights around campgrounds. The armadillo is another night creature of the 'glades, most likely to be seen squashed along the roadside. Look out at dawn and dusk for white-tailed deer grazing by the road. Animals that live a partially aquatic existence include the marsh rabbit and the elusive river otter (try Shark Valley for a sighting).

Your chance of spotting a dolphin in Florida Bay and Whitewater Bay are good, and manatees occasionally visit the Mangrove Wilderness, Everglades City.

Above: the most beautiful and most rare large animal in the state – the Florida panther

Below: never underestimate a 'gator in the wild – it may be your last mistake

Birds

Birdwatchers from all over the world come to the Everglades to view almost 300 species, but there is no need for binoculars to count a good many. Of all these, the species that seem perfectly designed for this watery wilderness are the stately wading birds, often so still (watching for fish) that they appear wooden. Tallest of these, at over 4 feet (1.2m) is the great blue heron. When in its white plumage, it is distinguishable from the slightly smaller great egret by its yellow legs. Other common waders include the little blue heron, the white ibis (red down-curved bill and face mask) and the snowy egret. One of the most popular Everglades sightings is the distinctive bright-pink roseate spoonbill (try Mrazek Pond, near Flamingo, in winter, or the shallows off US 1 just north of Key Largo). A more common sighting is the anhinga, frequently seen on a tree drying off its outstretched wings. Birds of prey include ospreys, kites and falcons. Soaring overhead, both black and turkey vultures are almost a permanent feature of the 'glades.

The anhinga bird is a common sight throughout the state

PRACTICAL CONSIDERATIONS

Visit in winter. Birds and animals become more visible as they gather round the receding sloughs (waterholes), and the infuriating mosquitoes are virtually absent between January and March. These are a real problem from May to November, even with the protection of insect repellent. If you must go then, cover up well. The only place to avoid them is on the airboats, as the wind prevents them from settling. To appreciate the area fully, you must leave your car and either walk, cycle or, best of all, canoe along ranger-recommended routes. Drive slowly at night to avoid killing small animals.

Flora

The Everglades are, thankfully, not all sharply barbed sawgrass, though this is the dominant plant of the region. Small hammocks – raised areas characterized by hardwood vegetation – punctuate the great river of grass, attracting a variety of plant and insect life. This typically includes palms, live oaks, mahogany trees, wild vines and the gumbo-limbo tree (known as the 'tourist tree' because in hot weather its bark turns red and peels off). Air plants thrive in the hammocks by simply attaching themselves to other trees and plants. Most conspicuous is the wild pine, which resembles the top leaves of a pineapple, to which it is related. Look out, too, for the bright red of the stiff-leaf wild pine among bald cypress trees.

Along the Coral Keys

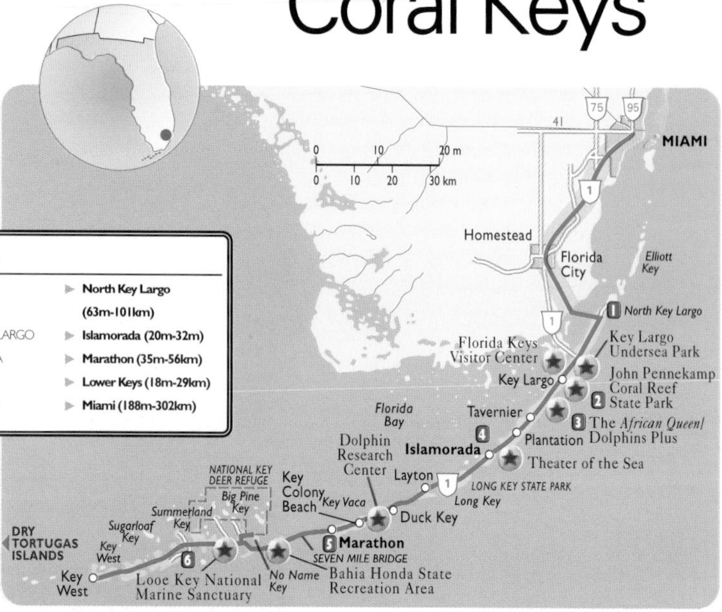

MIAMI
Homestead
Florida City
Elliott Key
North Key Largo
Florida Keys Visitor Center
Key Largo Undersea Park
Key Largo
John Pennekamp Coral Reef State Park
Tavernier
The *African Queen*/ Dolphins Plus
Florida Bay
Plantation
Dolphin Research Center
Islamorada
Theater of the Sea
Layton
LONG KEY STATE PARK
Long Key
NATIONAL KEY DEER REFUGE
Big Pine Key
Key Colony Beach
Key Vaca
Duck Key
Summerland Key
Sugarloaf Key
Marathon
SEVEN MILE BRIDGE
DRY TORTUGAS ISLANDS
Key West
Looe Key National Marine Sanctuary
No Name Key
Bahia Honda State Recreation Area
0 10 20 m
0 10 20 30 km

ITINERARY	
MIAMI	**North Key Largo (63m-101km)**
NORTH KEY LARGO	**Islamorada (20m-32m)**
ISLAMORADA	**Marathon (35m-56km)**
MARATHON	**Lower Keys (18m-29km)**
LOWER KEYS	**Miami (188m-302km)**

2 DAYS • 324 MILES • 520KM The Florida Keys are part of the largest living coral reef in the Western hemisphere, and it is thanks to this that Key Largo has become the diving capital of the world and Islamorada the sportfishing capital. The disadvantage of the reef is that the water along the shore is often too shallow for swimming and , because wave action is sorely missed, sandy beaches are scarce. For most visitors, however, the marvelous underwater opportunities outweigh simply bronzing on a beach.

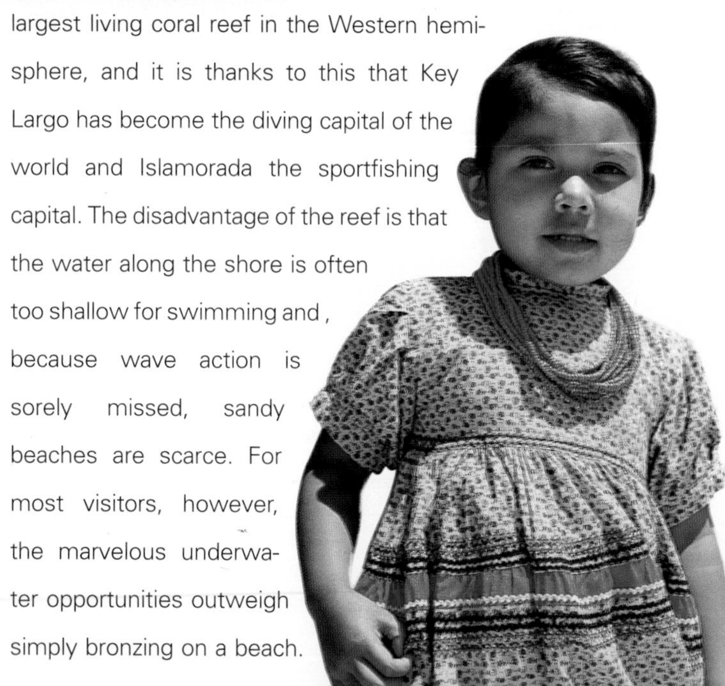

*From Miami take **I–95/US 1** south. Some 3½ miles (5.5km) past downtown Homestead, turn left on Card Sound Road. Cross the toll bridge to Key Largo. Note the mile-marker stones along the length of **US 1**. These start at **MM 127** just south of Florida City and finish at **MM 0** at Key West (on this route the first mile-marker you will see is **MM 105**).*

BACK TO NATURE

The whole of this trip will delight nature lovers, with fauna of West Indian origin, a marvelous concentration of corals and reef life and the delightful Key deer. The latter are unique to the Keys; do drive carefully as many of these tiny creatures are killed by cars.

1 North Key Largo

This is the wildest place in the Keys. The area immediately across the bridge is part of the Crocodile Lakes National Wildlife Refuge. You may well see some of its inhabitants from the roadside but don't venture too far out. Turn right onto SR 905 and you will pass through the Key Largo Hammock. This large area of West Indian hardwood also has its dangers. Not only are some of the trees here highly toxic, but this is a pick-up and drop-off point for drugs smugglering Humphrey Bogart and Lauren Bacall, and some scenes were shot in the Caribbean Club at MM 104. The origs.

Key Largo was immortalized in the 1948 film classic of the same name, starrinal building unfortunately burned down in the 1950s, but memorabilia in the current club on the same site recall the movie. The Key Largo Undersea Park (MM 103) offers an introduction to life below the waves, with conducted snorkeling and scuba dive tours.

i Key Largo Chamber of Commerce and Florida Keys Visitor Center, MM 106

2 John Pennekamp Coral Reef State Park, Key Largo (MM 102.5)

If you visit only one underwater park in the Keys, make sure it is this one. The park and the adjacent marine sanctuary boast 650 varieties of tropical fish and over 50 species of coral. There are lots of wrecks to explore, from a Spanish galleon to a World War II freighter sunk by a

The delights of John Pennekamp State Park are not confined to below the waves

Above: *The African Queen*
Right: the old Flagler Bridge on Highway A1A

U-boat. Ships have also been intentionally sunk in recent years to provide diving points of interest, and these also encourage marine life. Another popular feature is the 9-foot (2.7m) bronze statue 'Christ of the Deep'. See the visitor center, take a glass-bottom boat tour (booking is advisable – tel: 305 451–1621, then get really close to the reef on a snorkeling or scuba tour in the beautiful calm waters. If you would prefer to keep dry, there is still plenty to occupy you, including a huge aquarium, nature trails, boats for rent and a good sand beach. The Maritime Museum of the Florida Keys across from the park exhibits treasures salvaged from local wrecks and from around the world.

3 *The African Queen*/Dolphins Plus, Key Largo (MM 100-91)

Another Bogart film legend took its name from a boat, *The African Queen*. Here you will find the original vessel used in the Bogart–Hepburn film, built in 1912 for the African river trade. It is now based on the water at the Holiday Inn Resort (MM 100). Katherine Hepburn provides the link for another vessel here, *Thayer IV*, used for *On Golden Pond*, in which she starred alongside Henry Fonda. Also here is Dolphins Plus, a research center where you can swim with dolphins (tel: 305 451–1993 to make a reservation).

SPECIAL TO...

You can do just about anything underwater in the Florida Keys. Undersea weddings take place at the statue of Christ of the Deep in Pennekamp Park, and honeymooners can even stay below the waves at Jules' Undersea Lodge in Key Largo Undersea Park. Formerly a research laboratory, this is now the world's first underwater hotel and can accommodate up to six people.

Between ***MM 93*** *and* ***MM 91*** *lies the historic town of Tavernier, featuring some of the oldest buildings in the Keys, including an old post office and railroad buildings.*

4 Islamorada (MM 83)

Islamorada (pronounced I-lah-mor-AH-dah) means 'purple isle', possibly named after the purple orchids and bougainvillaea here, and it stretches for 16 miles (26km). The Theater of the Sea on Windley Key (MM 84.5) was established in 1946 and has been famous ever since for its performing dolphins. Audience interaction is an important part of its shows. After you have shaken 'hands' with a dolphin, board the glass-bottom boat for a colorful reef tour. It's possible to swim with the dolphins too, though it's expensive and you must book in advance (tel: 305/664 2431).

Islamorada is also known as the 'Sport Fishing Capital of the World', and was a favorite retreat of former president George Bush.

i *Islamorada Chamber of Commerce, MM 82.5*

FOR CHILDREN

The Florida Keys are primarily an adult playground for divers and anglers. Older children who want to pick up a rod or put on a snorkel are well catered for, but attractions for youngsters are limited. Key Largo is the best area to keep children amused, and on adjacent Windley Key the Theater of the Sea is a perennial family favorite.

5 Marathon and the Middle Keys (MM 65)

More dolphins can be encountered at the Dolphin Research Center on Grassy Key, MM 59. You can swim with them (tel: 305/289–1121 well in advance), though they are not captive and are free to come and go at will. The biological diversity of Crane Point Hammock (MM 50) makes it the most environmentally important piece of land in the Keys and includes a Museum of Natural History. At MM 47 is the start of the Old Seven Mile Bridge, which linked the Middle and the Lower Keys. Destroyed by a hurricane in 1935 and superseded by the New Seven Mile Bridge, it is now the world's largest fishing pier. It is still possible to drive on it as far as Pigeon Key, which is being restored to reflect its days as a railroad camp.

Craft from the Keys

i Greater Marathon Chamber of Commerce, MM 53.5

6 The Lower Keys (MM 40)

The fine mile-long (1.5km) sandy stretch at the Bahia Honda ('deep bay') State Recreation Area (MM 37) is the best beach in the Keys. Be careful on Big Pine Key to avoid stray Key deer. These beautiful, diminutive creatures, measuring just 2 feet (60cm) high, can be seen in the National Key Deer Refuge (take Key Deer Boulevard at MM 31.5 to Watson Boulevard). Continue on to No Name Key for even better sightings.

If you are searching for solitude, you can find it in many of the outlying Lower Keys, which are uninhabited and barely touched by tourism or the trappings of the 20th century. The reef at Looe Key National Marine Sanctuary (MM 27.5), rated by many divers and snorkelers as the most beautiful in the Keys, features many varieties of soft and hard coral and teems with a multitude of different sea creatures.

FOR HISTORY BUFFS

Fort Jefferson, located on the Dry Tortugas 68 miles (110km) off Key West, is a huge circular Civil War fortress. Its walls are some 50 feet (15m) high, 8 feet (2.4m) thick and guarded by over 140 cannons, yet it has never fired a shot in anger. Visitors must take a boat-trip or seaplane from Key West. The latter gives wonderful views through the shallow waters, including shoals of shark and Mel Fisher's treasure galleon, the *Atocha*.

SCENIC ROUTES

There are 42 bridges between the mainland and Key West, and each gives constantly changing views of beach, ocean and the scattered isles. The finest of these is the 1982 New Seven Mile Bridge, which is an unsurpassed vantage point for taking in the sheer sweep of the Straits of Florida and the Gulf of Mexico. It also gives a fine view of the Old Seven Mile Bridge.

RECOMMENDED WALKS

The geographical distinction of being the southernmost state recreation area means that Bahia Honda has a natural environment that is more Caribbean than North American and is a delightful place for a leisurely stroll. The Silver Palm Trail here contains many rare West Indian trees and plants that are not found anywhere else in the Keys.

i Welcome Center, Big Pine Key, MM 31

▶ *Continue to Key West, then return to Miami via* **US 1**.

Key West

Key West is no longer just a place, it has become a fashion statement. John James Audubon was inspired to produce some of the country's most beautiful art here, and Ernest Hemingway created a hell-raising legend while writing some of America's finest literature. Amid the bars and nightlife, this is also the state's oldest city, with dozens of beautifully kept historic houses. Within the few blocks that make up Key West Old Town is one of the biggest concentrations of specialty shops, restaurants and nightlife in Florida. Today, if you're bohemian, gay, hip, or simply an inquisitive tourist, Key West is Florida's new mecca.

2 DAYS

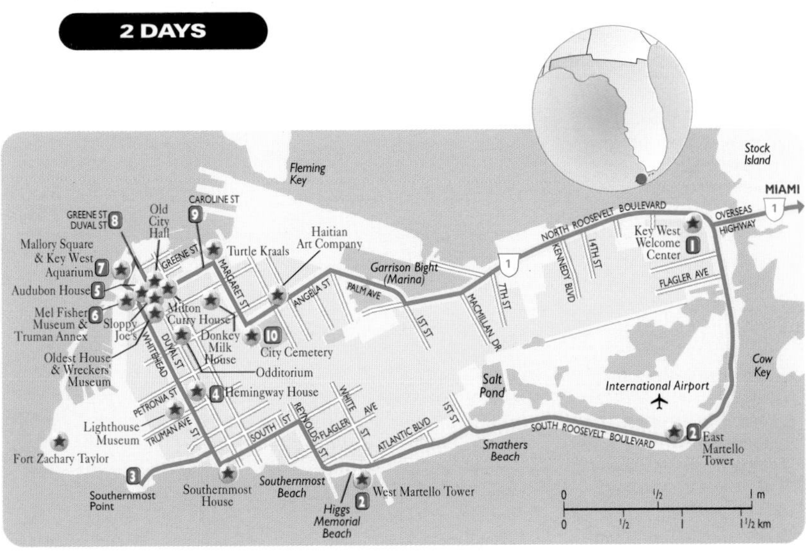

[i] Key West Welcome Center, North Roosevelt Boulevard; Chamber of Commerce, Mallory Square

▶ *Shortly after entering the island, the Overseas Highway* ***(US 1)*** *divides north and south. Turn right (north) onto North Roosevelt Boulevard.*

1 Key West Welcome Center

As well as a tourist information center, the Welcome Center is the base for the excellent Old Town Trolley Tour, which allows you to hop off and back on free of charge at 12 stops. The non-stopping Conch Tour Train (next door) will also welcome you aboard. Both tours last 90 minutes.

▶ *Turn around and head south on South Roosevelt Boulevard for just over a mile (1.6 km).*

2 Martello Towers and Beaches

These twin brick structures were built in the Civil War era as part of the island's defenses. The East Tower now houses a comprehensive and lively museum and art gallery. Drive past Smathers Beach to the West Tower. This is home to the Key West Garden Club who boast a beautifully well-tended tropical garden (closed Mondays and Tuesdays). Adjacent is the Higgs Memorial Beach.

▶ *Follow the road around to the right as it becomes Reynolds Street. Take the fourth left, South Street. Turn into Whitehead Street, then left, where signed, to Southernmost Point.*

3 Southernmost Point

A striped marker buoy and plaque claims that this is the southernmost point in the conti-

BACK TO NATURE

No single large area on this tiny island is devoted solely to nature, but there is an abundance of marine life, seabirds, prodigious hibiscus and bougainvillaea and only small-scale island development. There is a small wildlife sanctuary at Salt Pond (no visitor facilities) behind Smathers Beach, and the gardens of Hemingway House, Audubon House and the West Martello Tower are all very inviting.

Key West looks even better from a biplane – several companies offer excursions

nental US (in fact it isn't – there is an army base just beyond!). Adjacent is the Southernmost Beach and two contenders for the title of Southernmost House. Vendors ply their wares at this tourist photo-stop, and you will hear conch shells being blown. Pronounced 'konk', the name is applied to the shell, and to its edible flesh.

▶ *Return to Whitehead Street and turn left heading northwest.*

4 Hemingway House

No one person is associated more with the island than Ernest Hemingway. The hard-drinking, big-game-hunting, Nobel Prize-winning author bought this elegant Spanish Colonial mansion (built 1851) for $8,000 in 1931. He lived here until 1940 and wrote from his 'tree-house' study *A Farewell to Arms, For Whom the Bell Tolls* and *To Have and Have Not.* Some 40 or so cats live in the house, many of them descendants of 'Papa's' own six-toed feline companions. Their drinking trough is a former urinal from Sloppy Joe's Bar, and is said to be regarded with much reverence by Hemingway aficionados. Almost opposite is the 92-foot (28m) tall old Key West Lighthouse, built in 1847. This and the clapboard keeper's house next door have been turned into a museum.

▶ *Continue for about ½ mile (0.8km). Leave your car and continue on foot round this part of town.*

5 Audubon House

Curiously, this beautiful 19th-century house has no link at all with the famous artist and naturalist, John James Audubon, who visited Key West in 1832 to study and sketch the native birds. However, the period furnishings and antiques, together with Audubon's delightful drawings and engravings, recall peaceful days in old Key West.

▶ *Cross the street.*

6 Mel Fisher Maritime Heritage Society Museum and Truman Annex

More a treasure trove than a museum, this glittering collection centers on the wrecks of the Spanish galleon *Atocha* and her sister ship, *Santa Margarita,* both lost off Key West in 1622. In all, some 47 US tons (52 metric tons) of gold and silver were salvaged by Mel Fisher in 1985. Behind the museum is the Truman Annex. This development on the old site of a navy base includes original Victorian houses, a restaurant in the 1891 Custom House, a shopping village, and the Harry S Truman Little White House Museum. The latter house was home to the President on 11 working vacations.

▶ *Continue along Whitehead Street.*

7 Mallory Square

By day the square is a lively jumble of marketplace, shops, galleries, bars, restaurants and tour trollies. Here also are two of the island's four theaters, the Key West Aquarium and a small factory making handmade cigars. Every evening at sunset a bizarre circus ritual is played out against a glorious golden backdrop with jugglers, unicyclists, high-wire walkers, singers, mime artists, perhaps a cat-tamer, an escapologist and even a string quartet.

▶ *Whitehead Street runs parallel to Duval Street.*

> **SPECIAL TO...**
>
> In addition to the nightly perf stage festivals. Old Island Days is a three-month-long eclectic series of special events highlighted in the history, culture and architecture of the island (late January to late March); the Conch Republic celebrations in late April–early May recall the island's mock seccessionormances at Mallory Square, Key West still has plenty of energy to; Fantasy Fest, which mixes Halloween and Mardi Gras, and is the wildest of all!

8 Duval Street and Greene Street

Duval is famous for its specialty shopping, art galleries, European-style sidewalk cafés and bars. The most famous of these is Sloppy Joe's. Hemingway often drank here and the bar is now a shrine to

Sloppy Joe's, where the drinkers are laid back, but the drinking is serious

him. A short stumble away is Greene Street and Captain Tony's Saloon, another of the writer's favorite watering-holes. A little further down Duval Street is the Oldest House/ Wrecker's Museum. Here you can learn the 'rules of wrecking' (salvaging), which was one of the mainstays of the island's economy during the early 19th century. The house was built in 1829 and is worth a visit for its age and antiques alone. Moving from the sublime to the ridiculous, is the Odditorium (a branch of Ripley's Believe It Or Not!, see page 132) further along Duval Street. Walk back up the street and return to the nautical theme at the Shipwreck Museum, located in the Old City Hall (built 1891) on Greene Street.

▶ *Duval leads onto Caroline Street.*

9 Caroline Street

Enter Caroline Street from Duval (near Sloppy Joe's bar) and the Milton Curry House (Curry Mansion) is a few yards ahead. This is the grandest of Key West's many fine historic houses. It was built in 1905 and comprises 22 rooms of period antiques. Continue onto the old shrimp docks and Land's End Village, a collection of quaint shops and restaurants with a rustic atmosphere. The Turtle Kraals, where turtles were once landed for meat is now a restaurant.

▶ *Return to your car, regain Caroline Street, then turn down Margaret Street opposite the Turtle Kraals and continue for four blocks.*

10 City Cemetery

Owing to the difficulty of digging into the coral base of the island, this unusual graveyard is made up of aboveground vaults, laid out almost like a neighborhood in neat rows with street signs. The major memorial here is to the sailors killed in the sinking of the USS *Maine* in Havana in 1898, an act that precipitated the Spanish–American War. The character of Key West can be measured by some of the epitaphs here – 'I told you I was sick' and 'At least I know where he's sleeping tonight' are two favorites. As you leave the cemetery turn right onto Angela Street; on Frances Street, on the left, is the Haitian Art Company.

Turtles have a long association with the island

▶ *Continue on Angela Street until it joins Palm Avenue. Turn right, then left, as this becomes North Roosevelt Boulevard. This continues back to the Key West Welcome Center.*

RECOMMENDED WALKS

The Pelican Path is a historic walking trail through the original Old Town (the northwest tip of the island area bounded on the south by Angela Street and on the east by the cemetery). An excellent street map leaflet has been produced to guide visitors along the trail. An alternative series of tours is Solares Hill's *Walking and Biking Guide to Old Key West.*

THE SOUTHWEST

The area between Fort Myers and Naples is known as the Shell Coast, because of the prodigious number of collectible shells that are washed up on its shores. Shelling is a major pastime here and says a lot about what people who choose to visit this part of the state are looking for – serenity and a simple, natural break. Such a break certainly did no harm at all to Thomas Edison or Henry Ford, who did not actually go shelling, but did come to the area to refresh mind and body – and decades later the world is still reaping the benefits. Expounding on the tourism potential of the region, Edison once prophesied that 'There is only one Fort Myers and 90 million people are going to find it'. Fortunately for the peace of the area, this has never been realized and it is perhaps ironic that the Edison-Ford Complex is now the biggest man-made tourist attraction in southwest Florida. Fort Myers is booming, but it is doing so quietly, and if Edison were alive today it is unlikely that he would be displeased (despite his prediction) at how little things have changed in these parts. The region's other attractions are mostly natural, including some of the state's very best wildlife sanctuaries and miles of talcum-white sands dissolving into the blue and green of the Ten Thousand Islands. The name says it all, with apparently thousands of hammocks, in effect mini-jungle islands, scattered along the southwest coast like so much green confetti.

The resorts and cities of the region are generally low-key, and changes brought about by tourism trends are only being felt very gradually. While fashionable travelers flit to and from Miami and the Keys, Naples and Fort Myers welcome back old friends year in, year out, often at a fraction of the prices charged on the Atlantic coast. Few visitors here are short of a dollar, however.

The southwest is acquiring a reputation for attracting some of the country's wealthiest snowbirds, with Naples and Sanibel/Captiva the top destinations. The beautiful Caribbean-like island of Sanibel would be guaranteed a place on any tourist map, regardless of its marvelous shelling opportunities, and fortunately the scale and spacing of development have been sensitively carried out. In general, this is not an area that appeals to teenagers or those looking for 'fun', but for anyone with a more mature view or perhaps feeling a little world-weary, it is a perfect place to relax, re-charge the batteries and see a part of Old Florida.

Messing about in boats is a specialty of the Southwest

Tour 8
Naples is attractive, wealthy, understated and has miles of pristine sands. For that occasional rainy day the shopping is good, and there are also some fine small museums around the town. Caribbean Gardens is a good half-day outing, but to see nature at its best, explore to the east: you will find Corkscrew Swamp and Fakahatchee Strand as intriguing as their names. Head south to the Everglades to complete your safari.

The Ten Thousand Islands and their abundant wildlife are a nature-lover's joy, and the Everglades excursions and trails on this side of the coast are every bit as interesting as the more trodden paths into the 'glades from the east coast.

Tour 9
The tour starts at Fort Myers Beach, typical of the miles of unspoiled barrier islands along this coast, yet untypical because of the number of young singles it attracts (this is no Daytona Beach, however).

The attractions to the south include the Everglades Wonder Garden, as reliable for a good family outing as its years of experience suggest, and the thought-provoking Koreshan community site. The highlight of the area is the Edison Home – historic house, botanical garden and shrine to one of the country's true geniuses. The restored town center has other attractions, but if you feel like escaping from the madding crowd, then Pine Island is a perfect choice. If this seems too solitary, then the happy medium may be the islands of Sanibel and Captiva, where the beautiful tropical landscape is truly captivating.

Enjoy nature in the wild or pay a visit to one of several gardens in the region

TOUR
8

Naples & the Ten Thousand Islands

The jewel of the southwest, Naples boasts designer shops and manicured lawns, picturesque waterways and long golden beaches. The City Dock and Yacht Basin and the Old Marine Marketplace are the best places for waterside shopping, dining and drinking, while small boats depart from the latter to cruise the Ten Thousand Islands and inland waterways.

2 DAYS • 136 MILES • 218KM

ITINERARY

NAPLES	▶ **Caribbean Gardens (2m-3m)**
CARIBBEAN GARDENS	▶ **Corkscrew Swamp (28m-45km)**
CORKSCREW SWAMP	▶ **Fakahatchee (41m-66km)**
FAKAHATCHEE	▶ **Ochopee (7m-11km)**
OCHOPEE	▶ **Wooten's (2m-3km)**
WOOTEN'S	▶ **Everglades City (6m-10km)**
EVERGLADES CITY	▶ **Chokoloskee (4m-6km)**
CHOKOLOSKEE	▶ **Collier-Seminole (24m-39km)**
COLLIER - SEMINOLE	▶ **Marco Island (4m-6km)**
MARCO ISLAND	▶ **Naples (18m-29km)**

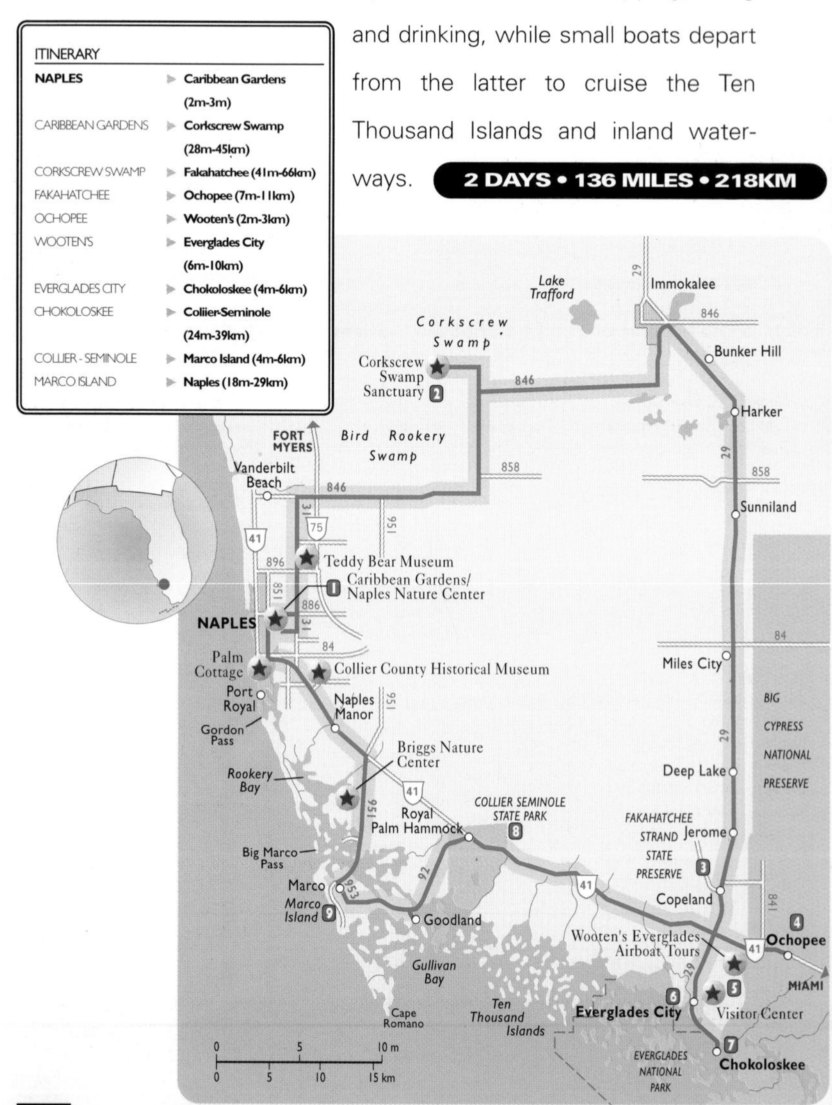

The city dock is a focal point for waterside refreshments

i *Naples Area Chamber of Commerce, 3620 N Tamiami Trail*

► *From the 5th Avenue bridge head north on Goodlette-Frank Road* ***(SR 851)*** *for 2 miles (3km).*

FOR HISTORY BUFFS

The Collier County Historical Museum, 2 miles (3km) south of the center of Naples on US 41, traces events from prehistoric times to the present. A 2-acre (0.8-hectare) historical park takes a look at a Seminole village and also features a steam locomotive. For history in situ, see Palm Cottage at 137 12th Avenue South. This 12-room house, built in 1895, is one of the last homes in southwest Florida made of tabby (an ancient shell-and-sand mixture).

1 Caribbean Gardens

Caribbean Gardens is Naples' main attraction, set in 52 acres (21 hectares) of tropical gardens amid stately banyan trees, rustling palms and towering bamboo. This is home to many exotic endangered animals and includes big cats such as Bengal tigers. See the entertaining and educational Scales and Tails Show and take the Primate Expedition cruise to see monkeys, apes and lemurs in near-natural surroundings. Sharing the site is the Naples Nature Center (although this is only accessible from 14th Avenue North). This features a small natural science museum with hands-on displays of the habitats and wildlife of South Florida, a wild animal rehabilitation clinic, plus nature trails.

► *Continue north and take the next right, Golden Gate Parkway* ***(SR 886).*** *Continue for 1½ miles (2.5km), turn left* ***(SR 31)****, then head north for 7¾ miles (12.5km) to* ***SR 846.*** *Follow this east, then north for 18½ miles (30km).*

2 Corkscrew Swamp Sanctuary

This 11,000-acre (4,450-hectare) park, maintained by the National Audubon Society, takes its name from a twisting creek that flows through it. Here you can see North America's largest surviving stand of virgin bald cypress forest, which includes trees over 500 years old and up to 100 feet (30m) tall. The sanctuary has the largest colony of wood storks in the country, and you may well see them nesting in the cypress trees from November through April when large wooden 'Quiet Please!' signposts are erected. Look down from the boardwalk trail and you could also spot alligators or even otters. A further 200 species of birds are to be found here and in spring and summer there is a beautiful display of orchids, wildflowers and ferns.

► *Continue east for approximately 10 miles (16km) on* ***SR 846.*** *At Immokalee head due south on* ***SR 29*** *for 31 miles (50km) to Copeland.*

The traditional way of seeing the 'glades is by airboat

3 Fakahatchee Strand State Preserve

Fakahatchee Strand is the major southwestern drainage channel of the aptly named Big Cypress Swamp. The vegetation here is outstanding, with the largest forest of native royal palms and the largest concentration and variety of epiphytic orchids in North America. Endangered wildlife includes the wood stork, the Florida black bear, the Everglades mink and the Florida panther. Facilities and activities here are limited, but there is a boardwalk providing access to an old growth cypress stand and opportunities for hiking are boundless.

> *Continue south for 3 miles (5km) and turn left onto **US 41**. Head east for 4 miles (6km).*

4 Ochopee

This tiny village's claim to fame is that it operates the smallest post office in the US. The simple wooden one-person shack measures just over 7 feet by 8 feet (2.1m by 2.4m). Send yourself a postcard from here to get its unique postmark!

> *Head back west on **US 41** for 2 miles (3km).*

5 Wooten's Everglades Airboat Tours

Wooten's is something of an evergreen in the 'glades, having operated here since 1953. It also claims to run the only tours that cover grasslands, mangroves and the Ten Thousand Islands. The airboats will take you on a fascinating 5-mile (8km) tour along the old Indian canoe trails used during the Seminole Wars and also into the mangrove jungles on the west coast. The firm also operates swamp buggies, which resemble the metal skeleton of a double-decker bus with huge tires for squelching through the wet terrain (seats are on the top deck only). These venture out to Halfway Creek Cypress Swamp, its waters stained a ruddy-brown by the tannin from the mangroves where airplants and orchids flourish. To complete your visit see the alligator farm containing some 200 residents and a collection of other Florida reptiles.

> *Head west for 2 miles (3km) on **US 41** and turn left on **SR 29** to enter Everglades National Park. Stop at the visitor center to pick up information. Continue south for 4 miles (6km).*

6 Everglades City

This small community is the embarkation point for Ten Thousand Islands trips and various sportfishing excursions. There are several companies offering various packages of boat or airboat tours combined with alligator farms, small zoos and Seminole Indian 'villages'. Most of these provide good value for money, but for the most authoritative trip aboard a quiet boat that will not have the indigenous wildlife scooting for cover, go to the National Park Information Center. The park's boats (some are double-decked) glide silently around the Ten Thousand Islands and, on the longer cruises, stop for shelling on a deserted key.

If you plan to stay overnight here, there are two outstanding resorts that are certainly worth seeing, if only for a drink. The Port of the Islands, considered one of the finest sportsmen's lodges in the country, is an attractive place in its own right, with a chickee (Indian-palm hut) waterfront bar overlooking a manatee sanctuary. The Everglades Rod and Gun Lodge is an even more famous sportsmen's retreat and has played host to a number of shootin' 'n' fishin' US presidents. Built in the mid-1800s and remodeled in 1920 it is well worth a look and perhaps a meal.

FOR CHILDREN

The Teddy Bear Museum of Naples claims the most comprehensive collection of teddy bears in America. Here, in a cottage in the woods on Pine Ridge Road, children will find tough teds in overalls and boots, chintz and cashmere bears, ursa majors measuring up to 6 feet (1.83m) and ursa minors that are just 1 inch (2.5cm) tall. Antiques from the likes of Steiff rub furry shoulders with bears belonging to famous celebrities and there is a display of bear memorabilia.

▶ *Continue on* ***SR 29*** *for 4 miles (6km).*

7 Chokoloskee

Take the second right past the Chokoloskee post office, then the first left to the historic Smallwood Store, perched above the water on stilts. This old Indian trading post and general store was built in 1906 by Ted Smallwood, who traded furs, turtles and venison with the Seminoles. Little has changed since those days except that the store is now a museum.

▶ *Return through Everglades City and turn left onto* ***US 41****. Continue west for 16 miles (26km).*

8 Collier Seminole State Park

To the right as you enter the park is a skeletal metal wheeled contraption, a 'walking dredge' used to construct the Tamiami Trail in the 1920s. The building a little way on to the left is a replica of a blockhouse used by US forces and local defenders during some of the final skirmishes of the Second Seminole War (late 1850s). Like the Fakahatchee Strand this park is also blessed with abundant stately royal palms and many endangered animal species, including brown pelicans, wood storks, bald eagles, red-cockaded woodpeckers, crocodiles, manatees, mangrove fox squirrels, Florida black bears and panthers. You can go on a ranger-guided tour along the nature trail, take to the water on a 13-mile (22km) canoe trip, or go the easy way, aboard the 38-foot (11.6m) *Seminole Princess*.

▶ *Head south on* ***SR 92*** *for 4 miles (6km).*

9 Marco Island

Turn left immediately after the bridge onto the island to the small fishing village of Goodland. Happily, very little of the modern construction that has completely obliterated the rest of the island's character has reached Goodland. Shops, restaurants and old homes, many on stilts, look peacefully out onto the water.

SCENIC ROUTES

The most scenic routes in this region can be seen only from the water. However, the southern end of SR 29 alongside the Big Cypress National Preserve is pleasant and there is a (slim) chance of seeing a Florida panther. At the southern end of this road are tall palms, houses on stilts and a countryside little touched by tourism.

▶ *Return to* ***SR 92****, turn left to reach the center of the island, then turn right onto* ***SR 951****. Head north for 8 miles (13km) to rejoin* ***US 41*** *which will take you back to Naples, 5th Avenue South (7 miles/11km).*

Seminole Indian dolls make good keepsakes and sponsor local craftworkers

TOUR
9

Lee Island Coast

This peaceful coast is one of the least developed part of habitable southern Florida. Sanibel and Captiva ('the American Tahiti') are the most desirable locations, Estero Island is famous for Lover's Key, while Fort Myer's Beach is a popular family choice. Back on the mainland the Edison-Ford Complex is a tribute to American genius.

1/2 DAYS • 139 MILES • 223KM

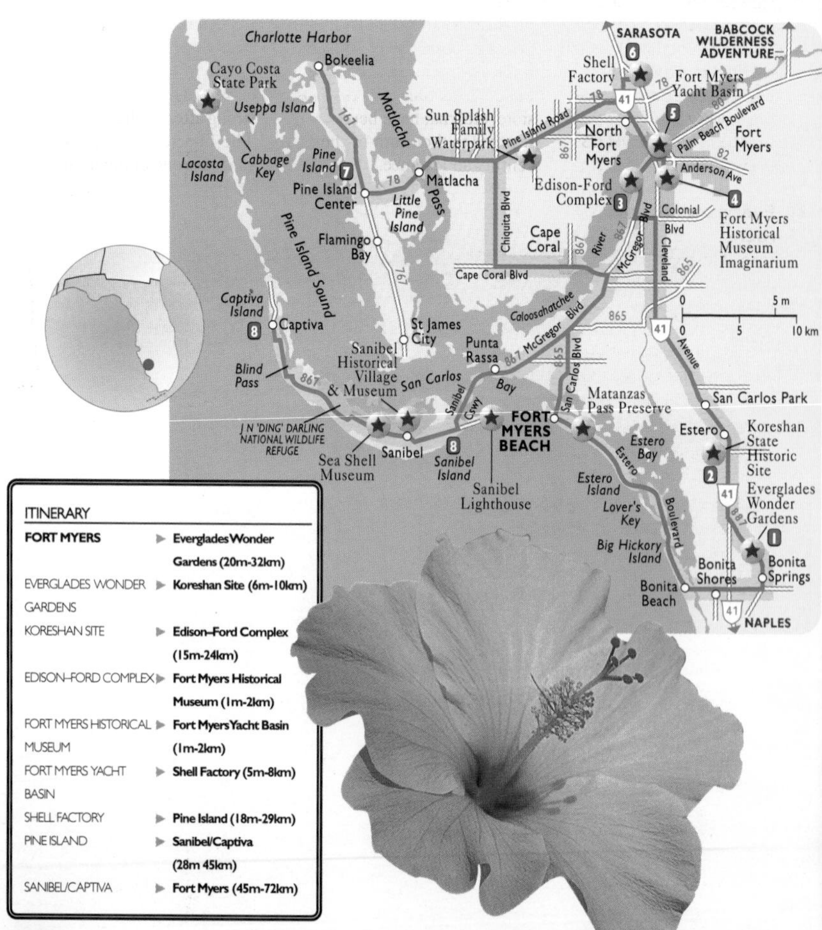

ITINERARY	
FORT MYERS	▶ **Everglades Wonder Gardens (20m-32km)**
EVERGLADES WONDER GARDENS	▶ **Koreshan Site (6m-10km)**
KORESHAN SITE	▶ **Edison–Ford Complex (15m-24km)**
EDISON–FORD COMPLEX	▶ **Fort Myers Historical Museum (1m-2km)**
FORT MYERS HISTORICAL MUSEUM	▶ **Fort Myers Yacht Basin (1m-2km)**
FORT MYERS YACHT BASIN	▶ **Shell Factory (5m-8km)**
SHELL FACTORY	▶ **Pine Island (18m-29km)**
PINE ISLAND	▶ **Sanibel/Captiva (28m 45km)**
SANIBEL/CAPTIVA	▶ **Fort Myers (45m-72km)**

Fort Myers Beach Chamber of Commerce, 17200 San Carlos Boulevard

SPECIAL TO...

There are no prizes for guessing whose birthday the 10-day Festival of Light commemorates during mid-February each year here. Thomas Edison's life is celebrated in a huge street parade, fashion shows, music and many other events. A Carnival King and Queen are crowned each year and members of the Edison family usually take part in the festivities.

*Head south for 14 miles (23km) on **SR 865**, through Lover's Key and Big Hickory Island. At Bonita Beach turn inland through Bonita Shores. Three miles (5km) past the latter, turn left onto **Old US 41 (SR 887)**.*

1 Everglades Wonder Gardens

This small lush garden zoo is southwest Florida's oldest attraction and, in places, could do with a coat of paint. However, the low admission price and the enthusiastic guides more than make up for any aesthetic shortcomings with an entertaining and educational tour of the gardens' residents. Among the many mammals, birds and reptiles, Big Joe the crocodile is king at 1,000 pounds (450kg), but the playful Everglades river otters are the show-stealers.

*Head north to join the Tamiami Trail **(US 41)** and continue for 5 miles (8km).*

2 Koreshan State Historic Site

In 1894 a religious visionary named Cyrus Reed Teed (who gave himself the biblical name Koresh) brought his followers from Chicago to a place he named Estero. His teachings advocated celibacy, communal living and communal ownership of property. The community and movement declined after his death in 1908, but you can take a guided tour to see the tropical gardens and several buildings (cottages, workshops, store, etc) that have been restored to their turn-of-the-century appearance.

(Note: there is no connection between these Koreshans and the infamous Waco cult which was led by the late David Koresh.)

*Continue north for 12 miles (20km) on **US41** and turn left onto Colonial Boulevard to reach McGregor Boulevard. Follow this road north for nearly 3 miles (5km).*

3 Edison-Ford Complex

Fort Myers is indelibly stamped with the genius of Thomas Alva Edison. Even McGregor Boulevard is a tribute to him, for it was he who first planted the stately royal palms that line 15 miles (24km) of road here, hence Fort Myers' nickname 'City of Palms'. Edison was the most prolific inventor the world has ever seen, and in total patented over 1,000 inventions, the best-known being the electric light bulb and the phonograph. His major achievement while at Fort Myers, which he made his winter home at the age of 38 in 1886, was the development of rubber from the goldenrod plant. The chemical lab in which he pioneered the modern synthetic rubber industry is perhaps the highlight of the tour, appearing today exactly as he left it, with the original light bulbs still going strong after all these decades! The 14-acre (6-hectare) tropical garden is one of the most complete in America and contains over a thousand plant varieties brought from all over the world for experimental purposes. King of them all is the incredible banyan, which Harvey Firestone brought here in 1925 as a sapling with a mere

The Edison banyan tree, with its circumference of 400 feet (120m), is the third largest banyan in the world

2-inch (5cm) diameter. It now shades the whole parking lot.

Henry Ford, who for a long time had been a close business associate and friend of Edison's, built his winter home next door in 1916. You can see the Model T that Ford gave Edison in 1907, still in running condition and with a goldenrod rubber spare tire. Despite being the world's first billionaire, Ford had modest tastes and his house is extremely pleasant without ever being grand. A museum is dedicated to his achievements during his 15 winters here. After Edison's death in 1931, Ford did not return to Fort Myers. (In order to catch the tours of both homes arrive by 3pm.)

FOR HISTORY BUFFS

The collection in the Edison Museum is not only a tribute to the genius of one man, it is a series of landmarks in 20th-century technological breakthroughs. Here you can see some of the world's earliest lighting, phonographic, cinematic and telegraphic equipment, as well as the more mundane domestic prototypes of electric fans, toasters, heaters, water softeners and much, much more.

► *As you leave the parking lot follow the signs to the Fort Myers Historical Museum, east along McGregor Boulevard and onto Dr Martin Luther King Boulevard.*

4 Fort Myers Historical Museum/Imaginarium

Housed in the 1924 Atlantic Coastline Railroad Depot, this is a local and regional museum. Hear in their own words the stories of different generations of local Indians, see models of early Fort Myers and admire the fine glass collection. Outside the museum is *The Esperanza*, the last and the largest Pullman private railroad car to be built.

About 1 mile (2km) due east on Dr Martin Luther King Jr Boulevard is Fort Myers' latest attraction, Imaginarium, an exciting 'hands-on' museum and aquarium.

► *Return to the Historical Museum. Head north on Jackson Street for about 1 mile (2km) and park.*

5 Fort Myers Yacht Basin and Downtown

This busy focal point offers several sightseeing cruises. It is a good place to have a drink and watch the busy Caloosahatchee ('river of the Calusa Indians'). First Street, one block back, runs through the middle of downtown, where there are several restored old-style shopping arcades and squares. Walk east three blocks and on the corner of Fowler Street you will see the splendid Burroughs Home, completed in 1901. Recently renovated, the house is open to visitors.

BACK TO NATURE

Well away from the main route (20 miles/32km north of Fort Myers on SR 31) is the Babcock Wilderness Adventure. A large elevated jeep-like swamp buggy will take you on a 90-minute journey into the beautiful forests and waters of this unspoilt backwoods. Knowledgeable tour guides will point out the abundant wildlife and you will learn about life on the range. Seats must be reserved in advance; tel: (941) 338–6367 information or (800) 500–5583 reservations.

At Manatee Park, on the SR 80, 1½ miles (2.5km) east of I–75 (Exit 25), visitors can see manatees in a non-captive natural environment, adjacent to a warm-water discharge from a power plant. Educational displays help explain the endangered world of these gentle native sea cows.

i *Lee Island Coast Visitors Bureau, 2180 West First Street*

► *Cross the river on* ***US 41*** *and continue north for 5 miles (8km).*

6 The Shell Factory

This 50-year-old tourist institution, spread over a massive 65,000 square feet (600sq m), claims the biggest selection of shells and coral for sale in the world. Tasteful it isn't, but for sheer scale and choice of merchandise (which includes foods, 'fashion items' and tourist trinkets) the place has a fascination all its own.

The Henry Ford Winter Home, where the great industrialist came to recharge his batteries

Return south for 1½ miles (2km) and turn right onto ***SR 78****. Head east for 13 miles (21km) to Matlacha, stop at the Pine Island Chamber of Commerce, then continue for a further 4 miles (6km) to Pine Island.*

7 Pine Island

If you want to see a little of the old Florida, then the hamlet of Bokeelia (turn right and go to the end of the island) is as good a place as any. Start at the Museum of the Islands (corner of Russell Road and Sesame Drive), then wander out on one of the fishing jetties, watch the pelicans wheeling and diving, enjoy a seafood meal in the simple home-style restaurant and you have exhausted most of the leisure options here. You can rent a boat to one of the other islands – Useppa, Cabbage Key or perhaps Lacosta – where you will find life little different. The latter island is home to Cayo Costa State Park, where the bird life is spectacular. Lacosta is also one of the few places in North America where mangoes are successfully cultivated. You don't have to go there to enjoy them, however, as they are sold at the friendly roadside stall at Pine Island Center, just as you enter the island.

Return via Matlacha. Four miles (6km) after rejoining the mainland, turn right on Chiquita Boulevard. Follow this south to Cape Coral Boulevard, turn left and follow the road for 4 miles (6km) to Cape Coral Bridge, which crosses the Caloosahatchee, onto McGregor Boulevard. Head south (right) to the Sanibel Causeway.

FOR CHILDREN

Aside from the attractions listed in the main text in Cape Coral, look for the Sun Splash Family Waterpark on Santa Barbara Boulevard, off Pine Road (closed mid-October to mid-March), and the excellent new Children's Science Center on NE Pine Island Road.

8 Sanibel and Captiva Island

Sanibel Island is world famous for its shell gathering. Its crescent shape, the smooth, gentle slope of the Gulf floor and its protected situation as a barrier island allow even the most fragile shells to be washed up on its shores intact. More varieties can be found here than on any other beach in North America; among the 400 types are such exotically named shells as golden tulip, sculpted lion's paw, tiger's eye, lady's ear and angel wing. Pick up a leaflet at the Chamber of Commerce, hop aboard a shelling charter boat, or take a guided shelling walk. Keen conchologists should pay a visit to the Bailey-Matthews Shell Museum (on the main Sanibel-Captiva Road), which is home to over a million shells.

Periwinkle Way/Sanibel-Captiva Road is the main road through the 12-mile (19km) length of this island. Turn left on this road just after entering the island to see the lighthouse, built in 1884. Turn around and continue for about 4 miles (6km) to visit the Sanibel Historical Village and Museum, adjacent to the city hall. Dedicated to the island pioneer families, it contains household furniture and artifacts from the 1900s (open Thursday to Saturday). Continue for 2 miles (3km) and turn right to the highly-acclaimed J N 'Ding' Darling National Wildlife Refuge. This comprises an informative visitor center, a 5-mile (8km) wildlife drive (closed Fridays), two red mangrove forest canoe trails and three walking trails.

From the wildlife drive exit, continue for 2 miles (3km); Captiva Island begins at Blind Pass, a favorite spot for doing the 'Sanibel Stoop' (as shelling is known here). Captiva is even prettier than Sanibel and hosts some world-class resorts.

i *Sanibel/Captiva Islands Chamber of Commerce, Causeway Road, Sanibel*

► *Return via McGregor Boulevard **(SR 867)**, turning right onto San Carlos Boulevard **(SR 865)** to Fort Myers Beach.*

Captiva Island – white sand beaches and gingerbread-trimmed antique shops

FL 9844 DR

GOLD COAST & TREASURE COAST

The gold and treasure that these shorelines were originally named after came mostly from the booty of wrecked Spanish galleons during the 17th century. In the late 19th century and early 20th century, the wealth created largely by just two men would have filled several armadas of galleons. The first man was Henry Morrison Flagler, the father of Florida tourism. There was little in the way of charity balls, polo clubs and championship golf courses when his railroad thundered past the yellow wooden shacks of Palm Beach in 1894. Only two years later the legendary Breakers Hotel was accumulating a formidable list of guest signatures, and by the time Flagler had built his great mansion, Whitehall – 'The Taj Mahal of North America' – in 1902, Palm Beach was an established mecca for every East Coast socialite. 'Get the big snobs', as Flagler might have said, 'and the little ones will follow.'

This was, in fact, Addison Mizner's business philosophy, and appropriately the famous architect arrived in Palm Beach in 1925 aboard Flagler's Orange Blossom Special. Mizner turned his attention to the beach resorts to the south and his 'Bastard-Spanish-Moorish-Romanesque-Gothic-Renaissance-Bull Market-Damn the Expense' style (as it was succinctly named) became the hallmark of the area. Perhaps the greatest legacy left behind by this flamboyant character is the Cloister Inn at Boca Raton – a giant pink wonder that remains one of the most costly hotels ever built.

Mizner also knew how to turn a dollar: during the height of the boom, his development company was said to be selling some $2 million worth of real-estate per week. Real-estate gold turned to fool's gold with the Great Depression in 1929, but the seeds were sown and Palm Beach County has never really gone out of fashion since. In Palm Beach, Rolls Royces are not just driven, they are submerged for the amusement of divers, and if you have to ask the price here, then it's probably better to move on. Perhaps to Fort Lauderdale, a fine middle-market family resort which may seem, at first sight, a little vulgar. Behind the souvenirs and bars on the beachfront, however, lie mansions which would not be at all out of place in Palm Beach itself. To the north of Palm Beach is the Treasure Coast. The main attraction for many visitors here is that there are no main attractions – simply peace, quiet, good facilities within easy reach, and miles of golden sand.

You'll need your own sunshade on Fort Lauderdale Beach

Tour 10
The tour starts in Fort Lauderdale. Nothing remains of the original fort built in 1838 during the Second Seminole War, but there is the settlement's first trading post, now Stranahan House, from which the city grew. The modern concrete development of downtown brings you up to date with a jolt before heading to Las Olas Boulevard for some shopping and a foretaste of style and price in Worth Avenue. This is also an indicator of the wealth of Fort Lauderdale; to appreciate this fully, take a river cruise to view the magnificent waterside homes.

Tour 11
North of Fort Lauderdale is the lively suburb of Pompano Beach, where there is plenty to keep all the family amused. Entering Palm Beach County you will encounter Mizner's Boca Raton and its sister resort of Delray Beach, which offers the unusual Japanese Morikami Museum. Next, stop off at Lake Worth for the area's best beach. West Palm Beach is unexpectedly good for children and is also home to the outstanding Norton Gallery of Art. In Palm Beach, stop at Whitehall for a history lesson from the horse's mouth, then padlock your wallet for fabulous Worth Avenue. Continue north through the turtle beaches of Juno and Jupiter and on to peaceful Hutchinson Island. The road leads back past the scenic Indian River, and the wild and lovely Loxahatchee River in Jonathan Dickinson State Park.

Above: The Breakers, built in 1926 in Italian Renaissance style to replace the original hotel which was destroyed by fire

Below: luxury beachside accommodation in Fort Lauderdale

Fort Lauderdale

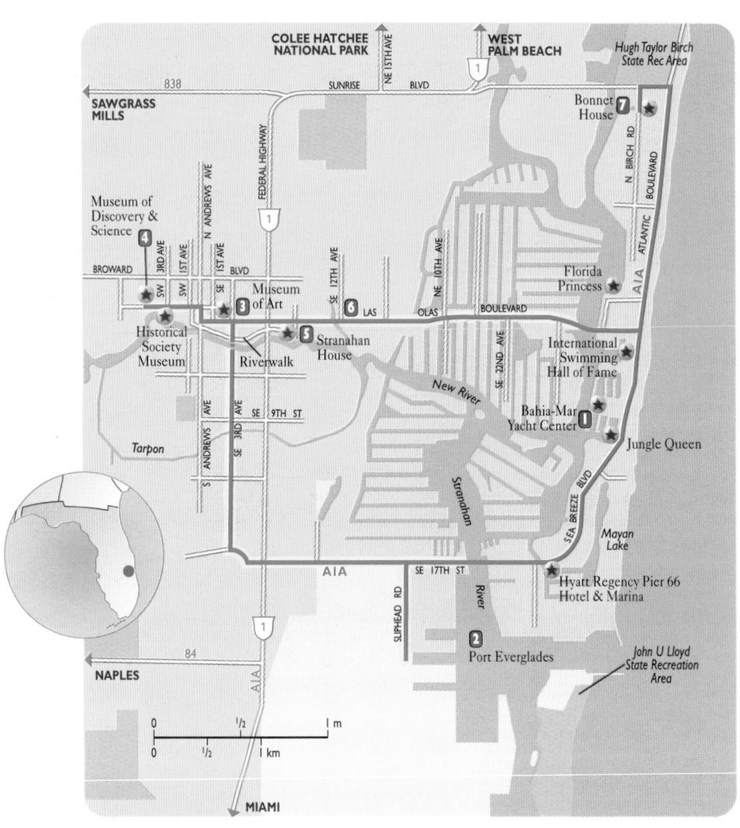

2 DAYS Fort Lauderdale is a lively modern resort with beaches comparable to those of Miami, glittering residences to match Palm Beach, and a well-balanced ambience all of its own. The city enjoys a buzzing nightlife and is renowned for its choice of eating establishments.

Municipal art – the colorful bus station at Fort Lauderdale

[i] *Greater Fort Lauderdale Convention and Visitors Bureau, 1850 Eller Drive, Suite 303*

▶ *Start at the Bahia-Mar Yacht Center.*

1 Bahia-Mar Yacht Center

Bahia-Mar is one of the largest marinas in the country. The front of the dock is always busy, and it is not uncommon to see deep-sea catch – shark, sailfish or marlin, weighing up to 300 pounds (136kg) – strung up fresh from fishing charter boats. Glass-bottom snorkeling boats are a great way to explore shallower waters and coral reefs, and an illuminated night excursion is particularly memorable. If your idea of a cruise is rather more relaxed, however, there are plenty of conventional sightseeing tours along the inland waterways. The *Jungle Queen* steamboat has been offering family excursions around Fort Lauderdale since 1945. Three-hour daytime tours cruise the New River, past 'Millionaires' Row', and stop at the *Jungle Queen's* very own jungle island complete with Indian village. The acclaimed and ever-popular dinner cruise adds to this a barbecue feast, a Vaudeville revue and the assurance of a lively sing-along evening. Just along the boulevard from Bahia-Mar is the Hyatt Regency Pier 66 Hotel and Marina. Prices here are as high as its famous 17th-floor revolving lounge, but it is well worth the cost of an early evening drink to watch the sunset and view the yachts. Just north of here is the International Swimming Hall of Fame, where a recently expanded museum contains Olympic memorabilia from over 100 countries.

▶ *Continue south on* ***SR A1A****. Turn left onto Sliphead Road.*

2 Port Everglades

This is the second largest cruiser terminal in the world after Miami, but in terms of luxury tonnage it is number one. If you would like to sample the world of cruising, book a full- or half-day trip on board SeaEscape or Discovery Cruises to the Bahamas, or to 'Nowhere'. For no more than the price of a good restaurant meal, the latter lets you experience all the trappings and entertainment you would expect on a luxury cruiser, including its own casino. ('Nowhere' is, of course, simply a sea voyage.)

▶ *Rejoin* ***SR A1A*** *and drive north to Las Olas Boulevard.*

BACK TO NATURE

There are two fine state recreation areas (SRAs) immediately to the north and south of the main town beach. The Hugh Taylor Birch SRA (north) comprises 180 acres (73 hectares) of undisturbed subtropical splendor with fishing, boating and canoeing facilities, while the larger 244-acre (99-hectare) John U Lloyd Beach SRA is particularly noted for its fishing from the rock jetties. A nature hike through the park's dunes, coastal hammock and mangroves is a refreshing contrast to downtown development, and you can swim, canoe or go boating here. Better still is Colee Hatchee National Park (2000 NE 15th Avenue). From boardwalks, visitors can see herons, raccoons and introduced parrots.

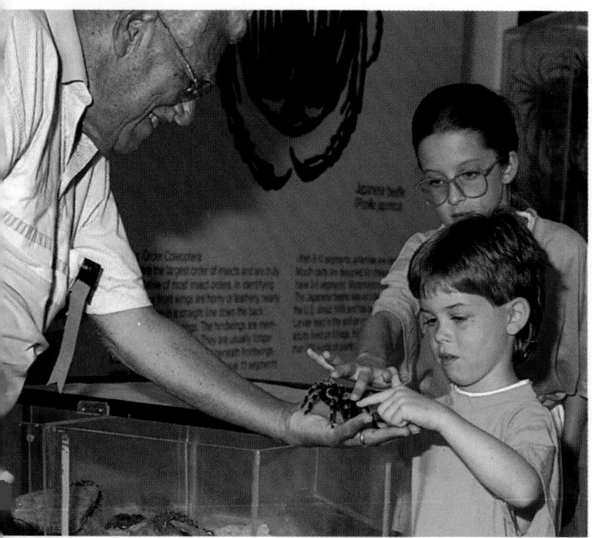

Hands on a tarantula at the Museum of Discovery

3 Museum of Art

The modern Museum of Art boasts Florida's largest art exhibition space and is the setting for two fine collections – the North European CoBrA (Copenhagen, Brussels, Amsterdam) school, and an ethnic range of American Indian, pre-Columbian, West African and Oceanic paintings and sculptures. One block north, the distinctive stepped profile of the Main Library is a striking addition to the modern cityscape.

> **RECOMMENDED WALKS**
>
> Close to the Museum of Art off SW 1st Avenue is the recently landscaped palm-lined Riverwalk. Here you can stroll in the riverside park and enjoy watching the boats sail by from sidewalk cafés. On the first Sunday of each month the Riverwalk features free outdoor jazz. Or to really get away from it all, take a ranger-guided walk at one of the state recreation areas.

▶ *Drive west on Las Olas Boulevard for a short way, turn right onto S Andrews Avenue, then left onto SW 2nd Street. Park at the Museum of Discovery and Science. (If you are feeling energetic leave your car at the Museum of Art and walk this route – it's only just over half a mile/1km.)*

4 Museum of Discovery and Science/Historic District

The highly acclaimed Museum of Discovery and Science not only features over 200 hands-on exhibits (on animals, ecology, space, health, sound, household science and much more), but also boasts a Blockbuster IMAX 3-D Theater which shows changing films.

A short walk east along SW 2nd Street is the town's eight-block historic district. The centerpiece is the Fort Lauderdale Historical Society Museum at 219 SW 2nd Avenue. This traces the history of Fort Lauderdale from its pioneering days up to 1945 by means of photographs, costumes and many other artifacts. A few yards away are two notable buildings; the 1907 King Cromartie House and the adjacent 1905 New River Inn – the city's very first hotel. Both of these houses are now part of the Historical Society Museum.

> **FOR CHILDREN**
>
> Fort Lauderdale is an excellent family resort with superb beaches and the Museum of Discovery and Science, and keen swimmers can dip into one of two Olympic-sized pools at the International Swimming Hall of Fame.

▶ *Return to your car and head back the same way you came; east on SW 2nd Street, right onto S Andrews Avenue, then left onto East Las Olas Boulevard, passing the Museum of Art. After about half a mile (1km) you will see Stranahan House (behind Hyde Park supermarkets on Las Olas Boulevard) on the right.*

5 Stranahan House

Modern Fort Lauderdale began on this site in 1901 when Frank Stranahan built a remote trading post on the New River. A year later it had become Stranahan House, a homely pioneer residence, and today it remains the oldest house in Broward County, containing much original Victorian furniture, mementoes and photographs.

> **FOR HISTORY BUFFS**
>
> A decade after Frank Stranahan had established his trading post, there were still only 143 white settlers registered in the whole of Broward County's 1,200 square miles (3,108sq km). Stranahan traded with the Indians and on occasions allowed them to camp out under his veranda. Sadly he was ruined by a property crash in the 1920s and drowned himself in the New River.

2

Modern art for sale at one of the numerous galleries lining Las Olas Boulevard

▶ *Continue along East Las Olas Boulevard.*

6 Las Olas Boulevard

This exclusive Spanish-Colonial shopping street is nationally renowned for its jewelry, haute couture and art and antique galleries, which stretch as far as SE 26th. Until very recently the boulevard went to sleep at 6pm and didn't wake until the 'Shop Open' signs reappeared the following morning. Now, however, a whole clutch of sidewalk cafés and restaurants, jazz bars and nightspots have transformed the boulevard into Fort Lauderdale's answer to Rodeo Drive, Beverly Hills. For a romantic night out on the boulevard, take a horse-and-carriage ride to one of its fine restaurants and do some window shopping by gaslight after dinner.

SPECIAL TO...

Sawgrass Mills, 12 miles (19km) northwest of the center of town, on Sunrise Boulevard, is claimed to be the world's largest discount shopping mall covering some 2 million square feet with nine major stores (including J C Penney, Donna Karan and Saks), over 275 other outlets, plus food courts and entertainment. You can, of course, shop 'til you drop, but the sheer scale of this tropically themed center makes it a sight in its own right.

▶ *Head back towards the ocean and turn left on* **SR A1A**. *Turn left at Sunrise Boulevard, then left onto North Birch Road.*

7 Bonnet House

This fine Florida-style mansion was built in the 1920s by artist and art collector Frederick Clay Bartlett. The 30 lovely rooms open to the public contain an eclectic and unconventional treasure trove of fine and decorative art. Open by reserved tour only, (usually Wednesday to Friday 10am, 1pm and weekends 1pm, 2pm) tel: (954) 563–5393. The house sits in 35 beautiful acres (14 hectares), with their hardwood hammock, mangroves and freshwater lagoon which you can tour in a surrey.

▶ *Head south on* **SR A1A** *to return to the Bahia-Mar Yacht Center.*

SCENIC ROUTES

The most scenic routes in Fort Lauderdale are water-bound, so take a day's rest from driving and climb aboard a riverboat excursion. Another option is to take an official Water-Taxi and ask the captain to take you on one of his very own scenic routes. These small craft can navigate picturesque creeks and inlets which are off-limits to larger craft.

Palm Beach County
& the Treasure Coast

2 DAYS • 211 MILES • 342KM

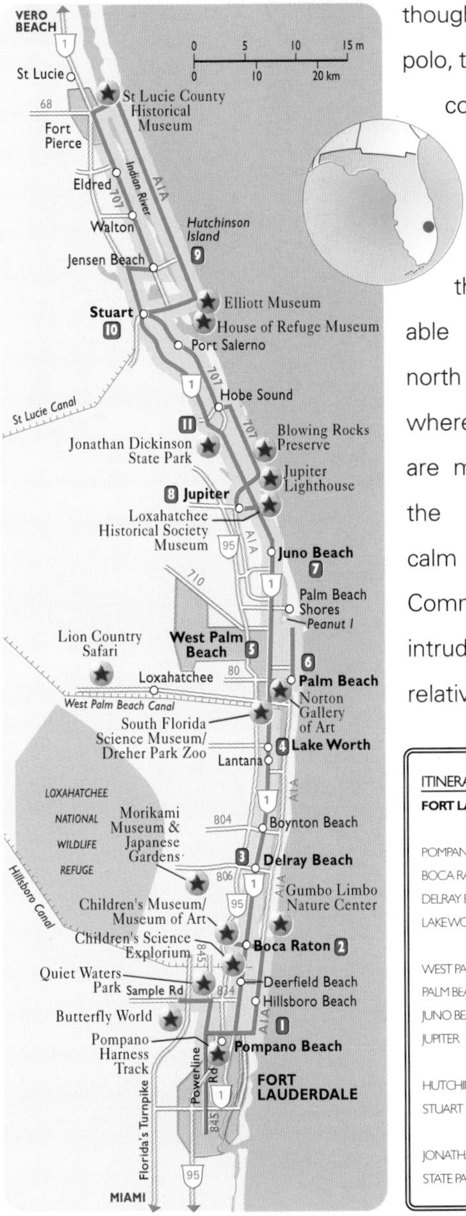

Mention Palm Beach and thoughts inevitably turn to polo, the 'beautiful people' and conspicuous consumption. Window-shopping and people-watching are free, however, and there are plenty of affordable attractions too. Head north to the Treasure Coast where the people and prices are more down-to-earth, yet the atmosphere is still calm and often elegant. Commercialism has yet to intrude in a big way along this relatively unknown stretch.

ITINERARY

FORT LAUDERDALE	▶ **Pompano Beach (6m-10km)**
POMPANO BEACH	▶ **Boca Raton (18m-29km)**
BOCA RATON	▶ **Delray Beach (8m-13km)**
DELRAY BEACH	▶ **Lake Worth (11m-18km)**
LAKE WORTH	▶ **West Palm Beach (6m-10km)**
WEST PALM BEACH	▶ **Palm Beach (2m-3km)**
PALM BEACH	**Juno Beach (8m-13km)**
JUNO BEACH	▶ **Jupiter (6m-10km)**
JUPITER	▶ **Hutchinson Island (24m-39km)**
HUTCHINSON ISLAND	▶ **Stuart (43m-69km)**
STUART	▶ **Jonathan Dickinson State Park (11m-18km)**
JONATHAN DICKINSON STATE PARK	▶ **Fort Lauderdale (68m-110km)**

Greater Fort Lauderdale Convention and Visitors Bureau, 1850 Eller Drive, Suite 303

▶ *From Fort Lauderdale head north either on Powerline Road* ***(SR 845)*** *or on the more scenic* ***AIA*** *for 6 miles (10km) to Atlantic Boulevard.*

1 Pompano Beach

The Pompano Harness Track offers the only opportunity in Florida to catch the elegant and exciting sport of harness racing (the harness, or sulky, is little more than a seat suspended between two wheels, and the race is carried out at a trot, not a gallop). Meetings starring the country's top drivers and horses are held from November through early April. Just north off Florida's Turnpike (SR 834) at W Sample Road is Butterfly World in Tradewinds Park. A lush indoor tropical rain forest has been created to house thousands of butterflies. Once inside, you will soon become part of this colorful world as its residents flutter around and settle on you (go in the afternoon to avoid school groups). There is also a hummingbird exhibit, botanical and water gardens, plus boat and bicycle rental.

Take W Sample Road east to where it rejoins Powerline Road. Watersports enthusiasts may wish to take a mile (1.5km) long diversion north to Quiet Waters Park, where – thanks to the Ski Rixen automatic cable-pull for water-skiing – the waters are rarely quiet. It is an excellent way to learn the sport and you can watch the more advanced skiers slalom, trick-ski and even ski barefoot. Return to Powerline Road and travel south towards Fort Lauderdale for 3 miles (5km) before turning left onto Atlantic Drive. Follow this east to the SR A1A coastal route and turn northwards. Towering above is the 136-foot (41m) skeletal steel tower of the Hillsboro Inlet lighthouse, built in 1907 (not open to the public).

▶ *Take* ***SR A1A*** *north through Deerfield Beach past its fishing pier.*

2 Boca Raton

The name of the city means 'mouth of the rat', and is a reference to the jagged rocks around the coast. This elegant, wealthy community was developed in the 1920s under the guidance of the colorful architect Addison Mizner and is distinguished by its fine Spanish Revival architecture. The highlight of Mizner's surviving work is the extravagant, huge pink Boca

Pastimes for the pampered – shopping at Mizner Park, Boca Raton, and polo at West Palm Beach

Raton Resort Hotel. This incorporates his famous 100-room Cloister Inn, built in 1926 as the last word in luxury. The whole complex advertized itself under the headline 'I am the greatest resort in the world.' There is a particularly well-kept beach here and a number of small museums to explore. Turn left on Park Road (SR 798), cross the bridge, then cross over US 1 to the Children's Museum (of Boca Raton at Singing Pines), with hands-on exhibits. A little further on is the Boca Raton Museum of Art.

Continue north on **US 1** *for 8 miles (13km).*

FOR CHILDREN

In addition to its Children's Museum, Boca Raton is also home to the Children's Science Explorium, where interactive exhibits provide hands-on fun and education for all ages.

3 Delray Beach

Similar in atmosphere to Boca Raton, this attractive resort has been kept deliberately low-key and low-rise. It too boasts a fine beach. Don't miss the beautiful Japanese art, culture and exotic plants at the peaceful Morikami Museum and Japanese Gardens (west on Atlantic Avenue/SR 806), a legacy of an early Japanese farming community.

RECOMMENDED WALKS

The best areas for walking on this tour are the relatively short nature trails at the Loxahatchee Refuge and the Gumbo Limbo Nature Center at Boca Raton. The latter is an Everglades-style boardwalk trail through dense tropical forest. The gumbo-limbo is a tree of Caribbean origin, nicknamed the 'tourist tree' because in summer its bark turns red and peels.

Continue north on **US 1** *through Boynton Beach and Lantana, and turn right at Lake Worth Road* **(SR 802),** *11 miles (18km).*

BACK TO NATURE

The Loxahatchee National Wildlife Refuge comprises over 221 square miles (572sq km) of unspoilt Everglades. Here you can see this beautiful wilderness from an airboat or you can hire your own motor boat or canoe.
There are two nature trails, one through a cypress swamp (look out for barrel owls), the other across a marsh to an observation tower. Bird watchers should look out for the rare snail kite, as well as rails, limpkins and herons, while anglers can enjoy some of the finest big bass fishing in the country. To get there take Atlantic Avenue (SR 806) west from Delray Beach.

Above: Whitehall, the great marble mansion built by Henry Morrison Flagler, served as a hotel from 1925 to 1959
Right: *Rambler*, Flagler's opulent personal railroad car, was built in 1886

4 Lake Worth

Cross the bridge and you will come to what is, according to locals, the best strip of sand in the whole Palm Beach area. Alternatively, check out the Palm Beach Community College Museum of Art (on Lake Avenue), featuring changing exhibitions of contemporary art.

▶ *Return to **US 1** and head north for 6 miles (10km).*

FOR CHILDREN

Lion Country Safari, on Southern Boulevard/SR 80, is the only self-drive safari park in Florida. Here over a thousand animals roam freely over 500 acres (200 hectares) of natural wildlife preserve. Close encounters with lions, elephants, rhinos, zebras, antelopes, giraffes, ostriches and inquisitive monkeys are all part of the excitement, but do remember to keep your windows wound up. An amusement park with rides, games, a petting zoo, a reptile exhibit, a river cruise and a nature trail completes the entertainment.

5 West Palm Beach

This is the mainland part of the famous city, originally built by Henry Flagler as a dormitory town for his railroad workers, and, compared to Palm Beach island, it is still relatively down-to-earth. Today it is a commercial center with a population of 70,000 and is the biggest city in the county. Before you reach downtown, just off US 1, is the South Florida Science Museum. Children can discover by touch in the Light and Sight Hall, explore the depths in the aquarium, chart the heavens in the observatory, enjoy an evening laser show and more. Adjacent is Dreher Park Zoo, where 22 acres (9 hectares) of lush botanical gardens are home to over

500 species of animals, and there is a boardwalk nature trail. Return to US 1 and continue north to the Norton Gallery of Art. This is one of America's most highly rated small museums. The core of the collection is major works by French Impressionists and modern masters including such artists as Monet, Gauguin, Matisse, Braque and Pollock. Priceless Chinese jades and bronzes and important sculptures by the likes of Moore, Picasso and Degas, set in a lovely patio garden, complete this outstanding gallery. You can see more outdoor sculptures and works of art at the Ann Norton Sculpture Gardens, half a mile (1km) south.

i Palm Beach County Convention and Visitor's Bureau, 1555 Palm Beach Lakes Boulevard

▶ *Continue north and turn right onto Royal Palm Way.*

6 Palm Beach

The stately colonnade of Royal Palm Way is a fitting processional route into one of the world's most monied communities. Turn left on Cocoanut Row to see the home of Henry Morrison Flagler, who created Palm Beach by bringing his railroad to southern Florida. Whitehall was the 73-room mansion that Flagler gave to his third wife as a wedding present in 1901, and since 1959 it has functioned as the Henry Morrison Flagler Museum. Its palatial great halls, music room, billiards room, library, dining rooms and bedrooms are decorated in historic European styles and give an idea of the lifestyle enjoyed in that pioneering era by Flagler and such illustrious guests as the Vanderbilts, Woodrow Wilson, John Jacob Astor and William Rockefeller. This is also the perfect place to learn more about the Florida East Coast Railroad, and you can even board Flagler's personal railroad car, 'Rambler'.

Continue on Cocoanut Row to Royal Poinciana Plaza. Among the exclusive shops here – a foretaste of Worth Avenue – is the Hibel Museum of Art. The only public non-profit gallery in the country dedicated to a living woman artist, it features the work of Edna Hibel, famous for her humanitarian efforts. Continue north, past the elegant Palm Beach Biltmore (now condominiums), built in 1927 at a cost of $7 million. The road becomes Lake Way, and parallel to it the Palm Beach Bicycle Trail runs for almost 5 miles (8km). The mansions along this route are some of the finest and most expensive in the county, and the trail is known as 'the world's most beautiful cycle path'. Continue to the end of the island and glance across to Peanut Island. Here is the site of the Kennedy's atomic bomb shelter, built during the Cuban missile crisis.

Return south on Ocean Boulevard. Just past the junction with Royal Poinciana Way – Palm Beach's other regal entrance route – is the beautiful church of Bethesda-by-the-Sea, built in 1927. Next is The Breakers, the legendary hotel built by Flagler in Italian Renaissance style in 1926 and still one of the benchmarks of high society today. On Sundays non-residents can sample The Breakers' lifestyle at the Beach Club Champagne Brunch, said to be the biggest in the state. Continue to the eastern end of Worth Avenue. This is one of the world's great shopping streets where Cartier, Hermes, Chanel, Gucci and Saks Fifth Avenue are just everyday names among the 250 or so glittering stores on and around the avenue. However, it is not just the names and prices that make Worth Avenue great – it is the atmosphere created by the manicured palms, the beautiful Addison Mizner Spanish-style architecture and the quaint, not to mention outrageously expensive shops and cafés tucked away in tiny alleyways.

FOR HISTORY BUFFS

The Breakers, probably the most famous hotel in Florida, encapsulates the pioneering spirit of the early days on the East Coast. A guided tour of the hotel is conducted every Wednesday. Tales of Flagler's legendary East Coast Railroad are, of course, de rigeur, but you will also hear about the hotel's use during Prohibition and how it served briefly as a hostel during World War II.

▶ *Cross back to the mainland by Royal Palm Way, turn right onto **US 1** and continue north for 8 miles (13km).*

Making friends with a turtle at the Loggerhead Park Marine Life Center, Juno Beach

7 Juno Beach

Juno, Jupiter and Jensen Beaches are all nesting grounds for sea turtles, and at the Loggerhead Park Marine Life Center in Juno Beach you can learn more about their habits. The center also features aquariums and various exhibits on local coastal life.

▶ *Take **US 1** north, turning left to Jupiter.*

8 Jupiter

The Jupiter Theatre was donated to the community by its most famous son, actor Burt Reynolds. Opened in 1979, it regularly plays host to stars of Broadway and Hollywood. Head west to US 1, turn right onto Jupiter Island and visit the Loxahatchee Historical Society Museum. You can't miss the bright red Jupiter Lighthouse, looming 105 feet (32m) above you. Completed in 1859, it is the county's oldest structure (open Sunday afternoons). Take SR 707 north to Blowing Rocks Preserve, a beachfront nature reserve of some 73 acres (30 hectares). At high tide, particularly during storms, the breaking waves are forced up through fissures and holes in the limestone rocks and 'blow' upwards creating dramatic plumes.

▶ *Continue north on **SR 707** through Jupiter Island and rejoin the mainland. Continue north to Stuart and turn right onto Hutchinson Island.*

9 Hutchinson Island

At the southern end of the island lies the (Gilbert's Bar) House of Refuge Museum (open 11am to 4.15 pm daily). The House of Refuge was built in 1875 to function as a coastguard station, including a lookout tower and dormitory accommodation for up to 24 shipwreck survivors. It is the only one of its kind left in Florida. The dormitory is closed to the public, but you can see the prettily restored rooms where the keeper and his wife lived. The old boathouse is now the front desk area, and there is a small aquarium below. Adjacent are picturesque rocky coves and a sandy beach, while just south of here is Bathtub Beach, a favorite bathing spot for families. A mile (1.5km) to the north of the House of Refuge is the eclectic and colorful Elliott Museum (11am to 4pm daily) which includes antique American shopfronts, period parlors from all over the world, and a fine collection of vintage cars. Follow the road north to the St Lucie County Historical Museum. Here you can see artifacts relating to Spanish shipwrecks and Seminole Indians, and a guide will take you round the adjacent 1907 Gardner House.

▶ *Cross over to the mainland and turn left, heading south on* **US 1**. *Pass through Fort Pierce and follow* **SR 707** *south, to Jensen Beach. Turn right to rejoin* **US1** *and head south.*

10 Stuart

The compact downtown area of this former fishing village has been renewed and revived with antique shops, specialty stores, the Court House Cultural Center and the Stuart Heritage Museum.

▶ *Continue south on* **US 1**.

11 Jonathan Dickinson State Park

At over 10,000 acres (4,047 hectares) this is one of south Florida's largest parks. The wild and scenic Loxahatchee River runs through the park, whose abundant wildlife, particularly birds, flourishes in a diversity of ecosystems. Ranger-guided tours and trips aboard the 30-seater *Loxahatchee Queen* are run year-round. Canoes and rowboats are available for rent.

▶ *Continue south on* **US 1** *to return to Fort Lauderdale.*

The landmark Jupiter lighthouse

CENTRAL GULF COAST

This is Florida's fastest growing tourist region, and comparisons with the rival traditional destinations of Miami and the Gold Coast are inevitable. Around a century ago both coasts were being developed apace by the two great railroad pioneers of the day, Henry Morrison Flagler and Henry Bradley Plant. As Flagler built his splendid Spanish-Mediterranean piles from St Augustine to Palm Beach, so Plant saw the potential on the west coast, brought his tracks south from Virginia, and created the magnificent Moorish-style Tampa Bay Hotel.

In 1891 Henry Plant sent an invitation to his rival to attend the grand opening of his new hotel in Tampa. Flagler's reply simply read 'Where's Tampa?' As far as the development of Florida went, Flagler again had the last word, for while Plant's tracks went no further south, Flagler's stretched the entire length of the Atlantic Coast.

It was not until the development of Busch Gardens in the last two decades that tourists have stopped asking 'Where's Tampa?' These days, however, the city of Tampa has much more to offer the visitor than just Busch Gardens, and the central west coast resorts, which stretch from Clearwater to Sarasota, have a number of advantages over their long-established east-coast counterparts; the beaches are better, the sea is warmer, the sunsets are more glorious and the climate is near perfect. Man-made attractions are almost as numerous as those on the east, while man-made intrusions (most notably, ugly canyons of condominiums) are far less common. Best of all for families, prices are lower here.

The first *Conquistadores* landed on the west coast in 1539, near Bradenton

The atmosphere on the Gulf Coast is also more relaxed and less fashion-conscious than the east coast. TV crews and fashion photographers will never beat a path to the west coast as they do to Miami Beach, but there are also few of the problems here that sadly come with that type of fast and glitzy life-style. But don't think for one moment that the Gulf Coast is all pensioners on park benches and children toting sand buckets. St Pete and Clearwater each have a bustling nightlife, while Sarasota is as stylish and attractive an all-round resort as you will find anywhere in the state. In summary, the Central Gulf Coast contains a little of everything required for a good vacation and, for most families, a perfect package.

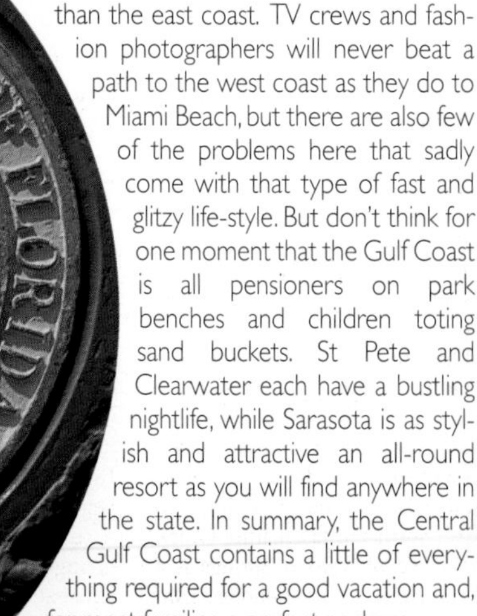

St Pete Beach is a broad, straight band of soft white sand, ideal for a relaxing break

Tour 12

The tour starts with the coastal vacation area known as the Pinellas. This is fast becoming the most popular choice among European holidaymakers for the second week of suntanning (after the obligatory week at Orlando) in the typical Florida family vacation. Clearwater and St Pete Beach are the best-equipped resorts, offering excellent beaches and plenty to do for all ages, both day and night. To the north the fascinating Greek enclave of Tarpon Springs is a unique day out in a sponge-fishing community.

Tour 13

Most Pinellas sun worshippers will take a day or two off the beach to explore the town of St Petersburg, if only to shop at the new malls and The Pier. The town is quiet, pleasant and almost belies its outstanding art galleries. The Salvador Dalí Museum could well turn out to be the most unexpected highlight of a whole fortnight in Florida.

Tour 14

Tampa is quite a contrast to St Petersburg, with its skyscrapers, central business district, diverse industries and ethnic influences, giving it the feel of a big city. As a magnet for tourism Tampa has long been associated with Busch Gardens, but with the revitalization of Ybor City and other major recent developments, it is beginning to woo tourists in its own right.

Tour 15

Across the magnificent Sunshine Skyway bridge it would seem that the only factor preventing Sarasota breaking into the big league of tourism is its lack of children's attractions. Aside from this it has wonderful beaches, the priceless Ringling complex, sophisticated shopping and dining and a cultural program that is second to none. For those who do not have to worry about amusing the children, it is a very attractive proposition.

TOUR
12

The Pinellas Suncoast

ITINERARY	
ST PETE BEACH	▶ **Treasure Island (4m-6km)**
TREASURE ISLAND	▶ **Madeira Beach (3m-5km)**
MADEIRA BEACH	▶ **Clearwater Beach (14m-23km)**
CLEARWATER BEACH	▶ **Dunedin (5m-8km)**
DUNEDIN	▶ **Tarpon Springs (8m-13km)**
TARPON SPRINGS	▶ **Boatyard Village (20m-32km)**
BOATYARD VILLAGE	▶ **Heritage Village (9m-14km)**
HERITAGE VILLAGE	▶ **St Pete Beach (15m-24km)**

2 DAYS • 78 MILES • 125KM With an average of 361 days sunshine per year, the Pinellas coast is not only the sunniest place on earth but also boasts some 28 miles (45km) of clean, safe white sand beaches. No wonder, then, that it is the most popular holiday destination on the west coast of Florida, particularly for families. Clearwater is the busiest beach and has the liveliest nightlife.

St Pete Beach Chamber of Commerce, 6990 Gulf Boulevard

Head north on Gulf Boulevard for 4 miles (6km).

SPECIAL TO...

There is no single outstanding festival in the Pinellas calendar, but the following are all recommended: April – Fun 'n' Sun in Clearwater, a carnival with a 40-year-old tradition; June – Sandcastle Contest on St Pete Beach, to witness some amazing sand creations: first week in July – Pirate Days and Invasion at Treasure Island; last weekend in October – John's Pass Seafood Festival, including music, arts and crafts.

1 Treasure Island/John's Pass Village

This area of beach – named for its long association with pirates – is slightly quieter than St Pete Beach and is about half its size, with older low-rise accommodation. Just across the bridge to Madeira Beach is John's Pass Village and Boardwalk. This old-time reconstruction of a 'fishermen's village' comprises some 60 ramshackle-looking tin-roofed wooden structures housing restaurants, shops and galleries, linked by a boardwalk perched high above the water. Fishing is both an important industry and a tourist attraction here, and boats can be chartered. If you prefer a pleasure cruise, the *Europa Fun Kruz* will take you out by day or night.

Treasure Island Chamber of Commerce, 152 108th Avenue

Continue on Gulf Boulevard for 3 miles (5km).

2 Madeira Beach/Suncoast Seabird Sanctuary

The name Madeira is derived from *madera*, referring (like *pinellas*) to pine woods. This long coastal stretch of some 7 miles (11km) is the least interesting of the Holiday Isles, with large characterless hotels and high-rise condominiums. Redington Pier, stretching over 1,000 feet (305m) into the Gulf, makes a welcome punctuation mark and is very popular with fishing folk. The Suncoast Seabird Sanctuary is certainly worth a visit. This is the largest wild bird hospital in the country, rehabilitating and releasing some 15 to 20 birds per day. Those that cannot survive on their own become residents; these can number up to 500, of which around a third are usually pelicans. Ask the staff what time the day's 'outpatients' are to be discharged and watch them return to the wild.

FOR HISTORY BUFFS

Fort De Soto, named after the Spanish discoverer of this coast, was built in 1898 to protect the Gulf shipping lanes during the Spanish-American War. Its intervention was never required, however. The Gulf Beaches Historical Museum at St Pete Beach will also show you that this strip has an interesting history.

St John's Pass Village is fun for shopping, strolling and watching (or boarding) the boats

"Welcome to Clearwater"
GUARDS
GULF TEMP.
TIDES-H-L.
WEATHER
NOTICE
LIFEGUARD ON DUTY
44

i *The Gulf Beaches Chamber of Commerce, 501 150th Avenue, Madeira Beach*

▶ *Continue north and cross the Clearwater Pass causeway, 14 miles (23km).*

3 Clearwater Beach

Clearwater is the liveliest of the Pinellas beaches, popular with young couples and teenagers, and is stocked with all the usual beachside facilities for their enjoyment. A number of cruises depart from Clearwater Beach Marina, and among these is Captain Memo's Pirate Cruise. Decorated and themed in buccaneer fashion the *Sea Hogge* cruises the scenic Intracoastal Waterway and sails out into the Gulf.

Turn east towards the mainland on the Garden Memorial Causeway (SR 60), turn left at Island Way, then left onto Windward Passage and continue for two blocks to the Clearwater Marine Aquarium. This coastal research station is dedicated to the rescue and rehabilitation of stranded sea mammals, otters and turtles. Among other residents you can meet Sam the bottle-nosed dolphins, and Big Mo, a 400-pound (180kg) loggerhead turtle. Return to the Memorial Causeway and continue east to US 19 (Alt). If you would like to see one of Florida's grandest hotels, make a diversion by turning right onto Fort Harrison Avenue US 19 (Alt), drive south 1 mile (1.5km) and turn right onto Belleview Boulevard. The Belleview Biltmore, creation of Henry B Plant (see Tampa), opened its ornate doors in 1897. It is claimed to be the world's largest lived-in wooden structure (the roof covers 2½ acres/1 hectare).

The sumptuous interior features Tiffany glass and crystal chandeliers and the guest list once included the Duke of Windsor. Renovated in recent times by its Japanese owners, it is now known as the Belleview Mido.

i *Clearwater Visitor Welcome Center, 40 Causeway Boulevard*

▶ *Turn right and continue north for 5 miles (8km) to the junction with Main Street **(SR 580).***

4 Dunedin

The Gaelic accent to this small old-fashioned town comes from its Scottish founders. The bagpipes can still be heard on the first Sunday of each month, and every March/April a festival of Highland Games is staged. Dunedin is also famous locally for its antiques shops and its romantically named offshore islands, Honeymoon and Caladesi (the latter meaning 'beautiful bayou'). You can drive to Honeymoon Island but for Caladesi Island you will have to catch the passenger ferry as no cars are allowed. It's worth the effort, however, if you're a sun-and-sand lover; in 1995 Caladesi Island was rated the third best beach in the entire US.

i *Chamber of Commerce, 301 Main Street*

▶ *Continue north for 8 miles (13km) to Tarpon Springs.*

5 Tarpon Springs

'America's Sponge Capital' really took off around 1905 with the discovery of high-quality sponge beds in the Gulf of

FOR CHILDREN

This whole area is geared for children, but for a change from sea 'n' sand try the Moccasin Lake Nature Park on Park Trail Lane. This is a wildlife preserve with several small animal exhibits, and an interpretive center.

Left: lifeguard on duty. Even paradise has its dangers
Below: soaking up the sun on the golden beach at Clearwater

BACK TO NATURE

Caladesi Island State Park is one of Florida's few undeveloped barrier islands. On the harbor side a mangrove swamp provides refuge for wading and shore birds, while the interior is virgin pine and oak hammocks. A 3-mile (5km) self-guided nature trail leads through here to an observation tower. Snowy egrets, herons, armadillos and 'gators are often seen along here.

Mexico quite close by. Expert Greek sponge-fishermen and divers were recruited from Key West and from Greece itself, and by the 1930s Tarpon Springs had become the biggest

Sponge shaping (below) and sponge shopping (right); ideal as gifts – useful, light and a bargain

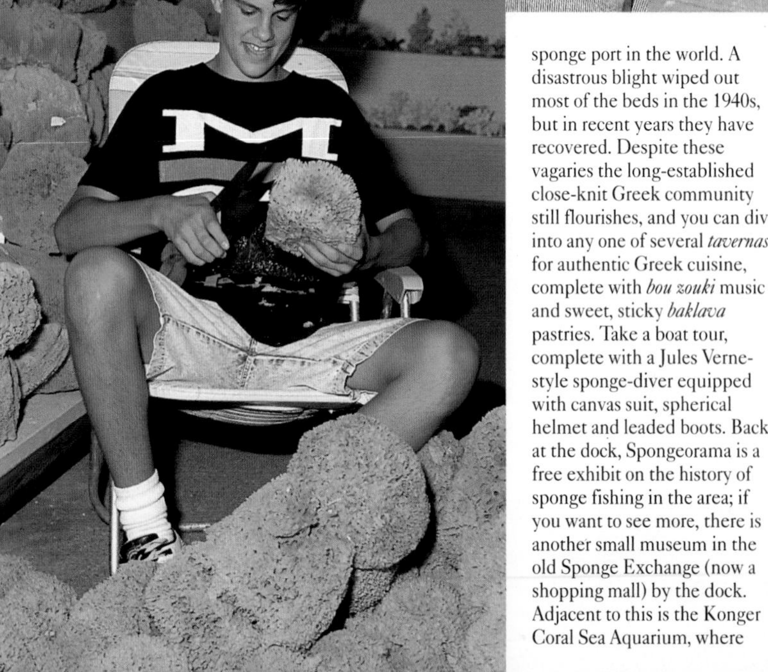

sponge port in the world. A disastrous blight wiped out most of the beds in the 1940s, but in recent years they have recovered. Despite these vagaries the long-established close-knit Greek community still flourishes, and you can dive into any one of several *tavernas* for authentic Greek cuisine, complete with *bou zouki* music and sweet, sticky *baklava* pastries. Take a boat tour, complete with a Jules Verne-style sponge-diver equipped with canvas suit, spherical helmet and leaded boots. Back at the dock, Spongeorama is a free exhibit on the history of sponge fishing in the area; if you want to see more, there is another small museum in the old Sponge Exchange (now a shopping mall) by the dock. Adjacent to this is the Konger Coral Sea Aquarium, where

huge open-air tanks teem with indigenous sea creatures and exotic species from the Caribbean Sea. You can take an interesting self-guided tour of Tarpon Springs by picking up a leaflet from the town's cultural center.

On your way out of town, stop on the main road to admire the marbled interior of the Greek Orthodox Church of St Nicholas, built in 1943 as a replica of the Byzantine church of Haghia Sophia in Istanbul. The highlight of the Tarpon Springs year is the Epiphany Celebration (6 January) when some 40,000 locals and visitors mark this religious festival with a feast of Greek food, wine, music and dancing.

[i] *Chamber of Commerce, 210 South Pinellas Avenue, US 19 (Alt)*

Instant heritage; even Disney would be proud of the rustic charm created at Boatyard Village

SCENIC ROUTES

The Sunshine Skyway is a suspension bridge finished in 1987 at a cost of $244 million. It measures 4.1 miles (6.6km) long and is suspended 183 feet (56m) above the water. The old bridge collapsed in 1980 with the loss of 30 lives after being rammed by a boat. It is currently being converted into Florida's longest fishing pier. Take the Sunshine Skyway for an excursion; returning in the evening you can admire the illuminated cables soaring high above you.

▶ *South of Tarpon Springs turn left onto* **SR 584** *and turn right to join* **US 19** *southbound. Continue for around 13 miles (21km) and turn left onto Roosevelt Boulevard* **(SR 686)**. *Turn left at 49th Street, then take the first right.*

6 Boatyard Village

Boatyard Village, at Tampa Bay, looks exactly like an authentic turn-of-the-century New England-style fishing village. In fact it is a clever re-creation, built of aged wood and tin from around the country. Within the rustic alleyways and rambling boardwalks you will find some fine shops, atmospheric restaurants and a theater.

▶ *Return to 49th Street and head south. Turn right on Ulmerton Road* **(SR 688)** *and continue for 5 miles (8km). Two blocks west of Missouri Boulevard/***US 19 (Alt 19)** *turn left onto 125th Street.*

7 Heritage Village

Twenty-one of the county's oldest structures have been brought to this 21-acre (8-hectare) leafy pine and palm park to give you an idea of what an early settlement may have looked like in its entirety. Visit the small museum to learn about Pinellas County history, then join a period-dressed guide who will show you around the properties. These include a railway station, a store, a church and the oldest surviving log house in Pinellas County. Basic pioneer skills such as spinning and weaving are often demonstrated.

▶ *Return one block east to Ridge Road, turn right and head south for 5 miles (8km) to Madeira Causeway/Bay Pines Boulevard,* **US 19 (Alt 19)**. *Turning right will take you back to the coast road and St Pete Beach; turning left will take you into the town of St Petersburg.*

TOUR
13

Around St Petersburg

The idyllic climate of St Pete (as the city is fondly known) has for many years attracted retired folks, but these days the city is in buoyant mood, capitalising on the Pinellas holiday trade. It features a lively pier, major new sports and retail complexes, and three outstanding museums – including the world-famous Salvador Dalì Museum featuring the world's largest collection of the king of the surrealists. Nevertheless, it remains at heart a quiet place, and makes a welcome break from the hustle and bustle of the beach.

1/2 DAYS

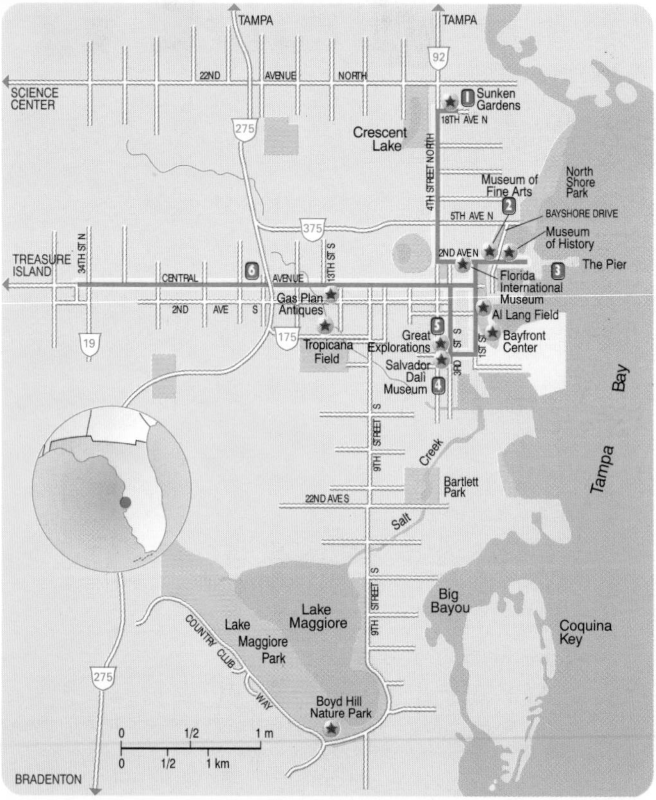

Replica of the *Bounty*, built in 1962 for MGM

i *Chamber of Commerce, 100 2nd Avenue North*

► *Start your tour at Sunken Gardens, driving due east from the beaches via 22nd Avenue North as far as 4th Street North, then south to 18th Avenue North.*

1 Sunken Gardens

These 5 acres (2 hectares) of luxurious tropical gardens are landscaped around a sinkhole and shallow lake, hence the name. Some 50,000 flowers (around 5,000 species) and rare orchids are planted here annually, and there are over 500 exotic birds and animals to admire with 'gator and bird shows. The walk-through aviary is a highlight of this tranquil spot.

► *Drive south on 4th Street North to 2nd Avenue North and turn left. Drop by the Chamber of Commerce (corner of 1st Street), and continue to Bayshore Drive and park your car.*

2 Museum of Fine Arts

This outstanding collection is housed in a handsome Palladian/ Mediterranean-style building near the Pier. Among the museum's most important holdings are outstanding European, pre-Columbian, ancient and Far Eastern art, contemporary photographs and complete Jacobean and Georgian rooms. The gallery of French Impressionism and the brilliantly displayed Steuben crystal are perennial favorites, while the traveling exhibits are frequently of international caliber. Take a free guided tour to get the most from your visit.

► *Walk along 2nd Avenue towards The Pier, noting 'Comfort Station Number 1' built in 1927.*

3 St Petersburg Museum of History/Florida International Museum/The Pier

Local and state history is covered in the tiny St Petersburg Museum, though there are some interesting larger exhibits such as Egyptian mummies and a replica of the world's first commercial airliner (which flew between St Pete and Tampa). Before you catch the complimentary trolley bus to The Pier, check out the much larger Florida International Museum, a short walk away on 2nd Street North. This hosts grand touring exhibitions, on loan from some of the world's finest museums. The Pier is a complex of specialty shops, restaurants and an aquarium housed in a five-story inverted pyramid. There are fine views from the observation platform, and in winter (November to May) HMS *Bounty* docks here.

► *Drive back onto 2nd Avenue North, turn left on 1st Street, past Al Lang Field (spring training camp of the St Louis Cardinals) and the multi-purpose Bayfront Center. Continue straight on as far as possible, to 7th Avenue South, then right, then next left onto 3rd Street South.*

4 Salvador Dalì Museum

Whatever your preconceptions may be of the work of the flawed genius, do not miss a visit to this intriguing collection. Free guided tours will take you through Dalì's earliest (quite conventional) works to the brilliant precision *trompe l'oeil* and double-image techniques of his surrealist period. You will also learn the meaning of his unforgettable 'soft watches' and lots more about his bizarre imagery. There is a total of 93 oils, over 100 watercolours and hundreds more works, displayed on a rotating basis. Most people's favorites are his 'masterworks', the five works that occupied him for a year or more and measure at least 5 feet (1.5m) in any one direction.

▶ *Turn left outside the museum and walk across the street.*

5 Great Explorations

All ages can explore this fascinating hands-on facility that focuses on the arts, science and personal health. Phenomenal

Different perspectives: a brilliant *trompe-l'oeil* painting by Salvador Dalì (left), and St Petersburg's famous 'inverted' pier (below)

Arts creates high-tech artistry by touch or audio-activation, the Touch Tunnel is a pitch-black maze for children to negotiate, and the Body Shop measures your fitness level. Avoid weekday mornings when school field trips arrive.

FOR CHILDREN

Great Explorations is the area's best hands-on discovery center, but the Science Center of Pinellas County may also provide a rewarding visit for older children with enquiring minds.

▶ *Return to your car, drive back north along 3rd Street for seven blocks and turn left.*

6 Central Avenue

St Petersburg's former main street is an interesting mixture of renovated 1920s buildings and modern developments. Seven blocks west of the front is Gas Plant Antiques which boasts the biggest collection of antiques and collectibles on the west coast of Florida. From here you can see the landmark Tropicana Field. This state-of-the-art sports and entertainment arena, home to the Tampa Devil Rays baseball team, is the first domed stadium in Florida, and if no event is in progress you are welcome to look inside.

▶ *Central Avenue leads directly west to Treasure Island.* ***SR 693,*** *off Central Avenue, leads to St Pete Beach.*

The candy-pink Don CeSar on St Pete Beach, built in 1927 in whimsical Moorish-Mediterranean style

TOUR
14

Tampa

Tampa is not only the regional business center, it boasts the country's seventh-largest seaport and is home to Busch Gardens, the best theme park in the west. Other first-rate attractions are Lowry Zoo, MOSI and the splendid new Florida Aquarium. Ybor City, the old cigar capital, is a preserved and revived district with good restaurants, bars and nightlife.

2 DAYS

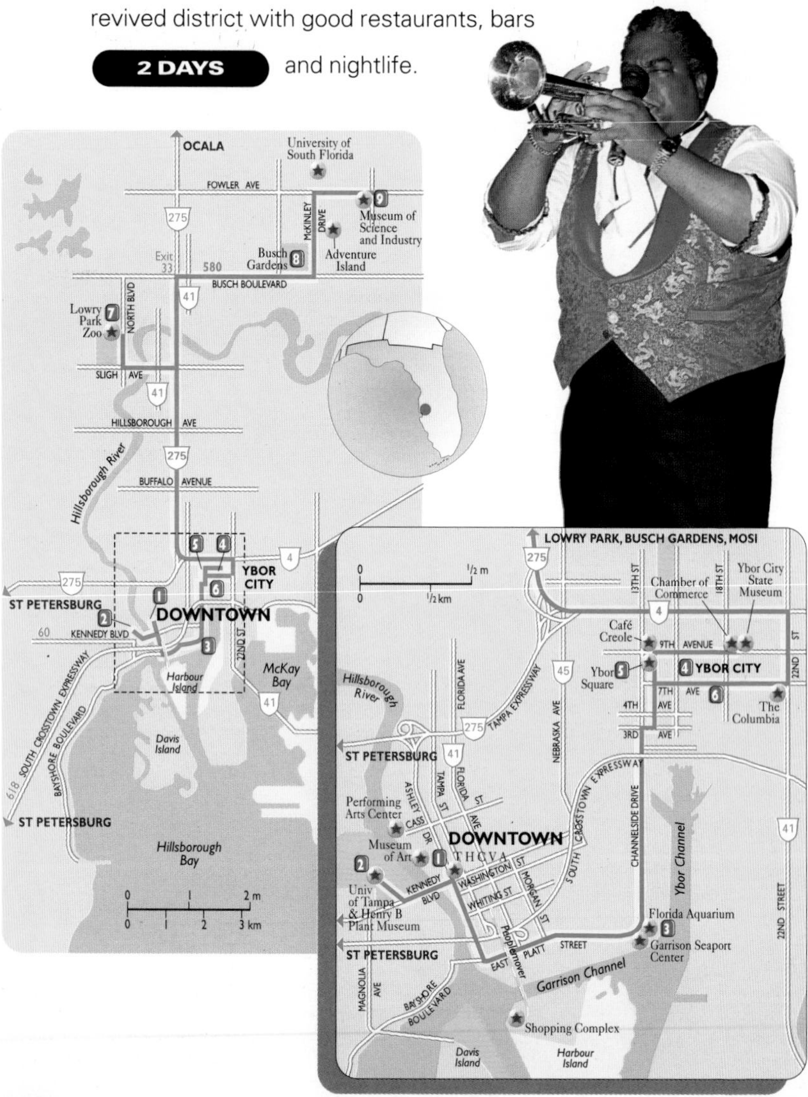

Downtown Tampa and *Fire Sticks* sculpture, as seen from the University

[i] *Tampa/Hillsborough Convention and Visitors Association (THCVA), 111 Madison Street*

SPECIAL TO...

In late January/early February the clock is turned back for a buccaneering festival, featuring an attack by the triple-masted galleon *Jose Gaspar*, and parades and concerts.

▶ *Downtown is easily accessible from* **I–275** *(exit 25, Ashley Drive) or the Crosstown Expressway (Florida Avenue exit). Park below the Tampa Museum of Art.*

1 Downtown

Tampa Museum of Art is acclaimed for one of the finest collections of Roman and Greek antiquities in the US. It also stages some high-quality touring exhibitions. Almost adjacent is the Tampa Bay Performing Arts Center, a magnificent state-of-the-art complex which stages world-class productions.

▶ *Turn right out of the museum and walk across the bridge.*

2 University Of Tampa/Henry B Plant Museum

Set in the beautifully landscaped gardens of the university is an amazing Moorish structure with 13 'onion-domed' silver minarets, each crowned with a crescent moon. This was originally the Tampa Bay Hotel, built in Arabian style by Henry B Plant in 1890, at a staggering cost of $2 million. Touring the world in search of furniture and art treasures for the hotel, Plant spent another $1 million. The hotel shut down in 1929, and the University of Tampa acquired the building in 1933. A museum set up in one wing exhibits Plant's sumptuous collection, and re-creates the hotel's glorious heyday.

▶ *Return to your car, drive south as far as you can go and turn east (left) onto Platt Street which becomes Channelside Drive.*

3 Florida Aquarium

The Florida Aquarium is one of the largest and most impressive aquariums in the United States. It offers a spectacular ecological voyage through Florida's wetlands, bays, beaches, coral reefs and oceans. Its upper galleries are light, airy and large-scale, set under a futuristic glass canopy while its huge tanks bring you eye to eye with the state's colorful marine life.

Look for beautiful Spanish *azulejos* (glazed tiles) in Ybor City

► *Continue north on Channelside Drive for about 1 mile (1.6km), then follow the road right into 4th Avenue. Take the first turn left into Avenida Republica de Cuba/14th Street. Continue north for six blocks, turn right onto 9th Avenue and head east for five blocks to 18th–19th Street.*

4 Ybor City

Start your tour of this historic district on 9th Avenue at the Ybor City State Museum, housed in the 1923 Ferlita Bakery (closed Sunday and Monday). This will give you a thorough introduction to the history of this colorful, predominantly Cuban community and its cigar-making industry. Free walking tours depart from here at 10.30am every Thursday and Saturday (also Tuesday January–April). Adjacent are six renovated turn-of-the-century cigarworkers' houses. One of these is open as a small museum, another houses the Ybor City Chamber of Commerce, which provides tourist information. Drive west along 9th Avenue for five blocks and directly across the road (Avenida Republica de Cuba) is the Spanish-American architecture of the former El Pasaje Hotel (now housing the Café Creole), built in 1896. Turn left and park at any of the three lots around the adjacent block which features Ybor Square.

5 Ybor Square

This impressive complex comprises three enormous three-story brick buildings, erected in 1886; the warehouse, the factory and the stemmery (where leaves and stems were separated). Collectively it was the world's largest cigar factory and for some 40 years employed around 4,000 workers. Today it is a fashionable dining and shopping complex. Of special note among the many specialty and antique stores is the Tampa Rico Cigar Company ('Thank You For Smoking'), which preserves the tradition of hand-rolling cigars.

► *Drive one block south to 7th Avenue and turn left.*

6 Ybor City Seventh Avenue

As the main street of Ybor City, 7th Avenue contains several historic buildings. Opposite each other on the corner of 15th Street are two survivors from 1917; Las Novedades, once a famous restaurant, and the superb Ritz Theater. Both now house nightclubs. Look out too for the 1914 Italian Club, on 18th Street. Four blocks down is one of the oldest and most famous restaurants in Florida, The Columbia, founded in 1905. It is both an aesthetic and gastronomic delight with ornate tilework inside and out, superb Spanish/Cuban food and famous flamenco dancing.

► *Head east on 7th Avenue to 22nd Street. Head north and turn left onto **I–4**, west. Bear right onto **I–275** north. Exit at Sligh Avenue, head west and turn right onto North Boulevard.*

7 Lowry Park Zoo

Recently renovated and lushly landscaped, this delightful zoo displays its residents in as near-to-natural settings as is possible. Boardwalks criss-cross the zoo giving excellent viewing. The highlights are a free-flight aviary with over 65 subtropical species of birds; Primate World; Asian Domain, including an extremely rare and very impressive Indian rhino, plus Sumatran tigers and Manatee Aquatic Center.

FOR CHILDREN

Kids love Busch Gardens and Adventure Island. However, if you have young children in tow and don't want to spend the whole day and/or a lot of money, then Lowry Park Zoo is an excellent alternative. The animals here are superbly presented, and there is also a petting zoo.

► *Return east to join **I–275**. Head north for 2 miles (3km), turn off at exit 33 (Busch Boulevard/**SR 580**) and continue for 2 miles (3km) to McKinley Drive (40th Street).*

8 Busch Gardens

Busch Gardens is the biggest and best theme park in Florida outside Orlando with some thrilling white-knuckle rides and cleverly themed areas which take you all over Africa – from Tut's Tomb to the intriguing architecture of Timbuktu. It also has the state's largest collection of animals, numbering over 2,800, several hundred of which wander freely across the 60-acre (24-hectare) Serengeti Plain which may be viewed by train, monorail, sky ride or special jeep safari (additional charge). Edge of Africa is an ingenious foot-safari adventure with several close encounters. More conventional creature shows are provided by the World of Birds and Dolphins of the Deep. The most impressive habitat is the Great Ape Domain where you can see chimpanzees and gorillas in a humid, misty tropical setting.

The park is also famous for its four roller-coasters, each one fiercer than the last. The latest is Montu, the world's tallest and longest inverted roller-coaster, soaring at over 60mph (96kph) – around the same speed as the park's Kumba, the largest and fastest conventional coaster in the southeast US.

Water rides are another Busch specialty with the Congo River Rapids, the Tanganyika Tidal Wave and the Stanley Falls Log Flume all making a very big splash (bring or buy a cheap plastic poncho to save a drenching!) There's plenty more to see and do with lots of live shows and the Land of the Dragons special fun area for little ones. Allow at least a day.

Opposite is Adventure Island, an excellent water park, which has enough thrills and spills for a good half day (open weekends only September and October; closed November to late March).

► *Continue north on McKinley Drive to Fowler Avenue. Turn right and head east.*

9 Museum of Science and Industry (MOSI)

This is Florida's largest science center featuring over 450 hands-on activities. Its latest claim to fame is the first IMAX Dome Theater in the state, opened in 1995. This is an 85-foot (26m) IMAX screen domed for an even greater cinematic effect. Other educational thrills include the Gulf Coast Hurricane, where you can be buffeted by 75mph (121km/h) winds in safety; Energy Pinball, where you can follow the country's largest pinball through a 700 foot (213m) journey, and Lightning Lab.

► *Return to downtown.*

SCENIC ROUTES

The 6-mile (10km) sidewalk of Bayshore Boulevard, on the other side of the Hillsborough River from downtown Tampa, is said to be the world's longest continuous walkway. You can walk it, but a slow drive with its fine views of Hillsborough Bay is much more preferable. At the north end of the boulevard, you can cross to elegant Davis Island, a residential neighborhood built on three man-made islands in the 1920s.

Trapped in the 1,200-foot (365m) long coils of the Python – and this is one of the less scary of Busch Gardens' famous roller-coasters!

Sarasota & Manatee Counties

Circus magnate John Ringling established Sarasota as a center for the arts with his own magnificent collection and the city continues to thrive as a major cultural center. Its greatest riches, however, are its exquisite beaches, comprising the finest white sand in the world.

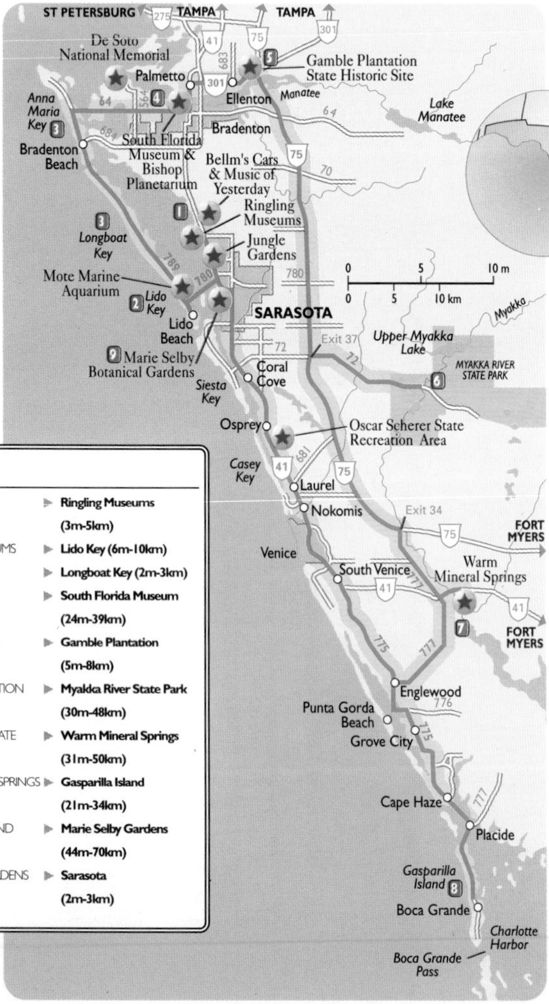

ITINERARY

SARASOTA	▶ **Ringling Museums (3m-5km)**
RINGLING MUSEUMS	▶ **Lido Key (6m-10km)**
LIDO KEY	▶ **Longboat Key (2m-3km)**
LONGBOAT KEY	▶ **South Florida Museum (24m-39km)**
SOUTH FLORIDA MUSEUM	▶ **Gamble Plantation (5m-8km)**
GAMBLE PLANTATION	▶ **Myakka River State Park (30m-48km)**
MYAKKA RIVER STATE PARK	▶ **Warm Mineral Springs (31m-50km)**
WARM MINERAL SPRINGS	▶ **Gasparilla Island (21m-34km)**
GASPARILLA ISLAND	▶ **Marie Selby Gardens (44m-70km)**
MARIE SELBY GARDENS	▶ **Sarasota (2m-3km)**

Sarasota Convention and Visitors Bureau, 655 N Tamiami Trail (US 41)

*Head north on **US 41** for 3 miles (5km).*

1 The Ringling Museums

The centerpiece of this magnificent 68-acre (28-hectare) estate is the John & Mable Ringling Museum of Art, one of the finest and largest collections of European paintings in America. The gallery was created in 1927 by John Ringling, who made a fortune in business to add to the wealth he created with his brothers in the famous Ringling Bros and Barnum and Bailey Circus. The collection is housed in a sumptuous Italian Renaissance-style villa replete with fountains, friezes, cartouches, vaults and columns. It holds some of the world's best grand baroque paintings with works by Rubens, Van Dyke, Velázquez, Hals, Poussin, Veronese and Tiepolo. Adjacent is the Asolo Theater, complete with an original 18th-century baroque interior. The Ringling Residence, Ca'd'Zan (House of John), is a 30-room Venetian Gothic mansion, built in the 1920s tradition of richly decorated historical houses for the wealthy and famous. Finally, don't miss the Circus Museum which displays a colorful collection of circus art and memorabilia. Here you'll see an animated miniature circus, a scale model of the Ringling Bros 1930s circus and lots of associated memorabilia.

Opposite the Ringling Estate is Bellm's Cars and Music of Yesterday. An entertaining guided tour of the 120-strong antique and classic car collection includes Ringling's Rolls-Royces and Pierce Arrows. You will also be guided round one of the world's largest collections of over 1,000 music machines (barrel-organs, nickelodeons, hurdy gurdies, phonoraphs, etc) and some of the more interesting examples are played.

Sarasota Jungle Gardens occupy a beautiful bayside location a mile to the south of Bellm's and two blocks west off US 41. This is a perfect spot for nature lovers with bird shows, reptile shows and a kiddie jungle to amuse children in tow.

The Ringling Museum is a pageant of over 500 years of European and American art

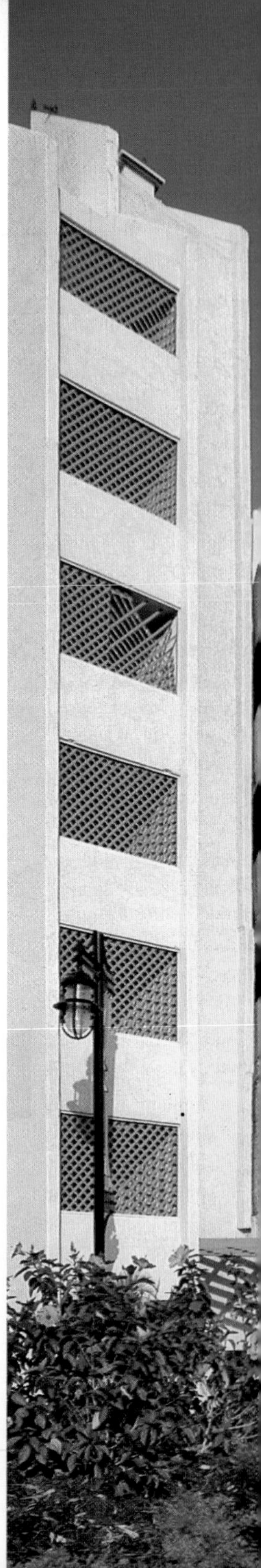

FOR CHILDREN

The luxurious Sarasota Jungle Gardens will appeal to all the family, with beautiful formal botanical exhibits, punctuated with bird and reptile shows, a petting zoo, plus monkeys, leopards, alligators, flamingos and many more animals.

▶ *Return south on **US 41** and after Sarasota Quay turn right onto John Ringling Boulevard.*

2 Lido Key

Ringling Causeway leads into St Armand's Circle, a huge traffic circle lined with over 100 well-heeled fashion, jewelry and specialty stores, plus restaurants and galleries. Continue straight on through the Circle and turn left to Lido Beach, one of the finest beaches in the area. Head back to St Armand's Circle and turn left for City Island and the Mote Marine Aquarium. As well as research projects and a shell exhibit, there are various tanks for marine life, a touch-tank and an outdoor shark tank with several awesome residents in excess of 8 feet (2.4m) and 400 pounds (180kg). Finish your visit with a cruise around Sarasota and Roberts Bays.

FOR HISTORY BUFFS

In 1539 Hernando de Soto and his *conquistadores* became the first Europeans to land on this part of Florida. Although the exact site is unknown, the historic event is commemorated at the De Soto National Memorial a few miles west of Bradenton (north on 75th Street off SR 64). There is a visitor center, and costumed guides demonstrate period weapons and tell you about the everyday problems facing this expeditionary force.

Bold art deco architecture in Sarasota

▶ *Return along City Island Road and turn right on **SR 789**.*

3 Longboat Key/Anna Maria Key

There is no sightseeing on these barrier islands, but there are good beaches at the northern tip of Longboat Key and on Anna Maria Key, at its southern tip and its junction with SR 64 some 4½ miles (7km) north.

i Anna Maria Island Chamber of Commerce, 501 Manatee Avenue West, Holmes Beach; Longboat Key Chamber of Commerce, 5360 Gulf of Mexico Drive, Longboat Key

SCENIC ROUTES

SR 789, which connects Anna Maria Key southwards to Lido Key, guarantees miles of blue-green Gulf water, beaches and some interesting beachfront houses and condominiums.

▶ *Follow **SR 64** east for 12 miles (19km), passing through downtown Bradenton to 10th Street West.*

4 South Florida Museum and Bishop Planetarium, Bradenton

This fine museum traces the area's history with dioramas of the Indian period, a Spanish courtyard and chapel, 'cracker'

RECOMMENDED WALKS

At De Soto National Memorial Park, near Bradenton, a scenic nature trail winds along the Manatee River to the ruins of a house from one of the first settlements in this part of the state, dating back to the 1880s.

(early white settlers) accommodation, an outstanding Civil War collection and much more. The star of the museum, however, is Snooty the manatee, who performs more like a sea-lion at feeding times. Combined with the museum is the Bishop Planetarium, featuring the usual astronomical displays plus state-of-the-art laser shows and music.

▶ *Continue on 10th Street West, turn north across the river and turn right on* ***US 301****. Follow this for 3 miles (5km).*

5 Gamble Plantation State Historic Site

Built in the late 1840s using oyster shells and molasses, this is the only pre-Civil War plantation house surviving in south Florida, and until 1856 it was the center of a sugar plantation and refinery covering 3,450 acres (1,396 hectares). Take a ranger-guided tour to see the house, restored and furnished to the style of its heyday.

▶ *Continue on* ***US 301*** *to* ***I–75****. Head south to exit 37, then east for 9 miles (14km) on* ***SR 72****.*

> **BACK TO NATURE**
>
> Myakka River State Park is a must, but if you would like to see more natural beauty visit Oscar Scherer State Recreation Area 2 miles (3km) south of Osprey. Here among the scrubby flatwoods you can fish and canoe in the tidal creek and swim in a fresh-water lake.
> Lake Manatee SRA, 15 miles (24km) east of Bradenton on SR 64, has similar character, wildlife and facilities.

6 Myakka River State Park

This scenic wildlife sanctuary is similar to the Everglades in places with its grassy marshes and hammocks. You can explore it on foot, by tram tour or aboard one of the world's largest airboats. Alligators, deer, wild turkeys, hawks and bald eagles are just some of the wildlife you may see in this beautiful area. There are over 37 miles (60km) of nature trails to enjoy.

▶ *Return to* ***I–75*** *and head south to exit 34. Take* ***SR 777*** *to* ***US 41*** *and head east, 21 miles (34km).*

7 Warm Mineral Springs

This is one of the state's most famous 'bottomless' waterholes, where some 10 million US gallons (38 million liters) of water flow daily at a constant 87°F (31°C). The mineral content of the water is claimed to be many times that of more famous spas worldwide, and a health resort has been established on the palm-fringed lake shore.

▶ *Return west on* ***US 41*** *for about 1 mile (1.5km) and turn left on* ***SR 777*** *to Englewood. At Englewood head south on* ***SR 775,*** *which runs into* ***SR 776*** *and* ***SR 771****.*

8 Gasparilla Island

It is said that this barrier island takes its name from José Gaspar

(see Tampa), the legendary 18th-century pirate, known as Gasparilla, who used it as a hideout. During the 1920s it was also a popular retreat for more legitimate businessmen such as John Jacob Astor and Henry Du Pont. They arrived by train, of course, and the railroad station at Boca Grande where they once alighted is now a colorfully converted café-restaurant. The small resort town has changed little in 80 years and the grand Gasparilla Inn, built in 1912, still retains a very exclusive guest list. Much of the island is a state recreation area and includes five beaches and an 1890 lighthouse.

► *Return to Sarasota on US 41.*

9 Marie Selby Botanical Gardens

The Marie Selby Botanical Gardens is acclaimed as one of the state's finest collections and enjoys a wonderful peaceful location on the bay. The star attraction is the collection of over 6,000 orchids, but its 11-acre (4.5-hectare) site has something for everyone.

► *Return to Sarasota on US 41.*

Simple pleasures at Boca Grande, Gasparilla Island

SPECIAL TO...

The southern part of this area is renowned for its fishing. In June and July the best tarpon fishing conditions in the world are found just off Boca Grande Pass.

The attractive small city of Venice, named for its miles of winding waterways, is the winter home of the Ringling Brothers and Barnum and Bailey Circus and even has a college for trainee clowns. It is also famous for the number of shark teeth washed up on its shores.

ORLANDO & CENTRAL FLORIDA

The Orlando area represents the world's most concentrated hive of tourism activity. The key to it all is, of course, Walt Disney World. This modern marvel of slick entertainment technology and ebullient, wholesome self-promotion attracts some 25 million visitors annually to the Orlando region. Indeed many tourists head for the magic beacons of Cinderella Castle and Epcot's great 'golf ball' even before unpacking. This is the world's greatest fantasy land and to a large extent sets the tone for most of central Florida's attractions. Step back into the Wild West, join King Henry's Feast, go Back to the Future, visit 11 countries in a day, see all manner of improbable wildlife performing unlikely acts – almost anything is possible here. There is a downside to this, however. Most parts of Orlando and Kissimmee are characterless, service is conveyor-belt slick and antiseptic, and at busy times of the year you can spend most of a week just waiting in line. However, while Walt Disney World is now very much the unofficial symbol of central Florida it is not typical of the region.

Below: Sea World Florida is one of the finest marine life attractions in the world

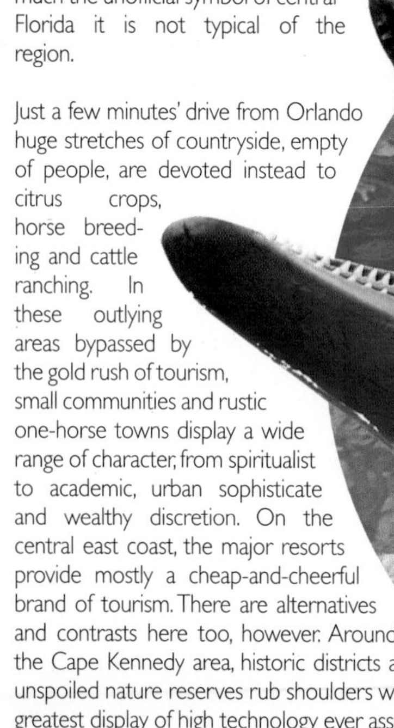

Just a few minutes' drive from Orlando huge stretches of countryside, empty of people, are devoted instead to citrus crops, horse breeding and cattle ranching. In these outlying areas bypassed by the gold rush of tourism, small communities and rustic one-horse towns display a wide range of character, from spiritualist to academic, urban sophisticate and wealthy discretion. On the central east coast, the major resorts provide mostly a cheap-and-cheerful brand of tourism. There are alternatives and contrasts here too, however. Around the Cape Kennedy area, historic districts and unspoiled nature reserves rub shoulders with the greatest display of high technology ever assembled by man, and there are quiet, understated beach resorts.

If you're seeking life in the fast lane, speed off to Daytona

Tour 16

Whether or not you explore Orlando, as opposed to just seeing Walt Disney World, is largely a matter of time, money and stamina. However, Disney aside, Orlando does boast some heavyweight attractions. The biggest and best of these are Sea World and Universal Studios. The family nightlife scene is also very lively in Orlando, and a visit to historic Church Street Station is a must.

Walt Disney World

Old-time, future-time and timeless entertainment of every conceivable kind is served up at Walt Disney World, and rare is the Florida visitor who passes it by. No family should miss it, and even those who profess to prefer the real world to the artificially conceived version will find something to delight them.

Tour 17 and Kennedy Space Center

After a week of Disney technology, you may feel in need of sand and surf. Take your 'R and R' where the early astronauts did after the high-tech rigors of Cape Canaveral, on the Space Coast beaches. Kennedy Space Center – the home of the space shuttle – is a great-value day out from Orlando.

Tour 18

The other most popular choice of coastal break away from Orlando is Daytona Beach. If you like a raucous night scene and think fast wheels are fun, you will probably love it; if you don't, you might easily hate it. Don't let that deter you from visiting the lovely area northwest of Orlando, however. Winter Park is a must for all Orlando visitors, and the Daytona area has several very cultured attractions.

Tour 19

The excursion to Ocala National Forest and Silver Springs features some of Florida's most beautiful woods and river scenery. Silver Springs' glass-bottom boats or a Juniper Springs' canoe trip are every bit as memorable as Disney – and are the real thing. There are several other rewarding springs on this route, and those in search of old Florida will not be disappointed.

Exhibit at the Kennedy Space Center, the centerpiece of the Space Coast

Tour 20

Old Florida even underlies the final tour, which focuses on the unabashedly tourist-oriented enclave of Kissimmee – though you will have to move away from the neon lights of US 192 to experience it. Just south of here, Cypress Gardens and Bok Tower Gardens are two of the area's most charming and peaceful attractions. Further south, where cattle outnumber people, the theme parks of Orlando seem a world away.

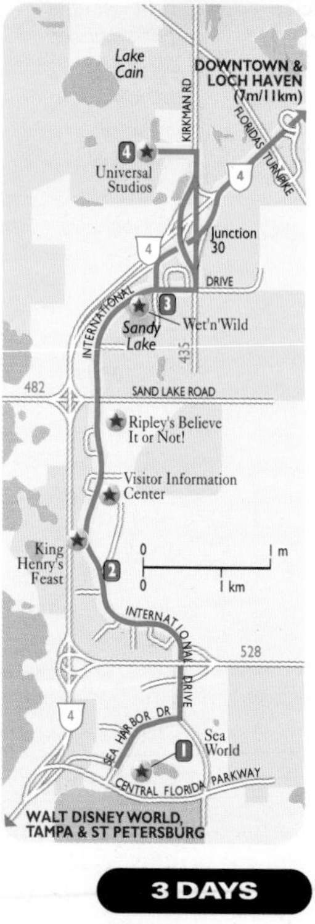

TOUR

16

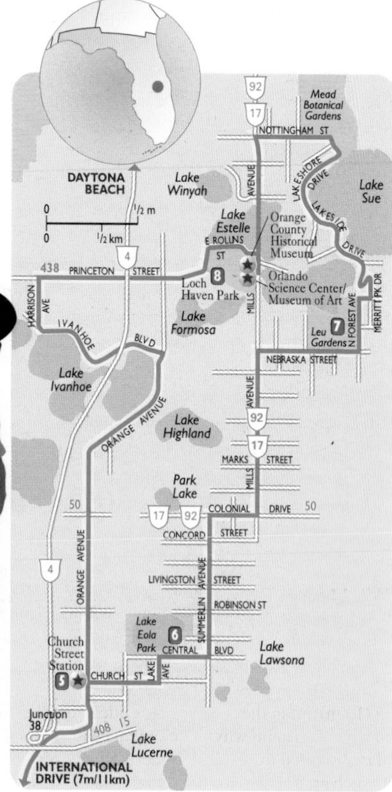

Lake Cain
DOWNTOWN & LOCH HAVEN (7m/11km)
KIRKMAN RD
FLORIDA'S TURNPIKE
4 Universal Studios
Junction 30
DRIVE
INTERNATIONAL
3 Wet'n'Wild
Sandy Lake
435
482
SAND LAKE ROAD
Ripley's Believe It or Not!
Visitor Information Center
King Henry's Feast
2
0 1 m
0 1 km
INTERNATIONAL DRIVE
528
SEA HARBOR DR
Sea World
1
CENTRAL FLORIDA PARKWAY
WALT DISNEY WORLD, TAMPA & ST PETERSBURG

Orlando

Still dominated by Disney, but also with a life very much its own, Orlando's attractions multiply at prodigious rate. Sea World and Universal Studios are unmissable while Wet 'n' Wild and Church Street Station continue to draw big crowds. And amid all the hokum, there's even room for traditional-style museums, as the excellent all-new Orlando Science Center is proving.

3 DAYS

i *Orlando Official Visitor Center, 8723 International Drive (corner with Austrian Court)*

SPECIAL TO...

There are two regular annual celebrations in town. In early November Light Up Orlando is a street carnival with bands, international foods and a celebration of one of its citrus crops, the kumquat. Arts in April is a self-explanatory series of visual and performing events. Look out at Church Street Station for festive celebrations, particularly at Halloween and Christmas.

1 Sea World

This is the most popular marine life park in the world – and when you see Shamu the 6,000-pound (2,700kg) killer whale leap 6 feet (1.8m) out of the water, you will understand why. Sea World is dedicated to marine research and educating the public by means of the most entertaining shows and best possible displays of marine life. The highlights are: any show featuring Shamu (and her babies); Key West Dolphin Fest show, with performing dolphins and false killer whales; Terrors of the Deep, where the world's largest underwater acrylic tunnel will transport you through deadly pufferfish, barracuda and sharks; Penguin Encounter, featuring 200 Antarctic penguins in the snow; Wild Arctic is a thrill ride adventure to a themed area featuring beluga whales, polar bears and walruses; Manatees: The Last Generation? offers total immersion into the world of Florida's very own gentle giants; Baywatch at Sea World features world-class water skiing; Pacific Point Preserve is a naturalistic setting for California sea lions and seals. Journey to Atlantis is the park's latest and largest ever project, combining high-speed water ride and roller-coaster elements with state-of-the-art special effects. Stay on for a spectacular after-dark Shamu show, a fireworks and music lasers extravaganza, the bohemian atmosphere and festivities of Key West at Sea World and a Polynesian feast.

▶ *Take Sea Harbor Drive to International Drive and turn left, heading north.*

2 International Drive (south)

International Drive is Orlando's Main Street – a high-energy strip of hotels, eating houses, dinner shows, entertainment complexes and visitor attractions. Look out for the following on International Drive's southern section: Pointe Orlando, the town's latest nightlife/cinema/shopping complex; Movie Rider (see page 125); King Henry's Feast dinner show, a long established Orlando favourite and Ripley's Believe It or Not! (see page 132).

▶ *Continue north on International Drive and turn right just after Wet 'n' Wild to park your car.*

Making a splash 'dolphin skiing' at Sea World

3 Wet 'n' Wild

This is probably the most exciting water park in the state, attracting over a million visitors a year. Every conceivable method of high-speed hydrosliding is explored here, from riding rapids seated on an inner tube, sledding head-first Cresta-Run fashion on a mat, or simply zooming unassisted through hundreds of feet of twisting, turning, enclosed tubing. Start on the gentler rides and work up. There's the exhilarating Black Hole (a roller-coasting ride in pitch darkness); the Surge, Florida's largest multi-passenger water ride; Bomb Bay, a virtual free-fall down a 76-foot (23m), 79-degree waterslide; Fuji Flyer, a four-passenger ride which towers six stories high and races down 450 feet (137m) of banked curves, plus many more thrills.

Watersports fans can catch a wave at the surf lagoon and try the cable-operated kneeboard rides. There is also a beach here and plenty of other peaceful water activities.

▶ *Continue on International Drive and turn left to join Kirkman Road **(SR 435)**.*

4 Universal Studios

This huge theme park is the largest working film and television studio outside Hollywood. It is four times the size of its Disney–MGM rival and features several more rides, theater shows illustrating the art of film-making, a tour of the sets and themed restaurants and shopping. Don't miss the following; Back to the Future –

the world's most exciting thrill ride; Jaws – a ride across the lagoon, waiting and watching; Kongfrontation – another technical masterpiece based on a movie monster; Terminator 2: 3D – the hottest ticket in Florida, featuring a stunning mix of 3-D film, state-of-the-art special effects and live action; The Lost World Behind-the-Scenes – a terrifying close-up of the life-sized creatures from Jurassic Park; Hercules and Xena: Wizards of the Screen – a multi-million dollar interactive attraction with live stunts and state-of-the art special effects; the FUNtastic World of Hanna-Barbera; Alfred Hitchcock 3-D Theater and Earthquake. ET Adventure is tame and popular with children. The street sets of New York, Hollywood and San Francisco are fun to wander through and every night there is the *Miami Vice*-style speedboat chase Dynamite Nights Stuntacular. Daytime restaurants include The Hard Rock Café, featuring the biggest collection of pop memorabilia in the world, and Mel's Diner from *American Graffiti*, while City Walk, Universal's new evening entertainment complex, features the Motown Café, the NASCAR café, the Downbeat Magazine Jazz Center, Bob Marley – A Tribute to Freedom, and more.

▶ *Return south along Kirkman Road and join* ***I–4*** *north to exit 38. Turn right onto Orange Avenue and right again onto Church Street.*

SCENIC ROUTES

The route outlined in the tour between Church Street Station and Loch Haven is deliberately chosen for its lake and garden scenery. To continue this drive, head west along East Rollins Street, by the lakeside, and turn left onto Camden Road, then onto Princeton Street. Go under I–4, turn left at Harrison Avenue to join Ivanhoe Boulevard (next to Lake Ivanhoe) and pick up Orange Avenue. This heads south back to downtown.

5 Church Street Station

A crumbling hotel and railroad depot has been brilliantly converted into downtown's premier evening entertainment complex. The theme spans the decades between the 1890s and the Roaring Twenties, and the highlights are the huge three-tiered Cheyenne Saloon & Opera House, Rosie O'Grady's Louisiana-style bar and the elegant wrought-iron 'crystal palace' Orchid Garden (a single admission price gets you into everything). Antique furnishings and fixtures throughout are of the highest quality. There is music and dancing for most tastes; Country and Western, Dixieland, Can-Can girls, mainstream dance and pop music, and Phineas Phogg's high-

Wet 'n' Wild claims more rides than any other water park in Florida

The Can-Can at Rosie O'Grady's

energy disco. Arrive late afternoon or early evening to make sure of seeing all the interesting shops. The area's latest attraction is a very different offering. Terror on Church Street (next to Church Street Station) is a spooky haunted house where costumed actors aim to give you the fright of your life.

▶ *Head east (away from **I–4**) on either Church Street or South Street (which run parallel at either end of the complex) and turn left onto Lake Avenue.*

6 Lake Eola Park

You can rent a swan-shaped paddle boat by day on this picturesque lake or come here by night in a horse and carriage from Church Street Station. Its fountain is lit by night and the illuminated skyscrapers make an impressive backdrop.

▶ *Head east on Central Boulevard, turn left onto Summerlin Avenue, turn right onto Colonial Drive **(US 50)** and second left onto Mills Avenue **(US 17/92)**. Turn right onto Nebraska Street, which leads to North Forest Avenue.*

7 Leu Gardens

Leu House is a restored turn-of-the-century mansion stuffed with artifacts that reflect the lifestyle of the wealthy farmers who cultivated this land between 1910 and 1930. It sits amid 22 acres (9 hectares) of peaceful gardens famous for their camellias, roses, orchids and a floral clock.

▶ *Continue on North Forest Avenue through Merrit Park, Lakeside and Lakeshore (with lakes to either side of you) to Mead Botanical Gardens on Nottingham Street. This leads back to Mills Avenue. Turn left and soon on your right is Loch Haven Park.*

8 Loch Haven Park

This is the often-overlooked center of culture and the arts in Orlando, home to science, art and history galleries. The Orlando Science Center has just been completely revamped and in any other town apart from Orlando would be hailed as its top attraction. In addition to four levels of the very latest in entertaining and educational hands-on exhibits, it also features the world's largest domed IMAX theater and planetarium. The adjacent Orlando Museum of Art is noted for its pre-Columbian South American permanent exhibits and also for the quality of the touring exhibitions it attracts.

The Orange County Historical Museum is a bright, airy place with re-creations of a general store, a pioneer parlor, a hotel lobby, and a restored fire station.

▶ *Return to Sea World (see Scenic Routes).*

RECOMMENDED WALKING

It is a fair bet that if you have been on your feet all day doing Walt Disney World, Sea World or Universal Studios, the last thing you will want to do is go for a walk. You will have to get away from International Drive if you want to escape the concrete and neon, and either Leu Gardens or Turkey Lake Park is a good choice.

FOR HISTORY BUFFS

Aside from the Orange County Historical Museum, which will take you through the development of the area from the time when it was known as Mosquito County, there are no other history exhibits. Visit downtown by day to see little bits of old Orlando still in situ – the handsome Kress Store and National Bank buildings were erected in the 1920s, and the Art Deco-like McCrory's Five & Dime actually dates from 1906. The original Church Street Station depot has also been renovated and comes complete with an impressive 19th-century steam locomotive.

WALT DISNEY WORLD

Walt Disney World (WDW) is the world's leading tourist attraction, boasting over 25 million visits per year. The complex occupies 45-square miles (116sq km) – around the size of Manchester (England) or twice the size of Manhattan Island – and comprises four major theme parks, three water parks, a nature island, a night-time entertainment complex, shopping villages, campgrounds and over 25 hotel resorts. The Magic Kingdom is the heart of WDW bringing back to life all those memories of childhood. This is the place for those who have not yet grown up, and for those who just don't want to grow up. Epcot combines educational and cosmopolitan elements in its attractions while Disney–MGM Studios is seventh heaven for all film buffs and movie lovers.

Disney's latest theme park is Disney's Animal Kingdom, starring animals from real life, fantasy and fables.

Adventures and Rides

While each park is very different, all feature themed rides, shows and adventures which often involve cinematic special effects (for example, simulation and 3-D techniques) and life-like animated models known as Audio-Animatronics®.

Magic Kingdom

As Cinderella Castle rises into view and the strains of *When You Wish Upon a Star* waft through the air, you will realize why this is called the Magic Kingdom. Your introduction to the Kingdom is Main Street, USA, an idealized re-creation of a turn-of-the-century Main Street in small-town America. Besides Main Street, there are six other themed 'lands' within the park – Adventureland, Frontierland, Fantasyland, Liberty Square, Tomorrowland and Mickey's Toontown Fair – containing over 40 rides, adventures and shows. Fantasyland and Mickey's Toontown Fair are geared for young children, while Tomorrowland shows the future (as dreamed by writers and sci-fi visionaries) that never came to be.

The following are the main showpiece attractions: Space Mountain – this hair-raising roller-coaster in the dark is a theme park legend. Pirates of the Caribbean – a boat ride through a series of sets depicting a port being sacked by pirates, is Disney Audio-Animatronics® at their best. The Haunted Mansion – frightening it isn't, but the special effects are first class. Big Thunder Mountain Railroad – a runaway train roller-coasters its way through old mining tunnels and a gold-digger's settlement. Splash Mountain – a watery

Main Street, USA and Cinderella Castle

thrill ride with Brer Rabbit, Brer Fox and their friends culminating in a Niagara Falls-like descent. Jungle Cruise – an ever-popular, gentle 10-minute cruise through waterfalls, jungles, the Nile Valley and the African veldt.

ExtraTERRORestrial Alien Encounter, where a teleportation goes horribly wrong and results in a terrifying encounter with a horrific alien (listen to the screams!). Also in Tommorrowland is the excellent new The Timekeeper show. Children will enjoy the stage show The Legend of the Lion King, Disney's latest 'imagineering' technique, and there's the perennial (excruciatingly twee) favorite of It's a Small World. The best stage show in the park is the Diamond Horseshoe Jamboree, for which you must book seats. Daily events include the Remember the Magic Parade, a carnival procession, and when park hours are extended, Fantasy in the Sky or Spectromagic, a carnival by night with spectacular lights, lasers and special effects.

Jungle Cruise features some excellent Audio-Animatronic® animals, and a few watery surprises!

Epcot

The Experimental Prototype Community of Tomorrow – Epcot for short – was conceived in 1966 by Walt Disney as a real-life multinational community. Although it proved impractical, the Future World section of Epcot still retains one of the original objectives of 'showing off the latest US technologies and the imagination of free enterprise'. Here the emphasis is less on rides for thrills than rides for learning, and because of the rapid changes in technology this whole area is constantly evolving. At the time of writing, however, highlights of Future World are: Universe of Energy which involves a very entertaining journey through the history of the Universe and its energy concerns.

Innoventions – an ever-changing exhibition of gadgets and gizmos of the near and not-too-distant future.

Wonders of Life, featuring an exciting simulator thrill-ride (Body Wars), and the amusing Cranium Command show. The Land pavilion features a cruise through various world climes to see how agriculture may look in the future and Circle of Life with characters from *The Lion King*.

The Living Seas – a sea-life exhibit with one of the world's largest man-made saltwater tanks holding over 80 species of tropical fish and mammals.

Test Track – Epcot's latest, longest and fastest attraction where you can ride in actual test vehicles to get first-hand experience on General Motors test procedures.

Journey into Imagination picks up the theme of the Disney hit film, *Honey, I Shrunk the Kids* (see Disney–MGM Studios), with its brilliant and very funny Honey, I Shrunk the Audience 3-D show.

Spaceship Earth is housed in Epcot's signature 'golf ball' geosphere and features a very popular ride through the history of communications, from cave-drawings to the information super highway.

The other half of Epcot is World Showcase, which resembles a permanent World Fair, Here 10 countries have done a remarkable job of transforming part of Florida into the buildings, sights, sounds, smells and tastes of a foreign country. Each pavilion has its own architectural showpiece (from a Mayan pyramid to the Eiffel Tower), shops and at least one restaurant – in fact there is a

surfeit of culinary excellence here.

The United States, Norway, Mexico, China, France and Canada also feature a ride and/or a striking Circle Vision film. Circle Vision is a cinematic technique in which a number of projectors and screens are used to surround the viewer (complete surround is referred to as 360-degree Circle Vision). The effect is akin to simulation and places you right in the center of the moving action. Entertainment is provided outside the pavilions by national street performers, who range from folk dancers and comedy players to bagpipers and Oriental drummers.

The end of every day at Epcot is celebrated by Illuminations, a pyrotechnic extravaganza of lights, lasers, fountains and music.

Disney–MGM Studios

Hollywood Boulevard replaces Main Street, USA, the theme tune from *Gone With the Wind* takes the place of *When You Wish Upon a Star* and Harrison Ford takes the starring role from Peter Pan in this magic kingdom for film lovers. If you have already seen the other Disney theme parks you will know what to expect in terms of animatronics, rides and special effects. This is also a genuine working studio, and the best possible introduction is to take both the Studio Backlot Tour and the Backstage Pass to 101 Dalmatians walking tour. If your tram survives Catastrophe Canyon, you will be shown a host of other mechanical and optical tricks, plus props and special effects equipment. To see how cartoons of all kinds are created, take the equally dynamic Magic of Disney Animation Tour featuring a brilliant Robin Williams/Walter Cronkite short film. Star Tours vies with Space Mountain as the fastest, most thrilling Disney ride. This is a space flight simulation, created by George Lucas, and has all the excitement of actually being inside the cockpit of a Star Wars craft during a hair-raising, hyperspeed adventure. The Indiana Jones™ Stunt Spectacular is a live production on a huge stage with our hero (a Harrison Ford look-alike) re-enacting scenes from the block-buster movies. The Twilight Zone™ Tower of Terror takes guests into a huge derelict hotel. A journey through a series of spooky special effects culminates in more than one heart-stopping 13-story plunge. Largest of all Disney's ride-through attractions is The Great Movie Ride, which reproduces some of the greatest moments in film history.

There is lots more to see here, including Honey, I Shrunk the Kids Movie Set Adventure, Jim Henson's Muppet Vision 3D, Voyage of the Little Mermaid, Disney's The Hunchback of Notre Dame: A Musical Adventure and Beauty and the Beast – Live on Stage. There are two audience participation shows; ABC Sound Studio demonstrating sound effects and SuperStar TV showing the craft of television production.

Disney's Animal Kingdom

Opening in spring 1998 this will be the largest Disney park in the world (five times the size of the Magic Kingdom!) and will involve close encounters with animals from the real and imaginary worlds, together with thrill rides and exotic landscapes. (At time of press its contents were a jealously guarded secret.)

Downtown Disney

Downtown Disney is another recent major expansion which adds to Pleasure Island and Disney Village Marketplace the new Disney's West Side complex. Pleasure Island is a vibrant evening entertainment zone which takes in two comedy clubs, a live country music club, a live rock-and-pop music venue, two pulsating discos and a more mellow jazz scene. Disney's West Side includes: two celebrity night-clubs, House of Blues and Bongos Cuban Café; several fashionable restaurants (including Planet Hollywood); the 1,650-seat Cirque du Soleil theater, plus shopping. All clubs open until the small hours and there is a 'New Year's Eve Street Party' every single night. There is an all-inclusive entry fee to Downtown Disney and persons under 18 must be accompanied by a parent or guardian (21 in some of the clubs). Note: Even if you are well over 21 you must still show proof of age (passport, driving licence) to obtain a wrist band at the entrance which allows you to purchase alcoholic drinks. Disney Village Marketplace is dedicated to shopping and restaurants.

Typhoon Lagoon, River Country and Blizzard Beach

River Country was designed as the idyllic Huckleberry Finn-style swimmin' hole, with rope swings, slides and flumes. The whole area is beautifully landscaped (complete with a lovely white-sand beach) and is also good for swimming. Typhoon Lagoon, four times the size of River Country, is probably the world's most innovative water theme park. Thrilling water slides and rapids rides spew out from a towering mountain topped by a stranded pirate galleon, but perhaps best of all is the amazing inland body-surfing lagoon (the world's largest), where you can catch 6-foot (1.8m) waves. A Caribbean reef offers snorkeling among exotic fish and, again, a perfect beach. Blizzard Beach is Disney's latest and largest water park – themed in a way which resembles an Alpine Ski resort where the pistes have melted.

Discovery Island

This beautifully landscaped zoological island is the perfect retreat when you have had enough of crowds, lines, animatronics and thrill rides.

The Space Coast

The Space Coast has two great attributes: the closest beaches to Disney, and it is the home of the Kennedy Space Center. The latter is not only one of the wonders of the technological world, but it is also Florida's best value day out.

1/2 DAYS • 201 MILES • 323KM

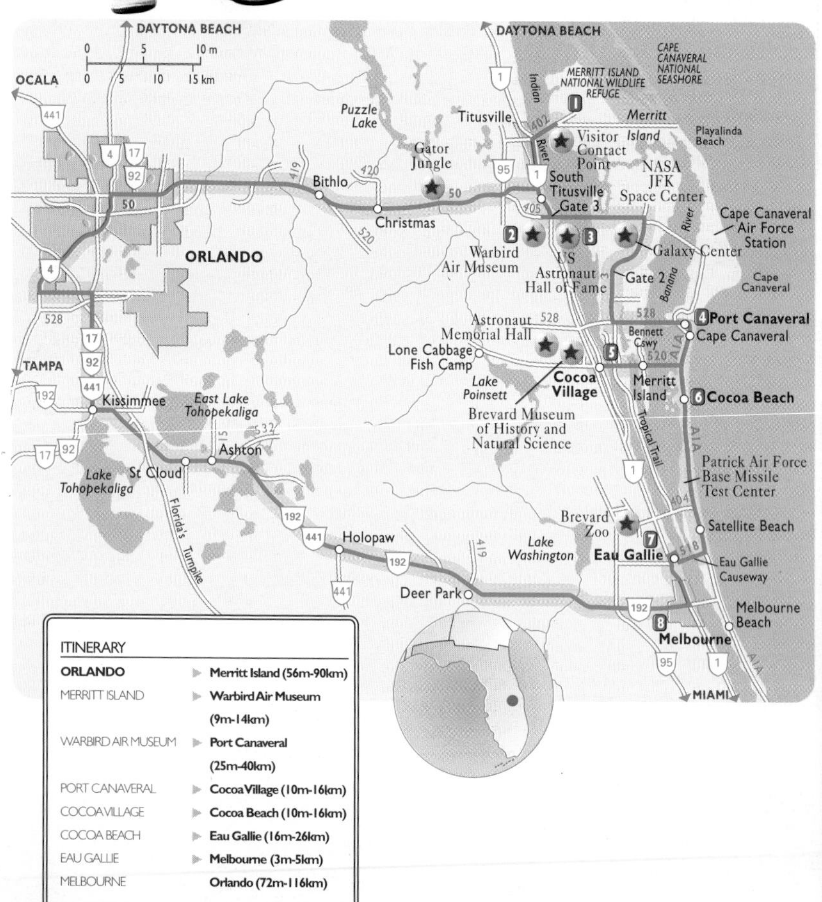

ITINERARY

ORLANDO	▶ Merritt Island (56m-90km)
MERRITT ISLAND	▶ Warbird Air Museum (9m-14km)
WARBIRD AIR MUSEUM	▶ Port Canaveral (25m-40km)
PORT CANAVERAL	▶ Cocoa Village (10m-16km)
COCOA VILLAGE	▶ Cocoa Beach (10m-16km)
COCOA BEACH	▶ Eau Gallie (16m-26km)
EAU GALLIE	▶ Melbourne (3m-5km)
MELBOURNE	Orlando (72m-116km)

[i] Orlando Official Visitor Center, International Drive (corner with Austrian Court)

▶ *From Orlando take the* ***I–4*** *north to exit 41 and head east for 40 miles (64km) on* ***SR 50****, crossing* ***I–95*** *to the Indian River/Intracoastal Waterway. Turn left onto* ***US 1*** *and head north for 4 miles (6km). Turn right to cross the river on* ***SR 402****.*

FOR CHILDREN

Gator Jungle, west of Titusville on East Highway (SR 50), is claimed to be the largest alligator farm in Florida, with over 10,000 crocs and 'gators raised for their meat and skins. You can see them in their natural habitat aboard a Jungle Cruise. Alternatively, visit Brevard Zoo, where you can stroll through the boardwalks of a Latin-American jungle.

1 Merritt Island National Wildlife Refuge

Adjacent to the Kennedy Space Center, this barrier island is an unspoiled wilderness stretching 25 miles (40km), home to 22 endangered and threatened species. At the Visitor Contact Point pick up a leaflet detailing the Black Point Wildlife Drive, a self-guided drive routed through areas of wading birds and other waterfowl. Take any of the three walking trails and you might see some of the refuge's land animals, including armadillos, deer, wild pigs, otters and turtles. The best times for viewing are early morning and later afternoon between October and March. Another option, renting a canoe, may get you up close to a manatee.

The Cape Canaveral National Seashore is one of the state's most untouched beaches. At the southern end, Playalinda is good for swimming and surfing, but to the north you are just as likely to see giant loggerheads and green turtles as other humans.

▶ *Return to and follow* ***US 1*** *south for 8 miles (13km), then turn right onto NASA Parkway West* ***(SR 405)*** *to the Space Center Executive Airport.*

RECOMMENDED WALKS

Merritt Island National Wildlife Refuge offers three walking trails. The Oak Hammock is a ½-mile (800m) trail through a subtropical forest, while the Palm Hammock includes boardwalks and stretches for 2 miles (3km). The Cruickshank circles a shallow-water marsh, and its observation tower is ideal for bird-watching.

2 Warbird Air Museum

This was the operations center and headquarters for the Valiant Air Command during World War II. It is now dedicated to preserving and restoring an outstanding collection of World War II and post-war military aircraft and displays many of them along with war memorabilia.

▶ *Head back east to enter the Kennedy Space Center by gate 3.*

Veteran biplane at the Warbird Air Museum

Mercury missions capsule at the US Astronaut Hall of Fame

3 US Astronaut Hall of Fame

A full-scale replica of the space shuttle holds a 72-seat theater where visitors take a 12-minute 'space trip' through a multi-story video ride. After that you can try landing a shuttle, roll 360 degrees in the most realistic flight simulator ever created, or do battle in an aerial dogfight. The Hall also features a museum dedicated to the Mercury and Gemini astronauts.

► *Turn left onto the Kennedy Parkway South **(SR 3)** and leave the NASA complex by Gate 2. After 2 miles (3km) turn left onto Bennett Causeway **(SR 528)**.*

4 Port Canaveral

You can visit here simply to admire the big boats that dock at this important cruise terminal, or you could take the Cape Canaveral Cruise Line to the Bahamas. The ship includes a casino, and a Las Vegas-style revue. Premier Cruise Lines also run a Bahamas cruise, and from 1998 Port Canaveral is the home of the Disney Cruise Line.

► *Drive south on **SR A1A** for 3 miles (5km) and turn right onto **SR 520**. Continue west for 2½ miles (4km) and cross the causeway.*

5 Cocoa Village

Historic Cocoa Village is a delight, a Victorian block of around 50 shops and restaurants, the earliest dating back to the 1880s, when the official population here numbered just 25. On Delannoy Avenue is Travis Hardware, built in 1907, and still operated by the same family. The original tin ceiling remains, as do the track ladders used to reach merchandise on its high shelves.

A mile (1.5km) west on SR 520 at Brevard Community College is the Astronaut Memorial Hall. There is a small museum here, but the real attraction is its planetarium, one of the biggest and most modern complexes in the world, where you can explore the universe through Florida's largest public telescope. Laser shows are staged on Tuesday, Friday and Saturday nights (everything closed Sunday). Close by, on Michigan Avenue, is the Brevard Museum of History and Natural Science. Exhibits include a large shell collection, pioneer antiques, a children's Discovery Room and nature trails that explore a 22-acre (9-hectare) nature preserve.

[i] *Cocoa Chamber of Commerce, Brevard Avenue, Cocoa Village*

SCENIC ROUTES

The routes directly along the Indian River are recommended. Take SR 515, which runs parallel to US 1 for 16 miles (26km), starting some 4 miles (6km) south of Kennedy Space Center Gate 3. The Tropical Trail, on the other side of the river, runs parallel to SR 3 and can be reached by turning right off SR 3 (heading south) 2½ miles (4km) south of SR 528.

FOR HISTORY BUFFS

Walking tours of historic Cocoa Village are conducted on a regular basis (ask at the Chamber of Commerce). The Porcher House on Delannoy Avenue is open to the public 10am to 1pm Tuesday through Friday. Built in 1916 in Classic Revival style, it has recently been renovated. The Porcher family was once the county's largest citrus grower.

► *From Cocoa Village cross back over the bridge on **SR 520,** through Merritt Island and turn right on **SR A1A** heading south.*

BACK TO NATURE

Opportunities to get close to nature are abundant on this relatively undeveloped coast. Merritt Island is a completely unspoiled nature-lover's paradise, while the Brevard Museum of History and Natural Science (Cocoa) provides an urban wildlife sanctuary. Look for herons, ibises, waders, terns and gulls. You can also take an airboat ride along the St John's River to see wild alligators and elegant cypress trees. The station is at Lone Cabbage Fish Camp on SR 520, 4 miles (6km) west of I–95.

Ron Jon's famous Cocoa Beach palace – for surf dudes and beach fashion victims

6 Cocoa Beach

There isn't a great deal to this traditional beach resort aside from its good, gently shelving beaches which are popular with families. Cocoa Beach Pier, with various facilities, extends 800 feet (244m) into the Atlantic, but the most striking landmark is the alarmingly gaudy Ron Jon Surf Shop. At the southern end of the beach is Patrick Air Force Base missile test center. From the road you can see a smaller version of the Kennedy Space Center rocket park, except that these were once deadly missiles.

i ***Cocoa Beach Area Chamber of Commerce, Fortenberry Road, Merritt Island (Chamber of Commerce also on SR 1A1 at Ron Jon Surf Shop)***

▶ *Continue for another 2½ miles (4km) south and turn right onto the Eau Gallie Causeway* ***(SR 518)****. Cross the river and take the second right, Highland Avenue.*

7 Eau Gallie

This historic suburb of the town of Melbourne is home to the acclaimed Brevard Museum of Art and Science. This large, attractive modern facility is renowned for its touring exhibitions from collections of national stature. Gallery tours are given in the afternoon, Tuesday through Friday. If you have ever wondered what a dinosaur egg feels like, how freeze-dried astronaut food tastes or what 'a million' really looks like explore the science section where there are dozens of hands-on stations plus visiting exhibits.

▶ *Turn left onto St Clair Street and then left onto Harbor City Boulevard* ***(US 1)****. Continue for 3 miles (5km) to the junction with New Haven Avenue* ***(US 192)****.*

8 Melbourne

The historic turn-of-the-century heart of Melbourne lies along Crane Creek. Here you will find many restored shops, galleries and restaurants. These include Nannie Lee's Strawberrry Mansion (on East New Haven Avenue/Strawbridge Avenue). Built in 1905, this was a social, religious and civic meeting house until its recent conversion into a restaurant. At the scenic harbor a few blocks away, you can sometimes see dolphins and manatees in the protected waterway.

▶ *Return to Orlando via Kissimmee on* ***US 192****, 72 miles (116km).*

SPECIAL TO...

The 12-mile (19km) stretch of sand south between Melbourne Beach and Sebastian Inlet is the largest sea turtle nesting area in the US. You can take guided walks to watch the turtles at Merritt Island National Wildlife Refuge (June–August), and Sebastian Inlet State Recreation Area (June–July). Ask at the chamber of commerce for more details.

KENNEDY SPACE CENTER

After the establishment of NASA (the National Aeronautics and Space Administration) in 1958, the early manned space missions, Mercury and Gemini, were launched from Cape Canaveral Air Force Station. In 1964 the NASA Kennedy Space Center headquarters was relocated the short distance away to its present home on Merritt Island. Following the historic Apollo missions the focus is now on the reusable space shuttle which can be sent into orbit time and time again.

Bus tours

Because this is an operational site access is restricted outside the main visitor complex to bus tours. As soon as you arrive book the Kennedy Space Center (KSC) Bus Tour and at least one of the IMAX films. There is another bus tour to Cape Canaveral which shows the pioneer sites, but unless you are a space history buff, the KSC tour is more interesting. (There is a small charge for the bus tour and for each IMAX film. Everything else in the center is free of charge.)

Your bus will pass the Vehicle Assembly Building (VAB), one of the world's largest structures (where rockets were once built and the Shuttle is now assembled), and adjacent is the gigantic Giant Crawler Shuttle Transporter which takes the shuttle from the VAB to the launch pad. After a brief photo-stop close to one of the actual launch pads you move on to the highlight of the tour, the Apollo/ Saturn V Center, where you exit the bus.

A film tells the story of the landmark Apollo 8 mission, then you enter the actual control/ firing room used on that mission in 1968. After leaving this room you pass into the main hall which is home to the breathtaking Saturn V, the rocket which carried man to the moon and is the largest and most powerful machine ever built by the US, measuring 363 feet (111m) long. There are several more interesting hardware exhibits to admire, including a capsule and a lunar vehicle, plus another entertaining film which tells the story of the first moon landing. You are free to spend as long as you like here, then hop onto the next bus back to the main center.

The main complex

For many visitors the highlight of the Kennedy Space Center is the IMAX film theater. IMAX stands for maximum image and is a very large-scale cinema technique that pulls you into the screen almost as a simulator does. The screen is a massive five stories high and an array of powerful hidden speakers adds a booming reality to the sound. The Space Center's original film, *The Dream Is Alive*, gives an awesome insider's view into the Space Shuttle program, with footage actually shot in space by the astronauts. This is highly recommended. Destiny in Space is a similar voyage which explores the far reaches of the universe, while L5: First City in Space takes the IMAX experience a stage further by the use of 3-D cinematography. The effect is quite remarkable.

There is lots more to see including the dramatic Rocket Garden where actual historic craft point to the stars, a life-size replica of the Space Shuttle, which you can enter, more films, and more space hardware to view. Allow a full day for your visit. To see if a shuttle is due for launch call NASA on 800 KSC–INFO (toll free within Florida).

Getting to know an astronaut (right); impressive rocketry on display (far right)

UE
E
USA

TOUR
18

Winter Park to Daytona Beach

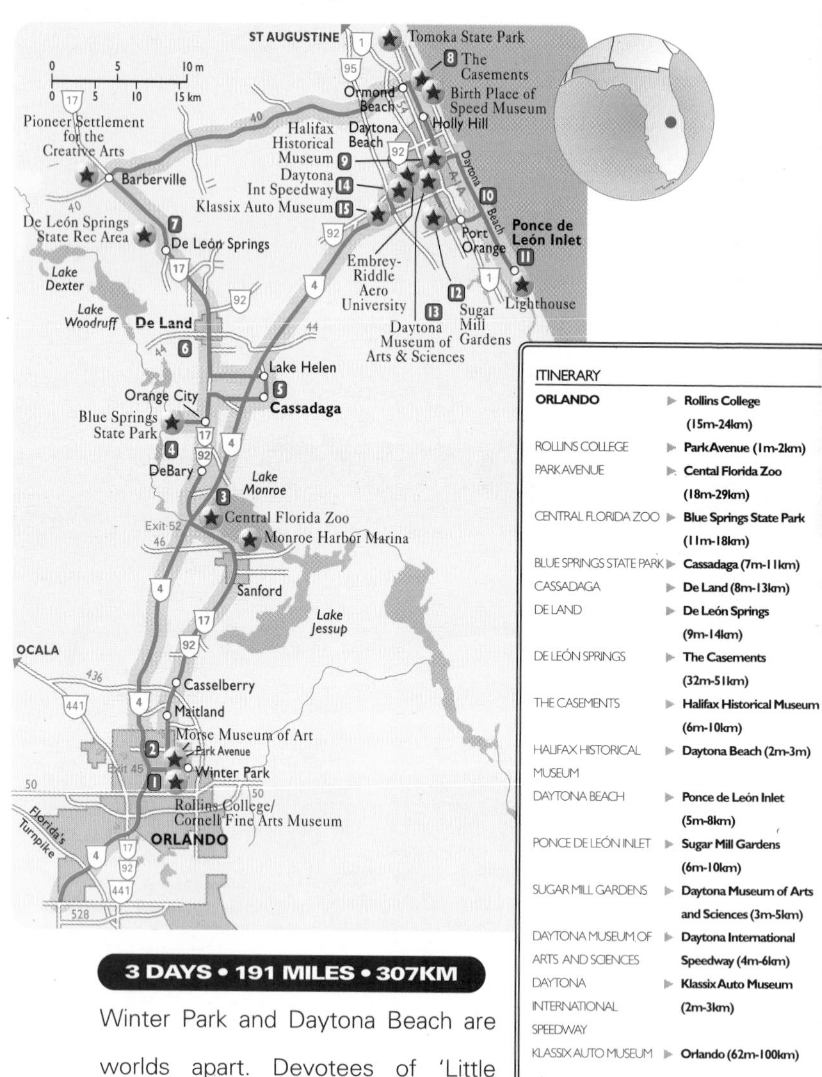

ITINERARY	
ORLANDO	▶ Rollins College (15m-24km)
ROLLINS COLLEGE	▶ Park Avenue (1m-2km)
PARK AVENUE	▶ Cental Florida Zoo (18m-29km)
CENTRAL FLORIDA ZOO	▶ Blue Springs State Park (11m-18km)
BLUE SPRINGS STATE PARK	▶ Cassadaga (7m-11km)
CASSADAGA	▶ De Land (8m-13km)
DE LAND	▶ De León Springs (9m-14km)
DE LEÓN SPRINGS	▶ The Casements (32m-51km)
THE CASEMENTS	▶ Halifax Historical Museum (6m-10km)
HALIFAX HISTORICAL MUSEUM	▶ Daytona Beach (2m-3m)
DAYTONA BEACH	▶ Ponce de León Inlet (5m-8km)
PONCE DE LEÓN INLET	▶ Sugar Mill Gardens (6m-10km)
SUGAR MILL GARDENS	▶ Daytona Museum of Arts and Sciences (3m-5km)
DAYTONA MUSEUM OF ARTS AND SCIENCES	▶ Daytona International Speedway (4m-6km)
DAYTONA INTERNATIONAL SPEEDWAY	▶ Klassix Auto Museum (2m-3km)
KLASSIX AUTO MUSEUM	▶ Orlando (62m-100km)

3 DAYS • 191 MILES • 307KM

Winter Park and Daytona Beach are worlds apart. Devotees of 'Little Europe' never go to 'the world's most famous beach' and vice-versa. However, en route to motor-mad Daytona you will find peace and quiet at Blue Springs and De León Springs and in Cassadaga and De Land more than just traces of 'old Florida'.

The beautiful glasswork of Louis Tiffany is a highlight of a visit to Winter Park

i *Orlando Official Visitor Center, International Drive (corner with Austrian Court)*

▶ *From Orlando take **I–4** north to exit 45. Turn right and follow Fairbanks Avenue east for nearly 2 miles (3km). At the seventh intersection after crossing **US 17–92,** Park Avenue, turn right on Holt Avenue, then left into the Rollins College campus.*

1 Rollins College/Cornell Fine Arts Museum

This delightful collection is one of central Florida's hidden treasures. Its outstanding paintings vary (on a temporary rotating exhibition basis) from works by Renaissance, baroque and European old masters, through 19th-century and contemporary American artists. Here, at Florida's oldest college, you are free to wander the elegant campus. You can see more of the lovely wooded grounds by taking a Scenic Boat Tour of the lakes (departs from East Morse Boulevard). This is also an excellent way of viewing the lakeside homes of some of Winter Park's millionaires.

> **RECOMMENDED WALKS**
>
> The Winter Park lakes are a lovely place to stretch your legs, so too is the campus of Rollins College.
> Stetson University campus at De Land is equally pleasant, and there are plenty of short nature walks available in the Daytona area.
> Try Sugar Mill Gardens, Tomoka State Park, Ponce de León Inlet Lighthouses area or the Ormond Beach Memorial Art Gallery grounds.

▶ *Return to Park Avenue.*

2 Park Avenue/Morse Museum of Art

Leafy Park Avenue, lined with European-style shops, fine restaurants, hidden gardens and antique and art galleries, is often quoted as the most beautiful shopping street in central Florida.

The jewel in its crown is the Charles Hosmer Morse Museum of American Art on Park Avenue North. This museum features the biggest and finest collection of the works of Louis Tiffany, world-famous for his Art Nouveau glass. Tiffany lamps, paintings, pottery, metalwork and furniture are also displayed, complemented by contemporary works of masters like Frank Lloyd Wright, Emile Gallé and Charles Rennie Mackintosh.

▶ *Continue north on Park Avenue and turn right onto Orlando Avenue **(US 17–92).** Continue north across **SR 436** heading towards **I–4,** exit 52.*

DeLand Hall on the University of Stetson campus

3 Central Florida Zoo

This relatively small but important zoo is home to hundreds of birds and animals. You will see cougars, siamangs, servals, margays and hear the laughing Australian kookaburra. Go at the weekend if possible to see the public feeding of the primates, hippos, otters and felines.

Sanford's other big attraction is cruising aboard the 1800s-style *Grand Romance* riverboat (reservations required). You can take a dinner-dance cruise or just go sightseeing along the scenic St John's River. To find the marina at Monroe Harbor, return south, turn left onto SR 46 and at the fourth light turn left.

▶ *From the zoo continue north on* ***US 17–92*** *for 9 miles (14km). At Orange City turn left on West French Avenue and head 2 miles (3km) west.*

4 Blue Springs State Park

This peaceful state park is famous as a winter home for manatees who seek refuge from the cold St John's River in the warm waters here – a constant 72°C (22°C). There is an observation platform, and from it you can usually see the outline of these gentle giants from November through March (February is particularly good). The spring is also good for snorkeling. Once a river port, the park presents its history in an 1870s mansion.

▶ *Return to Orange City. Head north on* ***US 17–92*** *for a short distance, turn right, then left, crossing* ***I–4****. Follow the signs to Cassadaga.*

5 Cassadaga

This tiny backwoods community is famous for being the center of spiritualism in Florida. Wandering around the village you will find that a number of mediums advertize their services, available on a walk-in basis, or you can just visit the Purple Rose Metaphysical Stuff Store. There is nothing remotely spooky about Cassadaga and this picturesque diversion gives a glimpse of old Florida.

▶ *Continue north and then west in a loop back to* ***US 17–92*** *via Lake Helen, and head north for 3 miles (5km).*

6 De Land

The University of Stetson, established by hat magnate John Stetson, is the major feature of this charming, quiet town, and visitors are quite welcome to look around the campus with its handsome porticos and pillars. DeLand Hall, facing the main street, dates back to 1884 and is the oldest building in Florida in continuous use for higher education.

Just off the main street, on West Michigan Avenue, is the Henry Addison DeLand House. You can tour this delightful property dating from the 1890s and see memorabilia relating to the city's founder.

▶ *On E Michigan Avenue you will find the Gillespie Museum of Minerals (closed weekends). Continue north on* ***US 17*** *for 9 miles (14km).*

7 De León Springs

A major spring, naturally pumping 19 million US gallons (72 million litres) of water each day, this is a wonderful place for swimming and canoeing.
A highlight of the park is the picturesque Old Spanish Sugar Mill, now a restaurant, complete with its huge water-driven wooden mill wheel. Each table has its own griddle, and patrons are given pitchers of batter, plus toppings, to create their own pancakes.

▶ *Continue north for 6 miles (10km) to Barberville and turn right. Head east on* ***SR 40*** *for 24 miles (39km). Cross the Ormond Bridge onto East Granada Boulevard and turn immediately right onto Riverside Drive.*

8 The Casements

This sturdy handsome wooden house, named after its numerous casement windows, was built in the early 1900s and from 1918 until his death in 1937 was the winter home of Standard Oil billionaire John D Rockefeller. It is now a cultural center, but tours are given of several rooms restored to Rockefeller's era (closed Sunday). The house is elegant but very modest for a man of Rockefeller's massive wealth and was a great source of

BACK TO NATURE

Any of the fine state parks or recreation areas on this route are recommended. The nearest to Daytona is the Tomoka State Park, 3 miles (5km) north of Ormond Beach, at the confluence of the Tomoka and Halifax rivers. In addition to nature trails you can take a boat trip or the 16-mile (26 km) canoe trail to explore the banks of the lovely Tomoka River.

friction with his family, who declined to visit such a humble abode. Rockefeller moved to Ormond Beach for health reasons. A block away, on East Granada Boulevard, is the Ormond Memorial Art Museum and Garden, featuring lush tropical grounds, with nature trails and fish ponds.

▶ *Return across Ormond Bridge and turn immediately left onto South Beach Street. Continue for 4½ miles (7km).*

9 Halifax Historical Museum

Step back and admire the splendid Classicist façade of the Merchants Bank building that houses the museum. Built in 1910, the bank lasted just 19 years before succumbing to the Great Depression. The museum (closed Sunday and Monday) is a small but interesting collection of historical exhibits and records relating to Volusia County.

▶ *Turn left onto Orange Avenue and follow this across Memorial Bridge all the way to the ocean front. The main center of activity is to the left.*

10 Daytona Beach

They call this the world's most famous beach in honor of its record-breaking speed legacy, but today the 23 miles (37km) of compacted white shoreline

Keeping a close eye on swimmers and beach revelers at Daytona Beach

SPECIAL TO...

Daytona Beach has been known as the speed capital of the world since 1902, when Henry Ford and R E Olds (of Oldsmobile fame) raced along the compacted sand beaches at the death-defying speed of 57mph (92km/h). Two years later the *Stanley Steamer* reached 197mph (315km/h) before crashing in spectacular fashion. Since then the greatest speed on earth has been recorded here 14 times on the Daytona/Ormond sands, one of the most famous occasions being in 1935, when Sir Malcolm Campbell reached 276mph (444km/h) in *Bluebird*.

usually resemble a huge parking lot. If you prefer beaches without internal combustion engines, head for Ormond Beach or Ormond-by-the-Sea. If you want to drive on the hallowed sands, you will have to pay for the privilege – and with a speed limit of 10mph (16km/h) you won't be setting any records. Proximity to Walt Disney World and cheap accommodation attracts families on a tight budget, regular motorcycle racing attracts hordes of leather-clad bikers, and each spring break, thousands of college revelers turn the town into one giant raucous party.

FOR CHILDREN

The Pier, claimed to be the longest on the whole of America's East Coast, is a good place for children, and the Ocean Center features good-quality live family entertainment shows. For the best view of the beach, take a ride on the gondola skyride to the end of the pier, take the elevator to the top of the Space Needle, enjoy the arcades and then ride or walk back. Castle Adventure is a giant castle maze, just east of Volusia Mall on U S 92.

[i] *Daytona Visitors Welcome Center, 1801 W International Speedway Boulevard*

▶ *Head south along Atlantic Avenue.*

11 Ponce de León Inlet

Ponce de León Inlet is a pleasant stretch of coastline which ends after some 5 miles (8km) at the Ponce de León Inlet Lighthouse. The red brick lighthouse, built in 1887 and towering 175 feet (53m), is the centerpiece of a small museum complex. After scaling the 203-step spiral staircase, visit the museums in the keeper's and assistant's cottages, a restored 1890s cottage and various other outbuildings.

▶ *Turn right onto South Peninsula Drive and head back north. Turn left onto Dunlawton Avenue and continue for a total of 2 miles (3km) across Port Orange Bridge to South Nova Road* ***(SR 5A).*** *Turn right here and head north for ¼ mile (0.4km) to Old Sugarmill Road.*

12 Sugar Mill Gardens

The ruins of an old English sugar plantation here are of historical interest, but most people come for the 12-acre (5-hectare) botanical gardens. There are flowering trees, holly, magnolia and over 40 species of ivy. Children will enjoy four huge dinosaur statues – reminders of the gardens' former life as Bongoland amusement park.

Daytona International Speedway, the world's most famous and most used racetrack

▶ *Continue north on Nova Road for 2½ miles (4km), turn left onto South Street, then immediately right onto Museum Boulevard.*

13 Daytona Museum of Arts and Sciences

The area's finest museum features two outstanding art collections – the Dow Gallery of American Art, the best of paintings, furniture, metal, glass and needlework from 1640 to 1920; and the Cuban Museum, two centuries of Latin folk art up to 1959, plus changing exhibits. The highlight of the prehistory wing is a unique 13-foot (4m) skeleton of a giant sloth found near by.

There is also a new 'Window in the Forest' Interpretive Center, an African Wing, a planetarium, nature trails and sculpture gardens in the grounds.

▶ *Return to South Nova Road and continue for 2 miles (3km) north to West International Speedway Boulevard* ***(SR 600/US 92).*** *Turn left and head west.*

14 Daytona International Speedway/Daytona USA

The 'World Center of Racing' opened in 1959. On days when there are no events, the track is open to the public. A Visitor's Center offers 30-minute guided tours, including the Gallery of Legends and a Daytona 500 Surround Sound audio presentation. Just opened on the same site is Daytona USA, a major interactive hands-on racing attraction which allows visitors to design and test race cars, watch the Daytona 500 on a giant IMAX screen, see historical displays and much more.

▶ *Continue on* ***US 92,*** *crossing under* ***I–95*** *and turn left into Tomoka Farms Road, 4 miles (6km).*

15 Klassix Auto Museum

A collection of Corvettes from every year since 1953 is the centerpiece here, though not surprisingly there is a lot of material devoted to the history of racing on Daytona Beach. Opposite is the Daytona Flea and Farmer's Market, with over 1,000 stalls.

▶ *Return to* ***US 92*** *and pick up the* ***I–4*** *for Orlando.*

TOUR
19

Backwoods & Springs

3 DAYS • 330 MILES • 529KM

ITINERARY	
ORLANDO	▶ **Wekiwa Springs (27m-43km)**
WEKIWA SPRINGS	▶ **Mount Dora (17m-27km)**
MOUNT DORA	▶ **Venetian Gardens (15m-24km)**
VENETIAN GARDENS	▶ **Don Garlits' Museum (25m-40km)**
DON GARLITS' MUSEUM	▶ **Ocala (15m-24km)**
OCALA	▶ **Appleton Museum of Art (4m-6km)**
APPLETON MUSEUM OF ART	▶ **Silver Springs (2m-3km)**
SILVER SPRINGS	▶ **Ocala National Forest (3m-5km)**
OCALA NATIONAL FOREST	▶ **Crystal River (105m-169km)**
CRYSTAL RIVER	▶ **Homosassa Springs (5m-8km)**
HOMOSASSA SPRINGS	▶ **Weeki Wachee Spring (24m-39km)**
WEEKI WACHEE SPRING	▶ **Brooksville (12m-19km)**
BROOKSVILLE	▶ **Clermont Citrus Tower (43m-69km)**
CLERMONT CITRUS TOWER	▶ **Orlando (33m-53km)**

A journey from the sleepy 19th-century village of Mount Dora, through the scenic backwoods trails into the Ocala National Forest is a trip back to Florida's pre-Disney age. Silver and Homosassa Springs are first-class visitor attractions, and you can stroll in the woods, paddle a canoe down a river or take a dip in the a swimming hole at Jupiter or Wekiwa Springs.

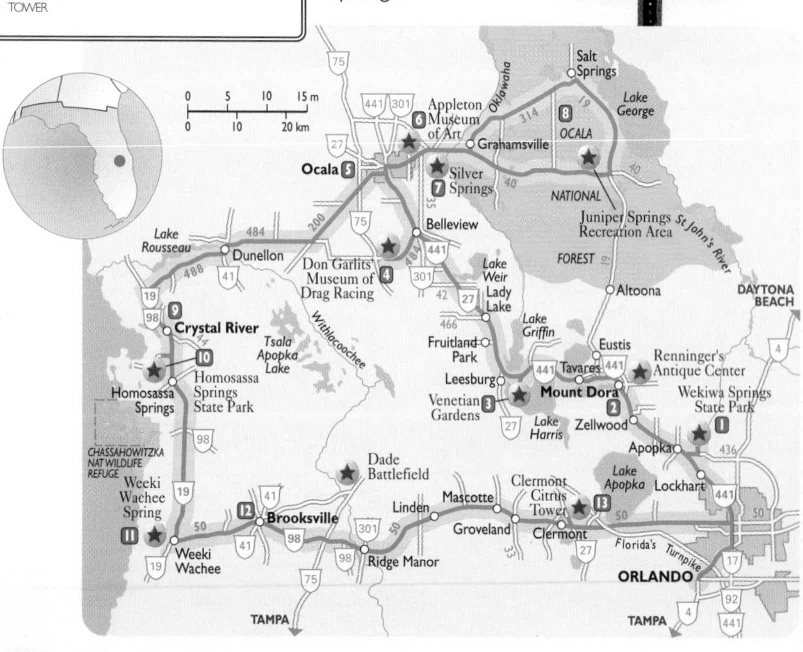

Orlando Official Visitor Center, International Drive (corner with Austrian Court)

*From Orlando head north on **I–4** to exit 33. Continue north on **US 17–92** to **US 441**. Turn off right onto **SR 436** and after 2½ miles (4km) turn left on Wekiwa Springs Road.*

1 Wekiwa Springs State Park

Wekiwa Springs is the head-water of the lush Wekiwa River, which flows into the St John's River. Activities here including swimming, canoe rental, 13 miles (21km) of hiking and nature trails and an 8-mile (13km) horseback-riding trail. The park is particularly good for bird-watching.

RECOMMENDED WALKS

Wekiwa Springs and Homosassa Springs both have fine nature trails. The Mount Dora Chamber of Commerce will also be happy to point out a historic walking trail to see this pretty little town on foot.

*Return to **US 441** and continue northwest for 11 miles (18km). Turn left following the signs to Mount Dora.*

2 Mount Dora

This delightful large village is closer in architectural character and atmosphere to New England than central Florida and is a world away from the neon strips of Orlando. Tourists have been staying at the Lakeside Inn since 1883, its most famous guest being President Calvin Coolidge, who wintered here in 1930. The porch of this charming hotel is the perfect place to appreciate the village's lovely lakeside setting. The oldest and most picturesque building here, however, is the Victorian Gothic Donelly House, built in 1882, and now a Masonic lodge (closed to the public). History buffs can visit the Historical Society's Museum, housed in the old jail (open Thursday–Sunday only) and browse the many antique shops in the quaint downtown district. Just southeast of Mount Dora is Renninger's Antique Center, which boasts 200 shops and claims the largest selection of antiques and collectibles in Florida (open Saturday and Sunday only).

Mount Dora Chamber of Commerce, 341 North Alexander Street

*Continue through Mount Dora for some 6 miles (10km) to Tavares to rejoin **US 441**. After another 8 miles (13km) turn left on Canal Street following the signs for Leesburg.*

SCENIC ROUTES

There are several scenic stretches on this route, most notably around Mount Dora, on SR 200 (southwest of Ocala) and to the west of Ocala National Forest.
The most scenic route from Mount Dora to Ocala is to head north on SR 19 via Eustis, Umatilla and Altoona (the Backwoods Trail) into Ocala National Forest.
Turn left onto SR 40 to Juniper Springs and continue on the indicated route. (Note: this excludes Venetian Gardens and the Don Garlits' Museum of Drag Racing).

Donelley House, a fine example of Mount Dora's architecture

3 Venetian Gardens

Set on the reedy shores of Lake Harris, this lovely park garden is a perfect spot for a picnic. You will soon be joined by a host of ducks, assorted wading birds and squirrels.

► *Rejoin **US 441** and head north for 21 miles (34km) to Belleview. Turn left onto **SR 484**.*

4 Don Garlits' Museum of Drag Racing

This is the world's only museum dedicated to the spectacular machines that tear along a ¼-mile (0.4km) straight in under seven seconds. There are over 75 drag-racing cars dating from the earliest 1940s models and, for cognoscenti of the sport, these include cars belonging to Tom McEwen, Shirley Muldowney, Art Malone and of course 'Big Daddy' Don Garlits.

► *Return to **US 441** and head north for 11 miles (18km).*

5 Ocala

Sited on the western edge of Ocala National Forest, Ocala is a medium-sized regional center best known for nearby Silver Springs and for the area's thoroughbred horse farms. Just south of town, on SW16th Avenue (I–75 exit 67) is the Garlits' Museum of Classic Cars with over 60 vehicles and one of the finest collections of early Fords in the world.

A calming influence: livestock on the thoroughbred horse farms of Ocala

SPECIAL TO...

Ocala is famous as the equine capital of the state, and around the town are some 400 horse farms. Many of these produce thoroughbreds and counted on their roll of honor are no less than seven Kentucky Derby champions. Some farms are open to the public at specified times, offering tours and rides to suit all levels of experience. For an up-to-date list ask at the Chamber of Commerce on East Silver Springs Boulevard.

The pristine waters and woods of Alexander Springs in the Ocala National Forest

i *Ocala–Marion County Chamber of Commerce, 110 E Silver Springs Boulevard*

► *Head northeast from Ocala centre on **SR 40** for 4 miles (6km).*

6 Appleton Museum of Art

Inside this modern glistening marble building is probably the best fine art collection in central Florida. Among its 6,000 diverse objects are splendid primitive tribal masks and artifacts, exquisite Indian and Oriental treasures, antiquities from Asia, Africa and pre-Columbian South America and fine 19th-century paintings from Europe and America. All items are beautifully displayed. An elegant courtyard café provides light meals and snacks.

► *Continue east for 2 miles (3km).*

7 Silver Springs

This multi-themed nature park enjoys one of the most beautiful settings in the state. At the heart of Silver Springs is the largest artesian limestone spring in the world, pumping an incredible 750 million US gallons (2.8 billion liters) of water each day.

The highlight of the visit is a glass-bottom boat ride along the crystal-clear waters of the Silver River into a primeval, exotic, natural world of ancient cypress, moss-draped hundred-year-old oaks and tropical palms. Peer down and you will see many of the 36 different varieties of fish that swim here; look to the side and you will enjoy some 30 species of water birds, plus alligators and turtles. Blink and you will miss something! Luckily there is an equally fascinating glass-bottom ride along the Lost River, where you will also see a 1,200-year-old Timucuan Indian canoe, amazingly preserved under the waters. Aboard Jungle Cruise (the third boat ride), you will see several wild monkeys – a legacy of six of the original *Tarzan* movies that were filmed here – free-roaming giraffes, emus, gazelles and other exotic creatures.

Jeep Safari is basically a land version of the boat cruises, visiting zebras, wild boars, many species of deer and birds, freely wandering through a natural wild habitat. Don't miss the White Alligator Exhibit, which features one of only 18 known existing white alligators in the world. The reptile lacks dark pigment and has blue eyes – but still packs a mean bite! In addition there is an excellent reptile show, bird and reptile displays, World of Bears (featuring five species of bear) and a petting zoo. Look out too for the live concerts at weekends which often feature famous names (free to park guests).

Adjacent to Silver Springs is Wild Waters, which features several water slides, flumes and a wave pool for body surfing.

▶ *Continue east on* ***SR 40*** *for 3 miles (5km).*

Close encounter with a gentle manatee

8 Ocala National Forest

The picturesque Oklawaha River is the eastern boundary of the forest. Turn left on SR 314. Continue northeast for 17 miles (27km) through the world's largest stand of sand pine. Turn right on SR 19 and head south for 15 miles (24km) following the shore of Lake George, Florida's second largest lake. Turn right at SR 40 and head west for 4 miles (6km) to Juniper Springs Recreation Area. There's a charming swimming hole here and a visitor center housed in a picturesque old mill house, where a huge water wheel rolls over 8 million US gallons (30 million litres) of water per day.

For many people the highlight of Ocala National Forest is the 7-mile (11km) canoe trip from here, paddling peacefully through palm, cypress and live oak spotting birds, mammals, turtles and alligators. A shuttle service will bring you back to the recreation area.

▶ *Continue west for 28 miles (45km) back to Ocala. Head southwest on* ***SR 200,*** *past several thoroughbred farms, for 14 miles (23km) and turn right on* ***SR 484*** *to Dunellon. Take* ***US 41*** *south for a short distance and turn right onto* ***SR 488****. After 2 miles (19km) turn left onto* ***US 19–98.*** *Head south for 6 miles (10km) and turn left onto* ***SR 44.***

9 Crystal River

During the winter months manatees gather around the 72°F (22°C) crystal-clear spring-fed waters here. You can jump right in with them (wetsuit, snorkel and flippers are for rent) or just hire a boat and watch them. Glass-bottom trips also set out from here. Near by, the Crystal River State Archeological Site marks what is probably the longest continuously occupied site in Florida. For 1,600 years (between 200 BC and AD 1400) this was a ceremonial center where American Indians buried their dead and conducted trade.

▶ *Return to* ***US 19*** *and head south for 7 miles (11km).*

10 Homosassa Springs State Park

Your visit starts with a 20-minute boat trip along beautiful Pepper Creek. The spring is famous for its manatee population and they can be viewed in a floating underwater observatory. The manatees come so close to the shore in the crystal water, however, that viewing is guaranteed and there is an excellent interpretive 'show' three times a day. Several other native and endangered species are showcased here, including American crocodile, black bear, otter, bobcats and many birds. Most are in natural surroundings, linked by a beautiful nature trail. Just southwest of the park is the Yulee Sugar Mill State Historic Site (exit and first right). The mill, now a ruin, stood at the center of a 5,100-

> **BACK TO NATURE**
>
> There are so many natural attractions on this route that it is hard to recommend an additional side trip. Some sites are more away from it all than others (for example, Juniper Springs is much less touristy than Silver Springs), but to get away altogether you may like to visit the Chassahowitzka National Wildlife Refuge. Home to bald eagles, manatees, turtles and peregrine falcons, the refuge is accessible only by boat, which can be rented from Chassahowitzka River Campground, just off US 19, 6 miles (10km) south of Homosassa Springs.

acre (2,062-hectare) sugar plantation, which was operated by around 1,000 slaves and supplied sugar products to Southern troops during the Civil War.

▶ *Return to **US 19** and head south for 23 miles (37km).*

11 Weeki Wachee Spring

This is a spring with a difference, featuring an all-singing, all-dancing underwater mermaid show. The performers, taking lungfuls of air from submerged air lines, mime and act out an adventure featuring the characters of *Pocahontas* and Hans Christian Andersen's *Little Mermaid* in the Underwater Spring Theater. Children love it, and adults are intrigued to see how it is done. The other highlight is the Wilderness River Cruise, where visitors can encounter Florida in its pristine unspoiled state. An exotic bird show, a birds of prey show and a petting zoo complete a half-day's entertainment. Spend the rest of the day cooling off and have a picnic in adjacent Buccaneer Bay. This is Florida's only natural spring water park, with three water slides and a small beach area (open March to September).

▶ *Head east on **SR 50** for 12 miles (19km).*

12 Brooksville

This attractive, sleepy village is home to a Heritage Museum (open Wednesday and Saturday) and Roger's Christmas House Village, with five themed houses that contain Christmas and gift items from around the world. Just on the right as you leave Brooksville is the delightful Blueberry Patch Tea Room, a picture-book cornflower-blue country cottage, furnished with antiques and serving homemade food.

▶ *Continue east on **US 98** for 13 miles (21km) before picking up eastbound **SR 50.** Continue for a further 29 miles (47km), then turn left onto **US 27** and head north for 1 mile (1.5km).*

Weird and wacky maybe, but the Weeki Wachee mermaid shows are compulsory viewing!

13 Clermont Citrus Tower

This towering landmark, which measures 226 feet (69m) high, is 543 feet (166m) above sea level, giving it the honor of being Florida's highest point. The tower was built as an observation deck so that tourists could enjoy the sight of the citrus groves stretching out over the rolling hills below. Adjacent to the tower is the House of Presidents Wax Museum where you can meet all the US Presidents from Washington to Clinton.

▶ *Return south to **US 50** and continue east to return to Orlando (**I–4** exit 41), 33 miles (53km).*

TOUR
20

Kissimmee & Cypress Gardens

3 DAYS • 214 MILES • 345KM Kissimmee, with its new beautification schemes and top-class attractions such as Splendid China, is striving to shake off its 'Disney-dormitory town' image. Head south to discover the old Florida of wide-open spaces and cattle ranches, and the beautiful Cypress Gardens.

ITINERARY

ORLANDO	▶ **Splendid China (11m-18km)**
SPLENDID CHINA	▶ **Cypress Gardens (33m-53km)**
CYPRESS GARDENS	▶ **Bok Tower Gardens (8m-13km)**
BOK TOWER GARDENS	▶ **Lake Wales (3m-5km)**
LAKE WALES	▶ **Lake Kissimmee State Park (15m-24km)**
LAKE KISSIMMEE STATE PARK	▶ **Gatorland (107m-172km)**
GATORLAND	▶ **US 192 (8m-13km)**
US 192	▶ **Old Town (6m-10km)**
OLD TOWN	▶ **Water Mania (0m-0km)**
WATER MANIA	▶ **Orlando (23m-37km)**

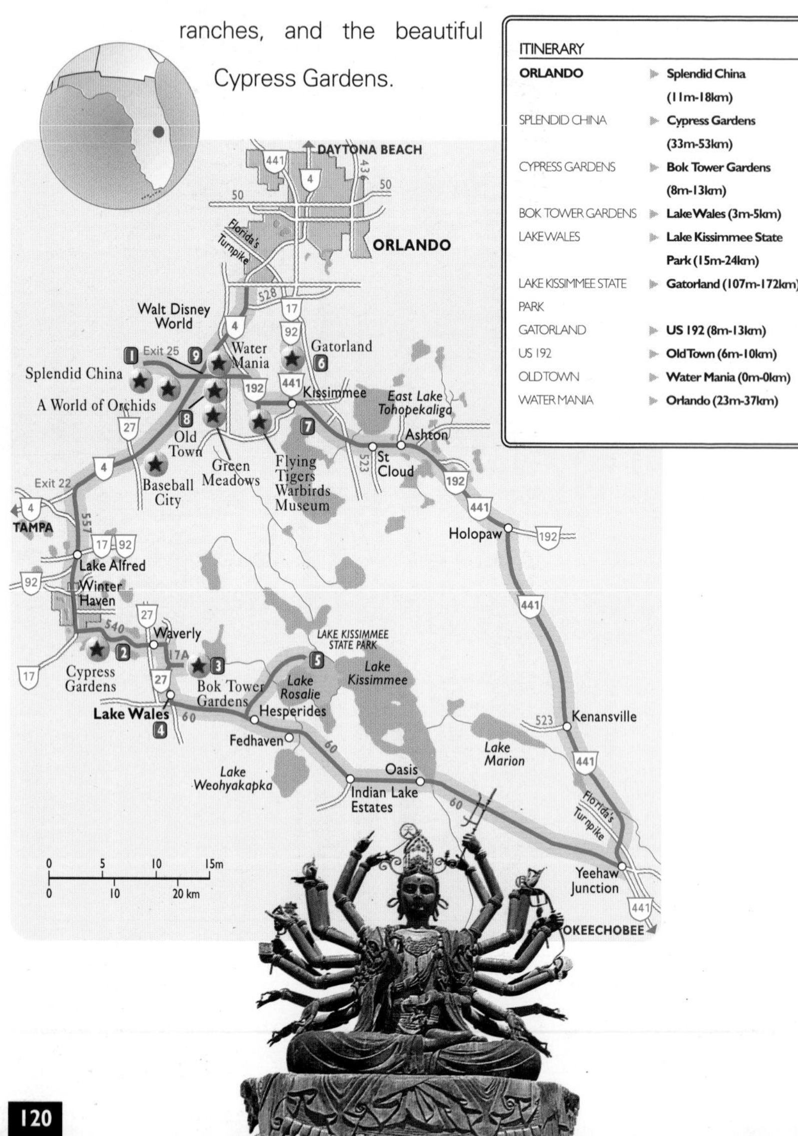

[i] *Orlando Official Visitor Center, International Drive (corner with Austrian Court)*

*From Sand Lake Road, Orlando (junction 29), head south on **I–4** for 9 miles (14km) to exit 25. Turn right onto **US 192** and drive for 3 miles (5km).*

0 Splendid China

Splendid China is a theme park in miniature and one of the world's greatest model village-style attractions. Set in beautifully landscaped grounds it features over 60 of the country's most renowned sights, all painstakingly re-created by Chinese craftsmen; China's most famous landmark, The Great Wall, alone was constructed from 6.5 million tiny bricks. Other highlights are the Leshan Grand Buddha Statue, the Terra Cotta Warriors and the Imperial Palace/

The Dazu Grotto Buddha at Splendid China

Forbidden City, but wherever you look you will find models of great beauty and full of intricate interest.

There are also eight theaters and show areas (don't miss the Snow Tiger show) featuring daily live entertainment. At the entrance to the park is Chinatown, an area of shops, restaurants and a theater. Admission is free and it's well worth a visit just for the excellent authentic food and free courtyard shows which are staged here daily.

SPECIAL TO...

A World of Orchids (a mile or so west of Splendid China, signposted) is a beautiful collection of over 2,000 rare and exotic orchids. It also features a lovely boardwalk trail and bird aviaries.

*Return to **I–4,** head south,exit left onto **SR 557** and just past Winter Haven turn left onto Cypress Boulevard **(SR 540)** and drive for 3 miles (5km).*

2 Cypress Gardens

Established in 1936, this is Florida's oldest theme park, though by today's standards it is hardly recognizable as such. Yet what it lacks in technological wizardry and thrill rides, it makes up for in natural beauty. Cypress Gardens has also long been famous for the quality of its water-skiers and the current SkiXtreme team features present and past national champions.

A Deep South theme pervades the park and is personified by the famous Southern Belles, who pose pretty as a picture, in their hooped antebellum skirts, among the beautifully manicured gardens and lawns. With over 8,000 varieties of exotic plants and flowers, Cypress Gardens is a photographer's paradise: the Spring Flower Festival runs from mid-March through mid-May; the Victorian Garden Party is one of the largest artistic topiary festivals in the world and runs from mid-June to early September; the Mum Festival features more than two and a half million chrysanthemums and is in bloom during November; the Poinsettia Festival showcases 10,000 plants in a dozen varieties and colors and runs from late November through to early January.

For the best overview of the grounds jump aboard the Island in the Sky, a revolving platform on a crane-like arm, which hauls its way up from ground level to 153 feet (47m) high.
To observe things at closer quarters, take the Botanical Gardens Cruise.

Other highlights include: the Reptile Discovery show; a birds of prey show; and Wings of Wonder, where over 1,000 brilliant butterflies fly freely in a rainforest jungle conservatory.

*Follow **SR 540** east crossing **US 27** to **US 27 (Alt)** and turn right (south). Turn left onto **SR 17A**, 8 miles (13km).*

3 Bok Tower Gardens

Bok Tower is located on the Florida peninsula's highest point, Iron Mountain, with an elevation of 298 feet (91m). The bell tower, which is the visual centerpiece of these beautiful gardens, is made up of pink and grey marble from Georgia, set off with brass, iron and ceramic friezes recalling the plant and animal motifs of Persia and India and images from Greece and China. Bearing Gothic and Art Deco influences, it was built between 1927 and 1928. Standing 205 feet (62m) high, it houses 57 bronze bells varying in weight from 17 pounds (7.7kg) to almost 12 US tons (10.8 metric tons). You can hear recitals daily at 3pm. The tower has never been open to the public, but an audiovisual program in the visitor center shows its inner machinery. The garden is one of Florida's most peaceful places.

Cypress Gardens' famous Southern Belles chat with guests and pose for pictures

FOR HISTORY BUFFS

Pinewood House and Garden is one of the finest examples of Mediterranean Revival landscape and residential design, including furnishings, in the whole state. Admission is by tour only.

*Return to **S 27 (Alt)** and continue south for 1½ miles (2km). At the traffic lights turn left onto North Avenue **(SR 17A)** and left onto Spook Hill.*

BACK TO NATURE

From the Bok Tower Gardens' Window by the Pond nature observatory, the lucky visitor might see belted kingfishers, purple gallinules, egrets and herons fishing a few feet away from the picture window.

4 Lake Wales

Spook Hill is certainly the most curious of this small town's attractions, though in Florida a steep hill of any kind is a curiosity in itself. Park on the white line facing up the steep side of the hill, release your brake and you apparently roll up the hill (don't expect to roll forwards up the really steep part of the hill – that really would be impossible!). An optical illusion? A Seminole Indian curse? Find out more about this fascinating phenomenon at the Chamber of Commerce on Central Avenue.

Spook Hill is a one-way street, so head back in a circle to the traffic lights and then continue a short distance further to The Depot, a restored railroad building which serves as the Lake Wales Museum and Cultural Center.

*Continue south on **US 27 (Alt)** and turn left to the junction with **SR 60.** Drive east to pick up Boy Scout Road heading north, then follow the signs on Camp Mack Road to Lake Kissimmee (15 miles/24km east of Lake Wales).*

A colorful character from Wild Bill's Wild West Dinner Show

5 Lake Kissimmee State Park

The park comprises 5,000 acres (2,024 hectares) bordering three lakes, and among its floodplain prairies, marshes and pine flatwoods roam white-tailed deer, bald eagles, sandhill cranes and wild turkeys. An observation platform provides a fine view over Lake Kissimmee, while canoes are available for a closer look at the park's waterways. The best time to visit is at the weekend when the park features a living-history 1876 Cow Camp. This was (and still is) cowboy country, and you can see one of the few remaining herds of scrub cattle still in existence. A cow camp consists of a holding pen where the cows are branded and a crude shelter for the cow hunters (as they call themselves), so don't expect to see a re-creation of Dodge City.

▶ *Return to **SR 60** and continue east for 37 miles (60km) to Yeehaw Junction. Turn left and head north on **US 441** for 35 miles (56km). Turn left at Holopaw onto **US 192–441** and follow this northwest for 24 miles (39km). Turn right onto the South Orange Blossom Trail **(US 441/17–92)**.*

SCENIC ROUTES

The lake area around Winter Haven provides for pleasant driving, and US 27 (Alt) south to Lake Wales is officially designated as a scenic route, though in fact there is not much to see. The area from Yeehaw Junction to Holopaw is regarded as old farming Florida ('Cracker Country'), and here you will see great stretches of fields and cattle pasture.

6 Gatorland

Boardwalks cross the habitat of this huge alligator farm, with over 5,000 scaly reptiles, ranging in length from a few inches to 15 feet (4.6m). Watch them leap out of the water at feeding time in the Gator Jumparoo Show. A narrow-gauge railroad takes you round the zoo. Snakes, exotic animals and birds are also residents here.

▶ *Return south to **US 192** (Irlo Bronson Memorial Highway) and turn right.*

7 US 192

Along with International Drive, Kissimmee is the most important accommodation area for Disney visitors, and there is no shortage of attractions along this strip. If you have not experienced an airboat ride or would like to pilot your own, stop at U-Drive Airboat Rentals for a look beyond the neon in Kissimmee. To the left off SR 531, towards Kissimmee Airport, is the Flying Tigers Warbirds Museum, where a fascinating guided tour demonstrates how World War II aircraft are lovingly restored from old pieces of scrap metal back to beautiful flying machines. Biplane flights are also on offer here, featuring several World War II survivors, restored to working condition.

Back on US 192 there's a whole host of dinner shows competing for custom: at Medieval Times watch jousting

FOR CHILDREN

The Kissimmee area is bursting with children's attractions. In addition to those on the itinerary, older children may enjoy Reptile World Serpentarium (on East US 192 towards St Cloud), an educational indoor display and scientific venom-production facility. Younger ones will love a hands-on day at Green Meadows Petting Farm (5 miles/8km south on S Poinciana Boulevard), and all ages can have fun on the go-karts at any one of several tracks in the area.

knights rescue damsels in distress: Arabian Nights, featuring a cast of some 60 horses and a chariot race; American Gladiators Orlando Live!; Capone's, a Broadway-style gangster-themed show; and Wild Bill's Wild West Dinner Extravaganza.

i *Kissimmee/St Cloud Visitor Information Center, 1925 E Irlo Bronson Memorial Highway (US 192)*

▶ *Further west on* **US 192** *is Old Town.*

SPECIAL TO...

The Silver Spurs Rodeo is held every February and July at the Silver Spurs Arena in Kissimmee. This features some of the South's top professional cowboys competing for a fistful of dollars in events such as calf roping, steer wrestling, saddle and bareback riding. Spectators are also treated to live music and the Silver Spurs Quadrille Team, which performs its brand of square dancing on horseback.

8 Old Town

Old Town is Kissimmee's answer to Disney's Main Street, USA, with some 70 shops, bars, eating and night-time places harking back to turn-of-the-century America. There's also a landmark vintage ferris wheel, a roller-coaster and the Haunted Grimm House (with actors playing the part of monsters and villains). Just east of here is Movie Rider, which offers two nerve-jangling roller-coaster-type simulator rides.

▶ *Almost opposite Old Town is Water Mania.*

9 Water Mania

This may be the smallest of Orlando's major water parks, but it offers plenty of thrills. Its top rides are: Wipe Out, an award-winning body board surf ride; Abyss, an enclosed tube ride in the dark; and the 72-foot (22m) Screamer. Family rides include the Anaconda, where a four-person raft twists and turns through 400 feet (122m), and the Banana Peel, a two-person water-chute plunge. There is also the second biggest wave pool in Florida, with eight different wave patterns, and the Double Beserker, where two people race each other to the bottom in directly adjacent slides. A sand beach, a shady picnic area, a maze and other dry amusements complete a lazy day's entertainment.

BACK TO NATURE

A treat for nature lovers close to the very urban center of Kissimmee is the new Cypress Island Wildlife Sanctuary in the middle of Lake Tohopekaliga.

RECOMMENDED WALKS

The most peaceful place far a walk is either at Bok Tower Gardens for a leisurely stroll or at Lake Kissimmee State Park for a more serious hike. At the former the North Walk is lined with many seasonal blossoming plants, including giant crinum with enormous lily-like flowers, while the rougher Pine Ridge Trail traverses the original vegetation of Iron Mountain. At the state park there are 13 miles (21km) of prairie and woodland hiking routes to choose from.

▶ *Rejoin* **I–4** *(exit 25) and return north to Orlando, 9 miles (14km).*

The vintage era of flight is well represented in Kissimmee

THE FIRST COAST

Florida saw the arrival of its first Europeans on Easter morning in 1513, when Juan Ponce de León landed near the site of St Augustine. Claiming the land for Spain, he named it after the Spanish Feast of Flowers at Easter, Pascua Florida. Ponce de León did not stay, however, and it was left to his fellow countryman, Pedro Menéndez de Avilés, to return in 1565 to found the first European settlement at St Augustine. The French followed hard on the Spaniard's heels, but rued their ambitions later that year when Menéndez wiped out their settlement and its inhabitants. Spain's other great contemporary rival, England, also had designs on the strategically important First Coast harbors, and in 1585 Sir Francis Drake burned St Augustine to the ground. It was not until 1763, however, that the British took Florida, and then it was a bloodless victory: the Spaniards handed over this territory peacefully in order to regain recently captured Havana.

Twenty years later it was the turn of the British to horse-trade territories, and the First Coast (and Florida) reverted to Spanish rule. Of course, the territorial period of Florida's history was not restricted just to the northeast, but nowhere was it more dramatic than here and nowhere in Florida is it better interpreted for the visitor than here.

The highlight is the beautiful, European-style old-world town of St Augustine. Although for some it has become a little too cocooned within its rich history, the tiny streets and alleyways and its charming lodgings are a breath of fresh air after the characterless malls and resort hotels found elsewhere in the state. Just north of Jacksonville, the pretty Victorian gingerbread mansions and shops of Amelia Island continue the history lesson, moving through the late 19th and early 20th century.

During the late 19th century, millionaire developer Henry Flagler started his East Coast ambitions at St Augustine by building three of his finest hotels. In terms of a lasting effect on tourism, however, the Flagler influence is much less marked here than further south. Significantly, none of Flagler's St Augustine hotels are still open as hotels. In many ways this lack of modern tourism development has been fortuitous for the First Coast, as the region retains a sense of history and a quiet charm far removed from the brash resorts of the southeast.

Five of the flags which have flown over the First Coast in its 500-year history

Above: old-fashioned transport in old-fashioned St Augustine

Tour 21

St Augustine, where it all began, is the most sensible starting point for a tour of the First Coast. It is also worth stressing that despite its deep historical roots, it is also the most complete all-round resort town in northeast Florida. A walking tour of the Old City will tell you all you want to know about the colonial period, but don't try to do it all in one day. There is too much to see, and you will soon overdose on 'oldest' houses, 'oldest' stores and 'oldest' claims of all kinds. The beach and its family attractions are a perfect antidote.

Tour 22

The Jacksonville beaches are every bit as good as their more famous rivals to the south, and visitors with a sense of history will appreciate the old ports, the even older forts and Florida's oldest plantation. The charming northeasternmost town of Fernandina Beach is arguably as rich in history and architecture as the state's southernmost point, Key West. It is an excellent all-round resort, and its relative lack of fame only adds to the enjoyment of those who are in the know.

Gainesville is another under-stated town which will reward the curious visitor. Here there are no skyscrapers, just elegant red-brick University of Florida buildings, an historic district and some fine outdoor attractions. Drive a little further south and it seems time has stood still. Paynes Prairie is almost primeval and the village of Micanopy seems locked in a 19th-century time capsule. It is not hard to see why novelist Marjorie Kinnan Rawlings loved Cross Creek so dearly. It, too, harkens back to a peaceful, almost disappeared, Florida.

Right: in the historic town center of Fernandina Beach, on Amelia Island

Tour 23

Thanks to some imaginative developments and first-rate visitor attractions, the city of Jacksonville is currently enjoying an upswing in its tourism fortunes. With its glittering skyscrapers and new waterside developments, it is like a smaller version of Miami, and city slickers are bound to enjoy it.

TOUR
21

St Augustine

St Augustine, founded in 1565, is the oldest permanent European settlement in the continental United States, and a walk down St George Street is like stepping back in time over two centuries and more. History here is living, vibrant and interpreted with enthusiasm and a smile.

2 DAYS

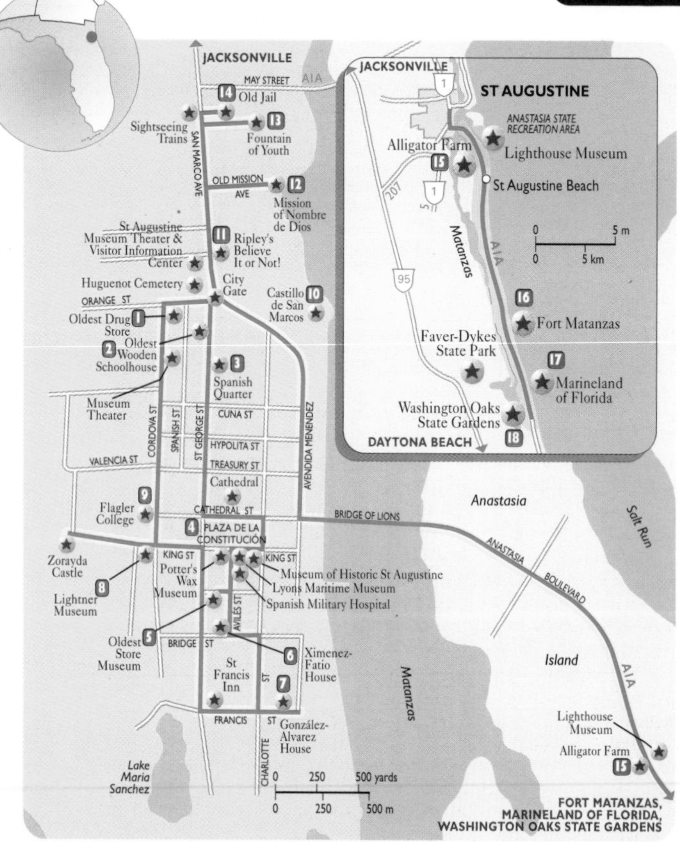

The González-Alvarez House (above and right) is claimed to be the oldest in the US

[i] *St Augustine/St John's County Visitor Information Center*

▶ *Park just outside the old city boundaries. Walk through the parking lot past the early 19th-century Huguenot Cemetery. Visit the Information Center and the Museum Theater, which presents an opportunity to see the history of St Augustine on film, then enter the old city through the stone gateposts. From here, turn immediately right onto Orange Street.*

1 Oldest Drug Store

This ancient-looking cypress-boarded building was originally built in 1739 to sell liquor, medicine and Indian remedies. It has been a pharmacy ever since 1887 and it now houses a fine display of memorabilia from its early days, up to the 1950s, with many original shop-fittings. Visitors are greeted by the 'shopkeeper' himself, who may well classify as 'the oldest animatronic'.

▶ *Return to the old city gate and follow St George Street.*

2 Oldest Wooden Schoolhouse

Another atmospheric red cedar and cypress-boarded building, this structure is held together by wooden pegs and hand-made nails. It was built some time before 1763 and is thought to be the country's oldest schoolhouse. You can ring the old school bell, see a 'class' in session and visit the spartan upstairs accommodation where the schoolmaster lived. The kitchen building to the rear is set in a charming garden.

▶ *Continue down St George Street.*

FOR CHILDREN

Most youngsters will enjoy seeing the conditions their peers were taught in some two centuries ago at the Oldest Wooden Schoolhouse. For a break from the city's history lessons, however, children (of all ages) will love the fun-house style and unexpected tricks of Ripleys Believe It or Not!, as well as marveling at its exhibits. On the beach side of town, Alligator Farm and Marineland are guaranteed child-pleasers.

3 Spanish Quarter (San Augustin Antiguo)

The centerpiece of the old city, this superb living history village depicts everyday colonial life in the mid-18th century. You can visit a Minorcan family house, a foot soldier's dwelling (incorporating a store), an officer's house, a blacksmith's shop, a spinning and weaving area and other houses. The enthusiastic costumed guides and craftspeople use only period tools and materials as part of their faithful re-creation of the past.

▶ *Continue along St George Street to the end of the pedestrianized section.*

4 Plaza de la Constitución

This was the business district during the Spanish heyday and across the square to your left stands a statue of Ponce de León, who claimed Florida for Spain in 1513. Immediately left is the handsome basilica Cathedral of St Augustine, built in 1797, though considerably reconstructed inside. Around the square are Potter's Wax Museum, the Lyons Maritime Museum and the Government House Museum of Historic St Augustine. Just off the plaza on

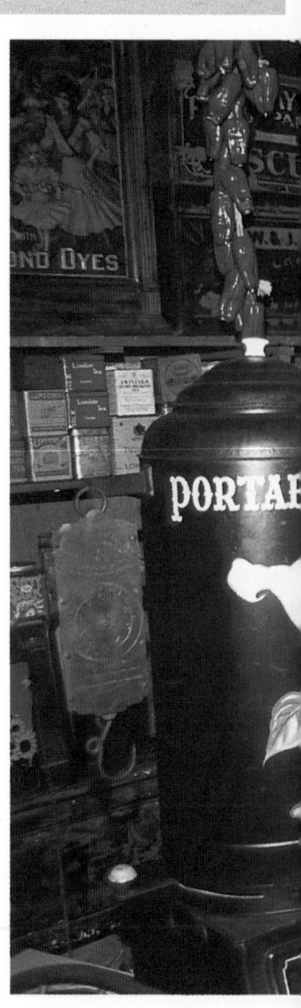

Above: the Old Mill in the Spanish Quarter
Right: the Oldest Store Museum

Avilés Street (by the Maritime Museum) is the Spanish Military Hospital, which is an outlying part of the Spanish Quarter. This is well worth a visit in order to see its apothecary and wards, presented as they were in 1791.

▶ *Continue along Avilés Street and turn right onto Artillery Street.*

5 Oldest Store Museum

This authentic turn-of-the-century general store is crammed full with over 10,000 nostalgic items evoking the days of high, stiff clip-on collars, lace-up corsets and Edison phonographs. It also holds a small museum of antique vehicles, high-wheeled bicycles and farm artifacts.

▶ *Return to and continue along Avilés Street.*

6 Ximinez-Fatio House

This beautiful historic house operated as a fashionable inn from 1855 to 1875. Its furnishings reflect this period, and a guided tour will point out the

English and Spanish design features. From the balcony you can look across to the 1763 Casa de Solana, which serves today's tourists bed and breakfast, and see how little has changed in old St Augustine.

► *Turn left on Bridge Street, right on Charlotte Street and left on St Francis Street.*

7 González-Alvarez House

This site has been continuously occupied since the early 1600s, and the present house is thought to date from the first decade of the 18th century. It reflects the simple lifestyle of the earliest Spanish settlers, the subsequent British influences, and the territorial American changes and additions. On the same site is a general history museum, a Museum of Florida's Army, and lovely ornamental gardens which contain plants typical of those grown by the occupants of the house.

► *Walk back up St Francis Street, turn right past the 1791 St Francis Inn onto St George Street. Follow it to the Plaza de la Constitución and turn left onto King Street.*

8 Lightner Museum

The stately Spanish Renaissance-style edifice in which the Lightner Museum resides was built by Henry Flagler in 1888 as the Alcazar Hotel. Monied guests once stayed in what now exhibits an

FOR HISTORY BUFFS

Needless to say, the whole area is a paradise for history lovers. González-Alvarez House (the oldest house), the Spanish Quarter and the Fountain of Youth are the bare essentials, but to get away from the crowds visit Flagler College, then pay your respects to Florida's greatest pioneer at the beautiful Memorial Presbyterian Church on Sevilla Street, behind the college. Designed in 1889 by Flagler in Venetian Renaissance style as a memorial to his daughter, this is also the last resting place of the great man himself.

outstanding collection of Victorian American and European art, antiques and furnishings, Oriental pieces, mechanical musical instruments (played once a day) and a sparkling display of American Brilliant Period cut crystal and Tiffany glass. Signs and photographs tell the story of the hotel, and the steam baths can still be seen in *situ*. Below the museum collection the former swimming pool now houses the Lightner Antique Shopping Mall and an elegant café-restaurant. Adjacent to the museum is Zorayda Castle, an architectural reproduction of part of the Moorish Alhambra Palace in Granada, Spain. Its artifacts are not without interest, but there is a disappointing lack of authentic atmosphere, hardly helped by American piped music. Next door is a Museum of Weapons and Early American History.

▶ *Cross the road opposite the Lightner to Flagler College.*

9 Flagler College

The Alcazar's sister hotel was the equally magnificent Ponce de León. The hotel closed its doors in 1967 and since 1971 has been home to the highly regarded liberal arts Flagler College. Only the marble lobby area is open to the public, allowing a mere glimpse of Florida's Gilded Age. A third Flagler hotel on the same square, the Cordova, now functions as the City Hall complex.

▶ *Follow Cordova Street north, past Victorian bed and breakfast inns, as far as Orange Street. Turn right to get back to the old city gates. Follow San Marco Avenue to the castle entrance.*

10 Castillo de San Marcos

Built between 1672 and 1695 to guard homeward-bound Spanish galleons against corsairs, this is the oldest stone fort in America. During its 300 years of constant active service it has played host to the British, during the American Revolution, to the unwilling Chief Osceola and his Seminole tribe, held captive here in 1835, and to troops from both the North and the South during the Civil War. The huge imposing walls made from coquina (a natural shellstone) measure some 33 feet (10m) high and are up to 14 feet (4.3m) thick at the base. Now a national monument, its rangers will provide you with an introductory history, then let you explore its rooms, exhibits and battlements.

▶ *Return to the parking lot at the information center. Opposite is Ripley's Believe it or Not!*

11 Ripley's Believe It or Not!

Robert Ripley, the self-billed 'modern Marco Polo', traveled to 198 countries during the early part of this century, and whenever he saw an oddity he collected it. This museum features some 750 objects from his extraordinary treasure trove and whether or not trivia, record-breakers and freaks appeal to you, there is never a dull moment here. Marvel at how the Mona Lisa was created from 63 slices of toasted bread, gasp at the 24-foot (7.3m) Eiffel Tower made up of 110,000 toothpicks, and shudder at the real shrunken human heads! The final 'believe it or not' is that Castle Warden, the grand building in which the museum is housed, was once home to the great American novelist Marjorie Kinnan Rawlings, of Cross Creek fame (see Cross Creek, Tour 22).

▶ *Follow San Marco Avenue five blocks north to Old Mission Avenue and turn right.*

12 Mission of Nombre de Dios

One of the most sacred and historic places in the country, the mission stands on the site where, in 1565, Pedro Menéndez de Avilés, admiral of the Spanish fleet, stepped ashore and the first Mass in America was celebrated. The place was called Nombre de Dios (Name of God), and a mission and the first Marian shrine, Nuestra Señora de la Leche, were established. A stainless steel cross towering 208 feet (63m) high marks the site of the founding of St Augustine.

▶ *Return to San Marco Avenue, continue north for three blocks and turn right onto Magnolia Avenue.*

13 Fountain of Youth

Predating the mission by 52 years in the history of European discovery is the Fountain of Youth site. This is the spot where Ponce de León first set foot on Florida soil in 1513, possibly searching for the fabled Fountain of Youth as well as for gold. An ancient spring does, in fact, still flow here, and you are given a free taste. The surrounding archeological park also contains a planetarium, an audiovisual display showing how de León navigated by the stars, excavations of a 2,000-year-old Timucuan Indian settlement, and the first Christian Indian burial ground in North America.

▶ *Return to San Marco Avenue, continue north one block and turn right.*

14 The Old Jail

This grim edifice, built in 1890, served as the St John's County Jail until 1953. The jokey courtyard displays of felons in black and white hooped prison suits contrast with the forbidding crumbling cell block and the collection of weapons taken away from criminals.

▶ *Return south on San Marco Avenue, collect your car, and cross the Bridge of Lions (so named after its stone beasts). Continue on **SR A1A** for 2 miles (3km).*

15 Alligator Farm
Established in 1893, this is the world's original alligator attraction. In addition to its hundreds of scaly residents, you can see the Snappin' Sam Show, the Mystic Alligator Swamp and the Florida Wildlife Show. An elevated boardwalk winds through a beautiful lagoon, and in late afternoon flocks of heron, egret and ibis return here to roost. Ironically the star of the farm is a huge crocodile, Gomek from New Guinea, said to be the largest captive reptile in the Western hemisphere.

Opposite the farm is the Lighthouse Museum. This landmark was built between 1871 and 1876. It now houses a coastal and maritime museum and a gallery featuring local artists. Climb to the top for a fine view of town and bay.

► *Continue south, to the resort of St Augustine Beach (information center on **SR A1A**) and on for a further 9 miles (14km).*

16 Fort Matanzas
Matanzas, Spanish for slaughter, refers to the attack at this site in 1565 in which 200 to 300 unarmed French Huguenots were put to the sword by the Spanish Catholic forces of Menéndez to counter French territorial encroachment and their perceived religious heresy. The well-preserved fort was built of coquina between 1740 and 1742 by Menéndez's successors to prevent any approach to St Augustine along the Intracoastal Waterway.

► *Continue south for 4 miles (6km).*

17 Marineland of Florida
This fine marine-life park, claimed to be the oldest in the world, has been delighting audiences for over 50 years without losing any of its originality or sparkle. You may well have seen leaping dolphins and barking sea lions before, but Marineland does it so well it is worth seeing again. Exceptional, too, is the underwater hand-feeding of sharks, barracuda and stingrays, and performing electric eels. Sea Dream is a 3-D movie where monsters of the deep seem to come right out of the screen; Wonders of the Spring is one of the country's largest freshwater aquariums, stocked with every type of Florida freshwater fish; and Secrets of the Reef exhibits exotic tropical fish.

► *Continue south for 3 miles (5km).*

18 Washington Oaks State Gardens
In contrast to the flat shores of St Augustine Beach, the ocean waves here have washed away the sand to create a picturesque boulder-strewn beach. Birdwatchers should arrive at low tide. Designated by the state parks authority as an underutilised 'gem', the gardens are a fine place for a picnic.

► *Return to St Augustine north on **SR A1A**.*

Demonstration at Alligator Farm

Florida's Crown

2/3 DAYS • 282 MILES • 454KM

In recognition of both historical and geographical factors, the northeastern tip of Florida is sometimes referred to as The Crown. While the Jacksonville beaches provide the gold, the jewel in the crown is Amelia Island. Almost hidden to the south lies Alachua County where life plods on much as it has done for centuries.

ITINERARY

ST AUGUSTINE	▶ **Jacksonville Beach (58m-93km)**
JACKSONVILLE BEACH	▶ **Mayport (8m-13km)**
MAYPORT	▶ **Kingsley Plantation (1m-2km)**
KINGSLEY PLANTATION	▶ **Little Talbot Island (3m-5km)**
LITTLE TALBOT ISLAND	▶ **Amelia Island (8m-13km)**
AMELIA ISLAND	▶ **Fernandina Beach (13m-21km)**
FERNANDINA BEACH	▶ **Jacksonville (33m-53km)**
JACKSONVILLE	▶ **Gainesville (66m-106km)**
GAINESVILLE	▶ **Paynes Prairie State Preserve (10m-16km)**
PAYNES PRAIRIE STATE PRESERVE	▶ **Cross Creek (8m-13km)**
CROSS CREEK	▶ **Ravine Gardens (44m-71km)**
RAVINE GARDENS	▶ **St Augustine (30m-48km)**

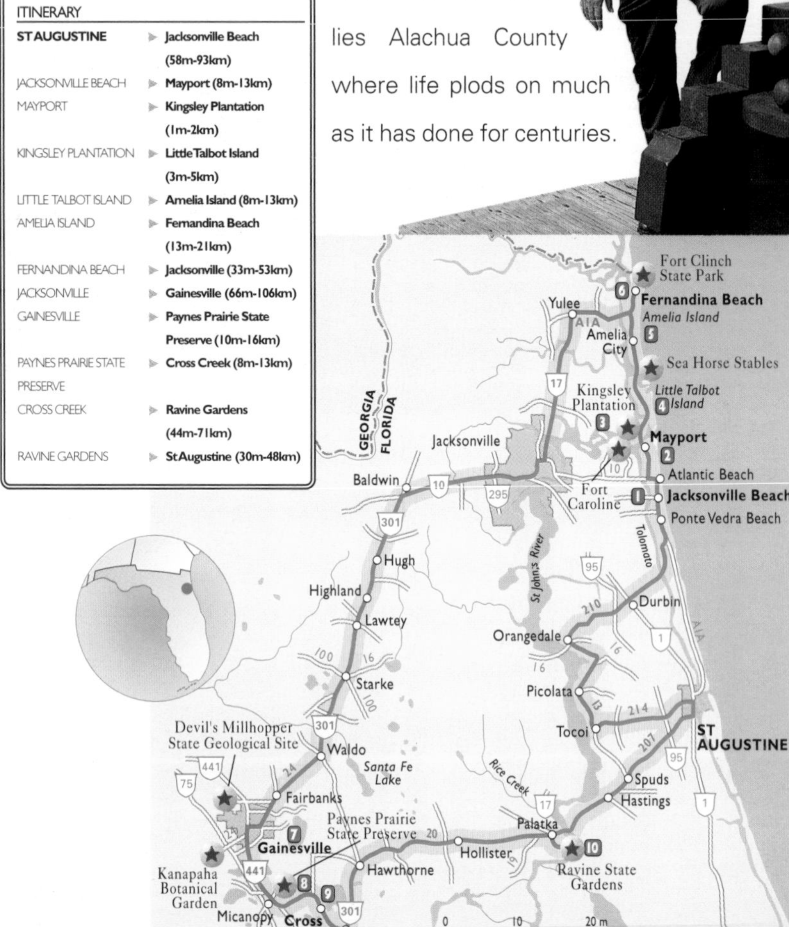

*From St Augustine follow **SR 214** west 14 miles (23km) to Tocoi on the St John's River. Follow the river north on **SR 13** for a further 17 miles (27km) to Orangedale. Turn right onto **SR 210** and follow it northeast to the coast where it joins **SR A1A**. Turn north for Jacksonville Beach. (For a more direct, though less scenic route, simply take **SR A1A** north from St Augustine for 29 miles/47km.)*

0 Jacksonville Beach

This is the centerpiece and liveliest of the four Jacksonville beaches, which stretch for some 7 miles (11km) as far as Ponte Vedra Beach (south of this are even more fine beaches, some of which are totally undeveloped). Just off the beach at North First Street is the Beaches Art and Craft Gallery, a co-operative showroom featuring the works of some 40 local artists. The Seawalk Plaza also regularly has art exhibits and festivals. On Beach Boulevard is the Beaches Antique Gallery, north Florida's largest antique mall with over 120 dealers, and Pablo Historical Park and Old House Museum. Here you can see turn-of-the-century railroad memorabilia, including a 31-US-ton (28,500kg) locomotive and the stationmaster's home, and a costumed guide will

The smooth white sands of Jacksonville Beach, gently lapped by Atlantic rollers

entertain you with tales of what life was like in the Old House back in the 1900s. History buffs may also enjoy the American Lighthouse Museum at North Third Street. The adjacent beaches of Neptune and Atlantic are quieter and good for surfing. The area's best beach is the Kathryn Abbey Hanna Park, north of Atlantic, with 1½ miles (2km) of lovely white sand and scenic nature trails.

▶ *Continue north on **SR A1A**.*

2 Mayport

Mayport Naval Station is the navy's fourth largest home port and the largest and busiest naval base in Florida. It is home to mine-sweepers, aircraft carriers, cruisers, frigates and destroyers. Free tours aboard certain ships are available to the public at the weekend. At the mouth of the St John's River is the 300-year-old Mayport fishing village, home to a large commercial shrimp boat fleet. Mayport is not exactly a pretty village, but there is plenty of authentic salty atmosphere to savor, particularly at Singleton's Seafood Shack (next to the ferry), where you can also sample the freshly landed catch.

▶ *Cross the river on the car ferry to Fort George Island.*

SCENIC ROUTES

Follow the bank of the St John's River between Tocoi and Picolata, with views of ancient live oaks with shaggy beards of Spanish moss. Just beyond the road are set some fine riverside mansions, and private fishing and boat jetties protrude into the peaceful river. Spanish moss is an apiphyte (it grows on another plant without harming it) and is related to the pineapple. Why is it called Spanish Moss? One explanation likens it to the beards of early Spanish settlers.

FOR HISTORY BUFFS

Fort Caroline was the site of the first confrontation between France and Spain for supermacy over Florida in 1565. The French sent a fleet out from the fort to attack the Spanish, but it was wrecked by storms. The Spanish sacked the fort, killing 140 of its inhabitants and capturing the other 70. The 200 to 300 shipwrecked French sailors were shown no mercy and the place where they were massacred (near St Augustine) still bears the name Mantanzas (Slaughter) Bay. A replica of the fort and a memorial stand on the original site some 10 miles (16km) east of Jacksonville.

3 Kingsley Plantation

Set well back from SR A1A, this is the oldest surviving plantation in Florida, dating back to 1792. Just before the entrance gates are some ruined outbuildings, made of tabby (a primitive oyster-shell concrete), where the plantation slaves lived and raised cotton, sugarcane, corn, black-eyed peas and sweet potatoes. The enthusiastic rangers will tell you about the conditions under which the slaves lived and worked and entertain you with colorful stories of the plantation owners, including the scholarly Zephaniah Kingsley and his African wife who, by all accounts, ruled her slaves with a rod of iron. You can see inside the main house, built in 1817, and around the plantation grounds.

▶ *Continue north on **SR A1A**.*

4 Little Talbot Island

Some 5 miles (8 km) of wide sand beaches, salt marshes and dunes have been preserved as a state park on this barrier island. Along the 4-mile (6km) nature trail or the ranger-led canoe trail you may catch a glimpse of armadillos, opossums, raccoons, gopher tortoises, frogs and cotton rats. The park is also a particularly good spot for bird watching, as nearly 200 species are known to inhabit Little Talbot Island.

▶ *Continue north on **SR A1A** to Amelia Island.*

5 Amelia Island

Amelia Island, in the northeasternmost corner of Florida, has the dubious distinction of being the only place in the state to have come under eight flags:

French (1562–65), Spanish (1565–1763 and 1783–1821), British (1763–83), Patriots (1812), Green Cross of Florida (1817), Mexican (1817–21), Confederate (1861–62) and American (1821–61 and 1862 to the present).

Equestrian types will love Sea Horse Stables, at the southern tip of the island. This is one of the places on the East Coast where you can ride horseback on the beach, and the wide near-deserted beaches are a perfect setting: by reservation only, tel: (904) 261–4878.

Continue on SR A1A, parallel to the ocean, past the Amelia Island Plantation Resort and some 13 miles (21km) of unspoiled beaches and dunes, and on to Fort Clinch State Park. Built in 1847 and occupied by both Northern and Southern troops during the Civil War, the fort is in an outstanding state of preservation. It features a living history interpretation in which the year is 1864 and the garrison soldiers are going about their daily duties.

For an even more atmospheric visit, book one of the candlelight tours given every Friday and Saturday during the summer (Saturday only during spring and fall); tel: (904) 277–7274. You will also find here some of the finest beaches on Amelia Island and a nature trail winding through a coastal

Fernandina Beach's cathedral

RECOMMENDED WALKS

Guided walking tours of the 50-block historic downtown district of Fernandina Beach are a must for anyone with an interest in American Victorian architecture. These depart from the Museum of History (Mon–Sat 11am, 2pm). Pick up a leaflet from the Chamber of Commerce.

hammock, where alligators and several varieties of wading birds can be seen.

[i] Amelia Island/Fernandina Beach Chamber of Commerce, 102 Centre Street, Fernandina Beach

▶ *Return to* ***SR A1A*** *and follow it to Centre Street.*

6 Fernandina Beach

Centre Street is the main artery of the picturesque historic town of Fernandina Beach, and it ends at the shrimp dock. A plaque on the waterfront tells you that this is the birthplace of Florida's shrimping industry. Come here at sunset for a wonderful photo-opportunity. By the dock is the old rail depot (opened in 1899), now the Chamber of Commerce. A walk along colorful Centre Street will soon give you a flavor of the town. Most of the buildings are shops, superbly restored to their original appearance of a century or more ago. Don't miss the Palace Saloon. Built in 1878, and a bar since 1903, it is Florida's oldest saloon still on its original site, resembling part Wild West saloon and part Victorian English pub with swing doors, a hand-carved bar, beveled glass windows and elaborate ceiling decoration. Here you can see the Patriot Flag, the shortest-lived of all eight banners to have been hoisted over the island, flying for just one day. Other Victorian gems on Centre Street include the Three Star Saloon, the City Mart (now home to Fantastic Fudge) and the Nassau County Courthouse. For a complete history tour visit the excellent Museum of History on S Third Street, housed in the old county jail. A lively presentation by a museum tour guide precedes a tour of the museum.

Centre Street, Fernandina Beach, is a charming place for strolling

SPECIAL TO...

If you are a seafood lover or harbor nautical interests, visit Amelia Island's Isle of Eight Flags Shrimp Festival on the first weekend in May. This two-and-a-half-day event draws over 175,000 people to a festival of arts, crafts and antiques, a pirate invasion, the Blessing of the Fleet, shrimping demonstrations, a best beard contest and firework displays. The festival is centered on Fernandina Beach's shrimp docks.

▶ *Leave Amelia Island on* ***SR A1A*** *traveling west, and after 11 miles (18km) turn left onto* ***US 17,*** *and head south to Jacksonville.*

▶ *Take the city tour of Jacksonville* *(see pages 140–143).*

BACK TO NATURE

Visit the Morningside Nature Center at East University Avenue, Gainesville, and you can experience the lifestyle of a local farmer around 100 years ago. The farm features an 1840 cabin, a turn-of-the-century kitchen, gardens and a barn. In addition there are trails and boardwalks through various habitats, with over 130 bird species and 225 types of wildflower. Look for woodland birds such as brown-headed nuthatch, pine warbler and red cockaded woodpecker.

▶ *From Jacksonville head west on* ***I–10*** *and turn off south at* ***US 301.*** *Continue for 34 miles (55km), then turn right onto* ***SR 24*** *(Waldo Road).*

7 Gainesville

This large, well-kept city is closely associated with the University of Florida, but it also features a fine historic district and, around the outskirts, some interesting natural features. As you enter the center of town, turn right onto SR 24/26 (Newberry Road) and right again on NE 6th Avenue to the historic district. The flagship house of the district is the beautifully restored Mediterranean Revival Historic Thomas Center, which puts on art exhibits, music and guided tours (closed Saturday). Continue on Newberry Road and turn left on US 441, which leads past the elegant red-brick buildings of the university. On the right is the Florida Museum of Natural History, the southeast USA's largest natural science exhibit. An interesting diversion 2 miles (3km) northwest of town (take US 441 north, then west on NW 53rd Avenue) takes in the Devil's

Millhopper State Geological Site. Formed by a collapsed underground cavern, this is basically a huge chasm, 120 feet (37m) deep and 500 feet (152m) wide with its own mini ecosystem, supporting animals more common to the ravines of the Appalachian Mountains and dozens of plant species found nowhere else in Florida. There is a vistor center and guided walks on Saturday mornings. More exotic plants can be enjoyed just south at Kanapaha Botanical Garden (SW 63rd Boulevard, just off I–75). Near here at Archer Road (SR 24) is the Fred Bear Museum. This is an unusual collection of archery and hunting artifacts from all over the world, together with natural history displays, several of these being hunting trophies (closed Monday and Tuesday).

► *From the Florida Museum of Natural History continue south on* ***US 441****.*

8 Paynes Prairie State Preserve

During the late 17th century this vast 18,000-acre (7,285-hectare) savannah was occupied by the largest cattle ranch in Spanish Florida. In the 18th century Seminole Indians settled here, and it is thought that the prairie is named after King Payne, a Seminole chief. There is a visitor center and an observation tower where you can watch waterfowl and wading birds. One mile (1.5km) southwest of the park is the small hamlet of Micanopy. A white trading post grew up here in 1821, making this one of the oldest settlements in Florida. Its main street is lined with moss-draped live oaks and historical buildings, of which around 20 are antique shops. In the fall some 200 dealers converge here for an annual antique fair.

FOR CHILDREN

A good bet for children is the Florida Museum of Natural History in Gainesville. Children can wander through a replicated prehistoric limestone cave, explore inside a Mayan temple, see a typical Timucuan Indian household and 'seek and find' at the Fossil Study Center.

► *Continue east from Micanopy on* ***SR 346*** *for 5 miles (8km). Turn right (south) onto* ***SR 325*** *and continue for 3½ miles (5km).*

9 Cross Creek

Marjorie Kinnan Rawlings, who won the 1939 Pulitzer Prize for her novel *The Yearling*, lived at Cross Creek from 1928 to 1941 continuously and intermittently until her death in 1953. Yet even if you have never heard of her, the countryside around here and her 1890s home (now a state historic site) are still lovely, unspoiled places to visit (closed Tuesdays and Wednesdays).

► *Continue southeast on* ***SR 325*** *for 5 miles (8km) to Island Grove, then turn left onto* ***US 301****. Head north to Hawthorne and turn right onto* ***SR 20****. Head east to Palatka.*

10 Ravine State Gardens, Palatka

The steep ravines created by waters flowing from the St John's River, now dry except for a spring-fed creek, are home to delightful wild gardens crossed by old wooden suspension bridges. A 3-mile (5km) loop road enables you to see the gardens without leaving your car, but walking is definitely recommended.

► *Follow* ***US 17*** *east across the river and turn left onto* ***SR 207*** *to return to St Augustine.*

FOR CHILDREN

Adventure Landing, on Beach Boulevard, features mini-golf, baseball batting cages, a go-kart track, arcade games and, perhaps best of all, Shipwreck Island water park. It boasts an intriguing ride called The Rage, which claims to be the state's only uphill water coaster!

TOUR
23

Jacksonville

Jacksonville will never be in the big league of Florida tourism, but that doesn't mean it's not worth a visit. Admire its thrusting skyline while dining or drinking on the banks of the St John's River. When it comes to visitor attractions, take a trip to its acclaimed zoo and enjoy the Cummer Museum of Art and the Museum of Science and History, the finest of its kind in Florida.

2 DAYS

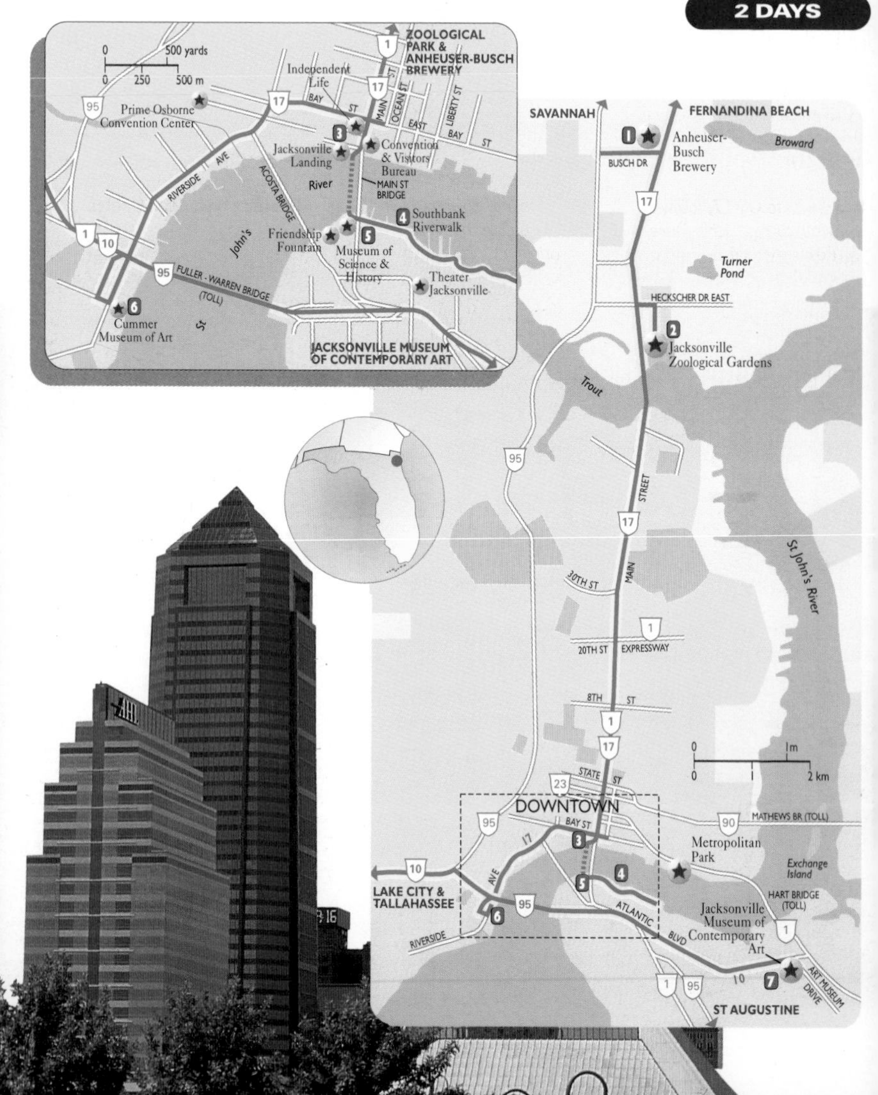

[i] Jacksonville and the Beaches Convention and Visitors Bureau, 3 Independent Drive

▶ *If you are continuing the tour of the northeast follow* **US 17** *for 21 miles (34km) south and turn right on Busch Drive. Or from the center of town head north on* **US 17** *and turn left on Busch Drive.*

1 Anheuser-Busch Brewery

If you have ever wondered what they put into your Budweiser and how, a free tour of this gigantic brewery should slake your thirst for knowledge (closed Sunday). After the tour, adults can sample the famous 'King of Beers' in the hospitality room (soft drinks also available for drivers and those under 21).

▶ *Return to* **US 17,** *follow it south to Heckscher Drive East (exit 124–A), turn right and then right again.*

2 Jacksonville Zoological Gardens

One of the oldest and most famous attractions in the city, the zoo (established in 1914) boasts over 600 species. Highlights include the 11-acre (4-hectare) African veldt where eland, kudu, Thomson gazelle and ostrich roam freely, the Okavango Trail, a boardwalk through pinewoods where animals native to southern Africa can be seen, a large outdoor aviary and rare white rhinos. Most of the animals can be viewed in a near-natural state, separated from the public by moats instead of cages. Chimpanorama, the baby animal nursery and elephant rides delight children, and train rides tour the full 61-acre (25-hectare) site.

▶ *Return to* **US 17** *and follow it south into downtown. Park just before the Main Street Bridge at Jacksonville Landing.*

3 Jacksonville Landing

This attractive riverside complex is home to dozens of specialty shops, fast food and fine dining, nightclubs and a one-room Maritime Museum chock-full of model ships. Behind the complex tower the giants of the city, including the 37-story Independent Life Building (tours available), while ahead is the busy St John's River. The splendid design of the Landing is by the Rouse Company, also responsible for Miami's Bayside Marketplace, Faneuil Hall in Boston and the Harborplace in Baltimore. Regular festivities and ever-present street entertainers ensure that there is never a dull moment. Immediately to the west, the dramatic Greek Revival-style building, with 14 massive columns and three pediments, is the Prime Osborne Convention Center.

Out of Africa – baby giraffes learning to walk tall at Jacksonville Zoo

City reflections; downtown Jacksonville from across the St John's River

Formerly the grandiose Union Terminal railroad station, built in 1919, it now functions as an exhibition and meeting hall.

▶ *Take a water-taxi across the river.*

4 Southbank Riverwalk

This old-fashioned boardwalk, just over a mile (2km) long and 20 feet (6m) wide, is lined with restaurants, food vendors, boat rentals and another branch of the Maritime Museum. Several major annual events are staged here, including an arts and crafts festival in May, when some 50,000 people tread the boards.

▶ *At the beginning of the Southbank Riverwalk is the city's premier museum.*

5 Museum of Science and History (MOSH)

This large museum is neatly divided into discreet sections. The Living World is home to the museum's live animal collection and includes a 1,200-US-gallon (4,540-liter) aquarium and an aviary overlooking the Hixon Courtyard, a piece of tropical hammock in the middle of downtown. The Science Center features the very latest in hands-on exhibits, with over 40 science PODS (personally operated discovery stations), plus the state-of-the-art Alexander Brest Planetarium. This is said to be the finest planetarium chamber in the US with the best possible sound system. You can not only hear but feel the launch of a shuttle

*Return to your car. Follow the north bank of the river south on Riverside Avenue and continue a few blocks south after passing **I–95** (the approach to the Fuller-Warren Bridge).*

6 Cummer Museum of Art

This outstanding fine arts museum and cultural center exhibits a permanent collection of over 2,000 items in 11 galleries. Of special note is one of the world's largest and rarest collections of early Meissen porcelain, plus some fine 17th-century Dutch and Flemish paintings and tapestries. Beautiful Florentine-style gardens lead to the river.

*Cross the Fuller-Warren Bridge **(I–95),** and after 1 mile (1.5km), turn left onto Atlantic Boulevard and right onto Art Museum Drive.*

7 Jacksonville Museum of Contemporary Art

Chinese porcelains, rare artifacts from the pre-Columbian era and a sculpture garden are highlights of the permanent collection here.

*Continue the northeast tour (see page 138) by recrossing the Fuller-Warren Bridge and picking up **I–10** west. Go south at **US 301**. Alternatively, return to St Augustine on **US 1** or the I–95.*

and the explosion of a star. For more life in space visit Asteroid Biosphere 3, which re-creates a space colony in the asteroid belt.

In addition to all this, there is Kidspace (see For Children), outstanding traveling exhibitions and a waterside café to relax in. Step outside the museum to see the spectacular Friendship Fountain. This sprays 17,000 US gallons (64,000 liters) of water 120 feet (37m) into the air every minute and is particularly impressive when lit at night.

FOR CHILDREN

Kidspace at the Museum of Science and History features its own phone system, face-painting stations, a treehouse where children can operate their own puppet theater, large soft-sculpture building blocks and a dynamic water table. Adults must be accompanied by a child up to 48 inches tall (1.22m). Older children will also enjoy the evening laser shows.

SPECIAL TO...

The three-day Jacksonville Jazz Festival in early October is the largest free jazz event in the US and draws crowds of 130,000 at Metropolitan Park.
The park is also a venue for a spring MusicFest in late April/early May, a country music festival in April and two weeks of Shakespeare's plays in September.

THE PANHANDLE

If peninsular Florida is the pan, then the long thin strip bordering Georgia and Alabama is the pan-handle. This is 'the other Florida', where glades and palms are replaced by rolling hills and pine and oak forests, which resemble the countryside of New York rather than the swamplands of southern Florida. Slick shopping malls give way to a countrified selection of collectibles, and the mention of Disney Animatronics will just get you a good ol' Southern guffaw. This Florida is not only a geographical extension of the southern states, it is also a cultural extension of southern Alabama and Georgia – the heart of old Dixie. Just look at the menu for confirmation – grits, hush puppies, catfish, black-eyed beans and chitlins, served in establishments with names such as Po' Folks (poor folks). Snowbirds and retirees are still thick on the ground in the northwest, but Europeans are largely absent and you are more likely to meet families from other Southern states and Canada.

The vacation seasons here are also different from southern Florida. As the rest of the state begins to swelter, the cooler panhandle summer season is just beginning. There are, of course, parallels with southern Florida: Panama City Beach is the Daytona Beach of the north, Pensacola rivals St Augustine for historical heritage, and Wakulla Springs resembles an earlier, less commercialized version of Silver Springs. The region's Southern accent is most pronounced around the green canopied roads of Tallahassee. Although this region still harbors the largest concentration of antebellum plantations in the US, don't expect to encounter many *Gone With The Wind* fantasies on the Florida side of the state line.

The Gulf Coast beaches of the Panhandle are often referred to as The Miracle Strip, a wry reference to the 'miraculous' price hikes experienced when the area's tourism potential was discovered in the years following World War II. The major resorts that have grown up here, however, are cheap and cheerful and the real treasure is the sugar-white sand – the result of quartz crystals from the Appalachian Mountains that have been broken down, washed, bleached, ground and polished by the action of the Gulf waters. The beaches and the barrier islands as far east as Destin are vigilantly protected by the National Park Service, and they too have a soubriquet – The Emerald Coast, a perfect name on a sunny summer day when the sparkling green-blue waters lap the snowy white shores.

Amusing attraction at Panama City

Tour 24
The tour starts at the state capital, Tallahassee. The Capitol Complex is the hub of modern-day Tallahassee's role as lawmaker and administrator to the state, and also gives a fine historical introduction to the region. The city itself is full of cultural and historical interest and is temptingly close to the lovely Georgia town of Thomasville. The route west passes through rolling green hills to pristine state parks, featuring caverns and a waterfall before heading to the coast. Panama City Beach is a lively, highly commercialized beach resort with plenty of action for youngsters and teenagers. Port St Joe and Apalachicola are in complete contrast to each other – the former is a sleepy, faded fishing village, the latter an important fishing port famed for its oysters. Wakulla Springs is an unforgettable trip down the river into Old Florida.

Tour 25
The old city of Pensacola is a must for history buffs, with its streets a living legacy of the period from Colonial times to the Depression. The city is not cocooned in its own past, however; the National Museum of Naval Aviation and the adjacent resort of Pensacola Beach provide ample outlets for those whose interests are more athletic than academic. More beautiful unspoiled beaches can be found along the protected Gulf Islands National Seashore, and the resort of Fort Walton Beach is another good all-round resort, with a US Air Force museum for fans of flying. The diversity of the beach communities of the South Walton area ranges from Seaside, a newly created, pretty Cape Cod-style resort, to Destin, a busy fishing charter port and vacation center over 150 years old.

Apalachicola town square

The much-restored village of Apalachicola is still an important fishing center and the source of the Florida oyster

TOUR
24

Tallahassee & Beyond

3 DAYS • 288 MILES • 463KM Remote, small, quiet, and more akin to Georgia than Miami or Orlando, Tallahassee is an unlikely choice for state capital. All the more intriguing then to explore and to see how it legitimizes its status. The countryside has retained its rich rolling greenery and deep south ambience while, west, the Miracle Strip caters for beach holidays.

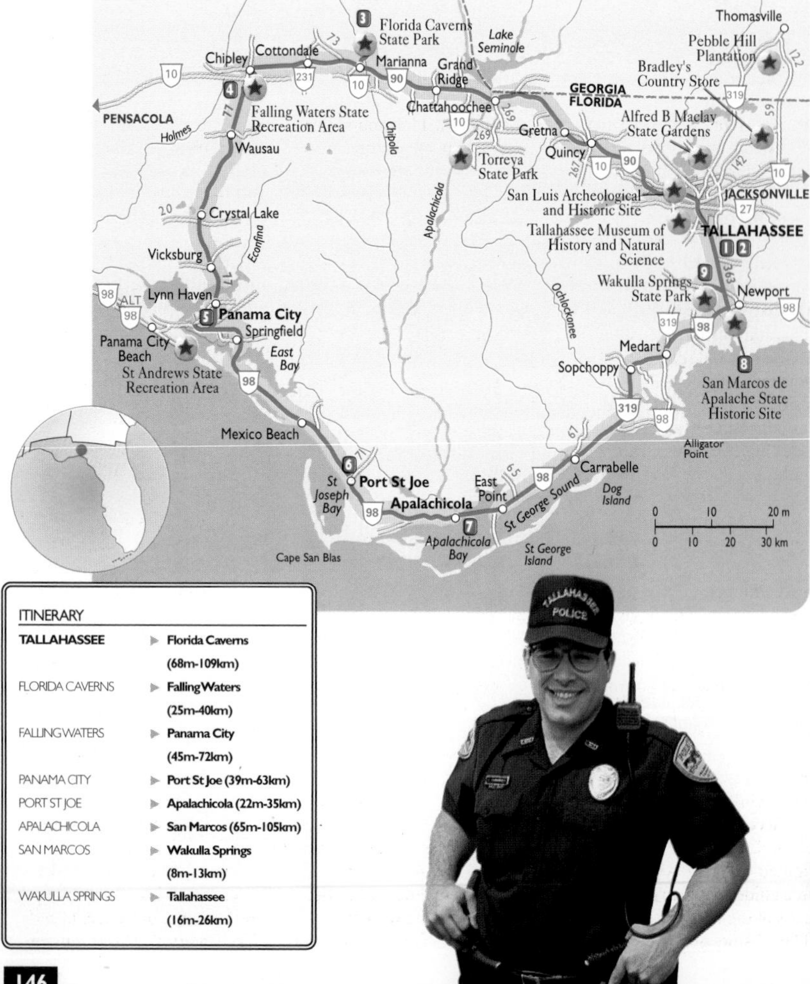

ITINERARY

TALLAHASSEE	► **Florida Caverns (68m-109km)**
FLORIDA CAVERNS	► **Falling Waters (25m-40km)**
FALLING WATERS	► **Panama City (45m-72km)**
PANAMA CITY	► **Port St Joe (39m-63km)**
PORT ST JOE	► **Apalachicola (22m-35km)**
APALACHICOLA	► **San Marcos (65m-105km)**
SAN MARCOS	► **Wakulla Springs (8m-13km)**
WAKULLA SPRINGS	► **Tallahassee (16m-26km)**

State troopers celebrating the 4th of July in Tallahassee

Park your car and you can explore most of downtown Tallahassee on foot. Alternatively, jump aboard a trolley car; the service runs a small circuit around central downtown.

1 Capitol Complex

This administrative complex, the historic old seat of Florida's government and its 22-story successor, makes for a good introduction to Tallahassee (which means 'old town'). The Old Capitol is just as you would expect, a handsome classical-style building with a green cupola. It was built in 1845 but has been restored, both externally and internally, to its 1902 appearance. It includes the Supreme Court, the House of Representatives and Senate Chambers and the Governor's Suite; all are open to the public. Other offices in the building have been converted into museum space and a visit is well worthwhile.

Access to the new State Capitol, erected in 1977, is limited to weekdays only with free guided tours to certain parts of the building every hour. The 22-story observation deck is open daily. The ground floor also holds an extensive statewide visitor information center. The Capitol really comes to life from April into June, which is when the legislative sessions take place. By law all such meetings are open to the public. Adjacent to the Capitol is the Veteran's Memorial, its twin granite towers flying the Stars and Stripes, erected in honor of Florida's Vietnam veterans.

Cross Monroe Street and a few yards away is the Union Bank.

2 Union Bank/LeMoyne Art Gallery

Built in 1841, this is Florida's oldest surviving bank building and today houses a museum of banking and daily life. Turn left at Gadsden Street and a block north is the LeMoyne Art Gallery, the city's center for the visual arts, housed in a small, well-proportioned 1853 mansion. One block west, turn right onto Calhoun Street; here you will find many of the city's oldest homes, most dating between 1830 and 1880. Park Avenue, heading west off Calhoun, also features many historic buildings (look on the left-hand side of the street). Walk up Park Avenue, turn left back towards the Capitol, and at the rear of the complex is the Museum of Florida History. This well-designed modern museum traces the story of Florida with exhibits like a 9-foot (2.7m) mastodon (from Wakulla Springs), Spanish galleon treasure, Civil War battle flags, a reconstructed steamboat, and the 'tin-can' camper tourists of the 1920s. Step outside the museum to the reconstructed center of historical downtown, Adams Street Commons.

Just along Duval Street is The Columns, the city's oldest building, dating from 1830. It is now the headquarters of the Chamber of Commerce, and is partly open to the public as a limited visitor information center. Tallahasse also boasts the Florida State University (FSU), and just west of the Capitol you can visit the FSU Gallery and Museum. Located at the corner of Copeland and Call streets, this hosts touring exhibitions, plus a permanent collection that includes 20th-century American and 16th-century Dutch paintings, Japanese prints and pre-Columbian pieces.

Five miles (8km) northeast of Tallahassee is the outstanding Alfred B Maclay State Gardens (1 mile/1.5km) north of I–10 on US 319). The star blooms are the 100 varieties of camellias and the 50 kinds of azaleas, but another 160 exotic species complement these. The season is from January through April, with the peak in mid- to late March. During this period the Maclay House, furnished as it was in the 1920s, is also open. The gardens encircle a beautifully landscaped lake where you can see alligators, turtles and migrating waterfowl, and in the park's woodlands over 150 species of wildlife have been recorded. You might like to combine a visit to the gardens with an excursion to Thomasville.

FOR CHILDREN

The Tallahassee Museum of History and Natural Science is not just for kids, it is a good place to escape from the bureaucratic atmosphere of downtown. It comprises an 1880s farm complex that is fully operational, a natural-habitat wildlife zoo housing animals native to Florida (including black bears, panthers and bobcats), an aquarium and an aviary, plus rural 19th-century historical buildings.

There is also a pleasant nature trail along the edge of Lake Hiawatha. The museum is located on SR 371.

▶ *From downtown head west on Brevard Avenue/Quincy Highway* ***(US 90)*** *through Quincy and Chattahoochee for some 65 miles (104km) to Marianna. Turn right onto* ***SR 167*** *and head north for 3 miles (5km).*

BACK TO NATURE

Aside from beautiful Maclay State Gardens and pristine Wakulla Springs, you may like to take a short detour off this route to Torreya State Park, some 17 miles (27km) south of Chatahoochee on US 90. The landscape here is more akin to the Georgian Appalachians than Florida, with verdant high bluffs rising 150 feet (46m) above the river. The park takes its name from a rare tree that only grows along these river bluffs. As a bonus, tours are conducted through the historic Gregory House, built in 1849.

3 Florida Caverns State Park

There are many similar limestone cave formations in Florida, but because of the state's high water table this is the only significant network of caves that is not flooded. The largest and most impressive caves are lit and open to the public for ranger-guided tours. Sodastraws, stalagmites, stalactites, draperies (resembling petrified curtains) and calcite formations of all shapes and sizes provide a memorable visit. The park also offers swimming, a horse trail (no rentals) and canoe rentals.

SCENIC ROUTES

The road from Tallahassee to Chipley, skirting the foothills of the Appalachian Mountains, is quite unlike anywhere else in Florida, with rolling wooded hills and green ravines. Tallahassee itself boasts a number of 'canopy roads', where moss-draped live oaks reach right across and touch over the street. The best of these are to the north and include Centerville Road, which is en route to Bradley's Country Store (see Special To).

▶ *Return to* ***US 90*** *and continue west for 19 miles (31km) to Chipley. Turn left onto* ***SR 77A*** *and head south for 3 miles (5km).*

4 Falling Waters State Recreation Area

The highlight of this park is a 67-foot (20m) waterfall, another geological feature rarely found in the state. It plunges into a sinkhole some 100 feet (30m) deep and 20 feet (6m) wide. This underutilized park also offers picnicking and nature trails that feature many uncommon plants and unusual geological formations.

▶ *Drive 1 mile (1.5km) west to pick up* ***SR 77*** *and head south for 42 miles (68km). Turn right onto* ***US 98*** *into Panama City.*

5 Panama City

Panama City Beach, some 5 miles (8km) south of the town proper, is the major resort on the northern Gulf Coast, a busy, brash place popular with college students and Southern families on a tight budget (hence its nickname 'The Redneck Riviera'). From May to September, the busy season, hotel rooms are fully booked and almost permanent traffic clogs US 98 (Alt), which leads to the beaches. Outside this period some attractions close down for the winter. The beaches along this strip of coastline are some of the very best in the state. Made up of 99 percent quartz crystal, the sand looks and feels like powdered sugar and actually squeaks as you walk on it.

Miracle Strip Amusement Park is the biggest man-made attraction in town, with some 30 fairground-style rides and one of the country's most heart-stopping roller coasters. Shipwreck Island, adjacent, is a large water park with a giant wave pool, a white-water tube ride, a 35mph (56km/h) racing slide, a 1,600-foot (488m) Lazy River ride and several themed areas in which to simply sunbathe. If you are more serious about your water thrills, there is every kind of watersport back on the beach, and the area is well known for its diving schools. The other major attraction here is the Gulf World marine park. Bottle-nosed dolphins and sea lions star in entertaining shows, and there is a shark pool, a penguin exhibit and a dolphin petting pool.

Finally there is the Museum of Man in the Sea. Here you can see some of the numerous imaginative devices that would-be sea explorers have devised over the centuries to allow themselves to breathe, move and work beneath the waves. The most scenic beach is St Andrews State Recreation Area, located at the end of Thomas Road/US 98 (Alt), where you can also fish or wander along the nature trail. Boats leave from here for an uninhabited natural barrier island, named Shell Island after the numerous types of shells buried beneath its silvery sands. Other charters will take you sea fishing, dolphin feeding and viewing the crystal waters of the Gulf Islands National Seashore by glass-bottom boat.

The sugar-sand beach of Panama City, to the south of the town, stretches away to infinity

The local harvest of the ocean, oysters by the boatload, served fresh to local restaurants

[i] Visitors Information Center, West Front Beach Road

FOR CHILDREN

Over 350 animals, many of them rare or endangered species, make up Zoo World Zoological and Botanical Gardens on Front Beach Road, in Panama City. There's a walk-through aviary and a petting zoo, in addition to the big cats, reptiles, orangutans and other primates on display.

▶ *Head southeast on **US 98** for 39 miles (63km).*

6 Port St Joe

St Joseph, as it used to be called, was created in 1835 and grew to be a booming port with a population of some 12,000. In 1838 it secured some degree of immortality by being the place where the first Florida state constitution was drafted, but by 1844 – wracked by yellow fever, economic problems and finally an almighty hurricane – the town had dwindled. Visit the Constitutional Convention State Museum to learn about this historic charter, and the sad story of how proud St Joseph was reduced to plain St Joe.

▶ *Continue east on **US 98** for 22 miles (35km).*

7 Apalachicola

An important Confederate port during the Civil War, this much restored fishing village has a New England flavor to it and is famous for its oyster beds. The vast majority of Florida's oysters come from here, as does half the state's shellfish, so you are always assured of the freshest seafood in the local restaurants. The beautifully renovated Gibson Hotel, dating from 1910, is a local landmark and probably the most characterful place to stay on this route. If you are just passing through, try the restaurant and lounge to sample the local oysters and its romantic turn-of-the-century ambience. The town's other claim to fame lies with Dr John Gorrie, who, during the early 1800s, served not only as town physician but also as postmaster, city treasurer, councilman and bank director. His concern for his patients suffering from yellow fever led him to invent an ice-making machine for cooling rooms, thus paving the way for air-conditioning. A replica of his invention is housed in the John Gorrie State Museum on 6th Street, off US 98.

▶ *Continue east for 33 miles (53km) on **US 98**, then fork left, away from the coast, heading north on **US 319**. Continue north, then east for 17 miles (27km), before rejoining **US 98**. Continue northeast on **US 98** for 13 miles (21km), then turn right onto **SR 363** and head south for 2miles (3km).*

8 San Marcos de Apalache State Historic Site

This area was first discovered by Europeans in 1528, when Panfilo de Narvaez arrived at what is now St Mark's with 300 Conquistadores. Here he established a boatyard and launched the first ships made by white men in the New World. The

fort, first built on the site in 1679, was destroyed and twice rebuilt; the most recent stone fort was occupied by Confederate forces in 1861. The museum here displays finds from the area and relates the colorful history of San Marcos.

*Return north on **SR 363** for 2 miles (3km), cross **US 98** and continue on **SR 363** for a further 3 miles (5km), then turn left onto **SR 267**.*

9 Wakulla Springs State Park

Variously and romantically translated as 'breast of life' or 'mysteries of strange waters', Wakulla claims one of the largest and deepest freshwater springs in the world. Peak flow has been measured at over 14,000 US gallons (53,000 liters) per second. Glass-bottom boats are the major visitor attraction here, and when the water is clear you can peer down through the crystal waters to the entrance of the spring cavern some 100 feet (30m) below. The cave has been explored to a distance of 4,200 feet (1,280m), and finds include the remains of a giant mastodon (now in Tallahassee's Museum of Florida History). The two scenic boat tours, similar to those at better-known Silver Springs (see Tour 19) cruise through a breathtaking primeval Florida riverscape. It was here that several of the early Johnny Weissmuller *Tarzan* movies were filmed. *The Creature from the Black Lagoon* was also shot here, though today the only creature likely to alarm you is 'Henry the Pole-Vaulting Fish', who leaps out of the water on command as one of the boat captain's *tours de force*. The river is a bird-watchers delight, with herons and egrets, black and turkey vultures, anhingas, kites, ospreys, bald eagles, limpkins and purple gallinules; turtles and alligators abound. Do not miss visiting Wakulla Springs Lodge and Conference Center. Built in 1937, it includes many original Spanish features, notably its tiled doorway and arches and Moorish grilled doors. The dining room, seemingly caught in a 1950s time warp, is acclaimed for its choice of traditional regional dishes. Its Southern cooking is well worth sampling, particularly as your park admission fee will then be waived (boat tours charged separately).

Apalachicola – the name means 'the land beyond the river'

*Return to **SR 363,** and head north for 13 miles (21km) to return to Tallahassee.*

SPECIAL TO...

To catch a glimpse of the gracious antebellum *Gone With the Wind* Deep South, you will have to cross the state border into Georgia. Check this does not invalidate your car rental insurance policy. Fortunately, one of Georgia's finest small towns, Thomasville, is only 35 miles (56km) north of Tallahassee.

Even closer – just 20 miles (32km) north – is the elegant Pebble Hill Plantation. Return via SR 59 to Centerville Road and Bradley's Country Store for it southern food specialties.

TOUR
25

The Pensacola Gulf Coast

2 DAYS • 183 MILES • 293KM

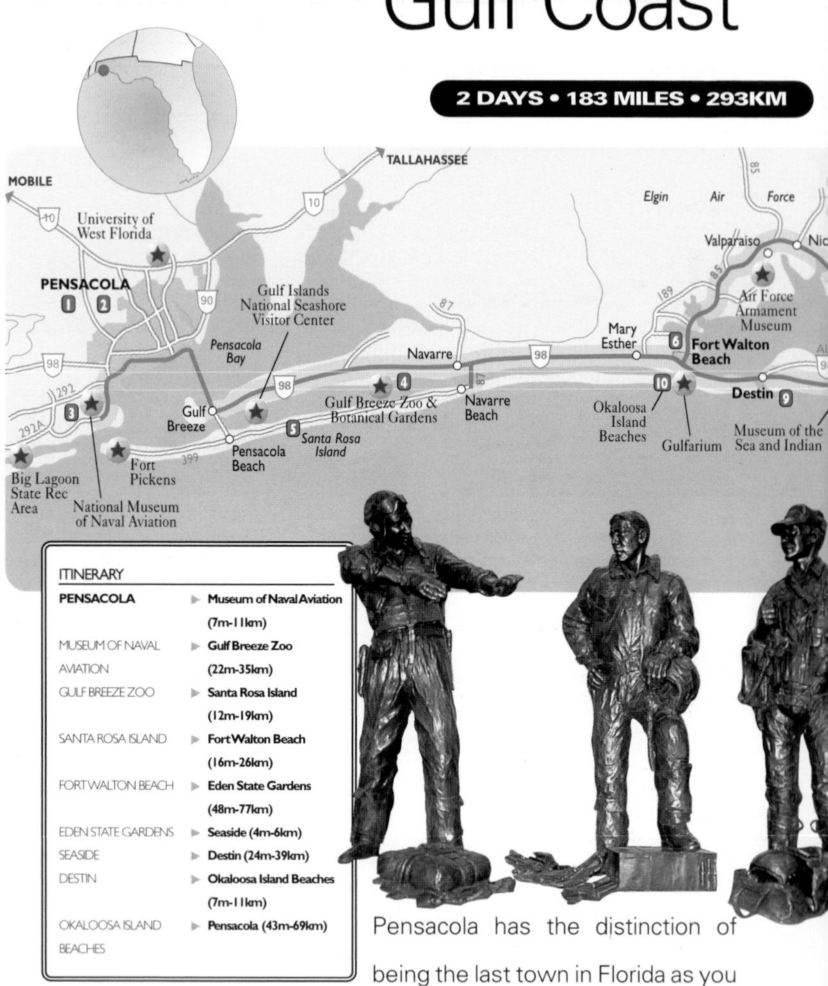

ITINERARY	
PENSACOLA	▶ **Museum of Naval Aviation (7m-11km)**
MUSEUM OF NAVAL AVIATION	▶ **Gulf Breeze Zoo (22m-35km)**
GULF BREEZE ZOO	▶ **Santa Rosa Island (12m-19km)**
SANTA ROSA ISLAND	▶ **Fort Walton Beach (16m-26km)**
FORT WALTON BEACH	▶ **Eden State Gardens (48m-77km)**
EDEN STATE GARDENS	▶ **Seaside (4m-6km)**
SEASIDE	▶ **Destin (24m-39km)**
DESTIN	▶ **Okaloosa Island Beaches (7m-11km)**
OKALOOSA ISLAND BEACHES	▶ **Pensacola (43m-69km)**

Pensacola has the distinction of being the last town in Florida as you head west into Alabama. Discovered in 1559 (but subsequently destroyed by a hurricane) it goes back even further than St Augustine. Its numerous museums and historic districts interpret its long history, while its modern naval air links make it home to one of the world's finest air and space museums. Away from the city and its brash beach resort lies some of Florida's finest, whitest sands.

Pensacola Visitor Information Center, East Gregory St (north end of Pensacola Bay Bridge)

Pensacola's three historic districts are best explored on foot. Leave your car at the Historic Pensacola Village parking lot on East Zaragoza Street.

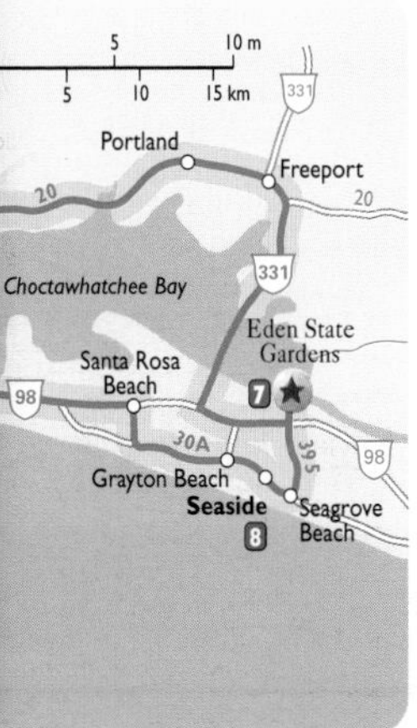

SPECIAL TO...

Each spring (late February/ early March) Pensacola stages a fortnight of Mardi Gras festivities. Spectacular costume-and-mask parades take to the streets to the sound of jazz and samba and culminate in a grand Mardi Gras Ball.
In June the city celebrates the Fiesta of Five Flags, which marks the settlement of the city in 1559 by Tristan de Luna. Locals don period costume and hold street fairs, and an old galleon sails into port.

1 Historic Pensacola Village

This fine collection of museums and interpretive houses lies at the heart of the Seville Square Historic District. If you would like to visit the museums, buy an all-inclusive admission ticket before starting your tour. Walk west along Church Street to the outstanding T T Wentworth Jr Florida State Museum, which is housed in an imposing Italian Renaissance Revival structure built in 1908 as the Pensacola City Hall. It contains some 30,000 items of local and regional interest and is the largest collection ever donated to the State of Florida by an individual. Walk back along Church Street to the Museum of Industry, which features 19th-century local industry memorabilia, and in particular relates to the west Florida lumber boom of the 1890s. Opposite is the Museum of Commerce, with an 1890s streetscape comprising a barber's shop, a toy store, a print shop, a hardware store and a pharmacy.

Diagonally opposite on Barrack Street is the early 19th-century Julee Cottage. This was owned by Julee Panton, one of the region's pioneering free black women, and is now home to a Museum of Black History. From the same period, across the street, is the French Colonial Creole Charles Lavallé House. Step inside to admire its handmade antiques and provincial furniture and a fully equipped cooking hearth. Opposite here is Old Christ Church, built in 1832, now serving as a local museum. Straight ahead is Seville Square, where several shops, restaurants and offices occupy old properties and continue the quarter's historic traditions. On the Adam Street side, look in at Dorr House, built in 1871 for a wealthy lumber merchant and fully furnished with ornate Victorian antiques.

You can complete seeing the main properties in the Seville Historic District one block east of Seville Square.

2 Seville, Palafox and North Hill Districts

Here are the Musician's Union Building (c 1880) and Lee House (1866), both on South Alcaniz Street, the William Fordham House (c 1892) and Mary Perry House (c 1883), both on East Zaragoza Street, and the Barkley House (c 1825) on South Florida Blanca Street.

Walk back towards the parking lot on Zaragoza Street and at the corner of Jefferson Street is the Pensacola Museum of Art, housed in the old City Jail, built in 1908. Continue and turn right onto Palafox Street. This was the main thoroughfare of old Pensacola's commercial area. Buildings of interest (from south to north) include: the Escambia County Courthouse, an elaborate 1887 Renaissance Revival structure; the Empire Building, Florida's tallest skyscraper (at 10 stories) when completed in 1909; and the Saenger Theatre, a 1925 Vaudeville theater.

Continue north on Palafox Street for four blocks, and at Wright Street you enter the North Hill Preservation District. The 500 homes in this upper-middle-class residential quarter, developed between the 1870s and the 1930s, comprise one of the state's most complete historic districts.

Continue past the site of old Fort George at La Rua Street to Lee Square, where a 50-foot (15m) obelisk was dedicated to the Confederacy in 1891. Continue north for two blocks, turn left on Strong Street and right onto North Baylen Street. The 1896 Charles H Turner House and the superb Queen Anne-style McCreary House (1900) lie almost opposite each other. Follow Baylen Street south to return to your car.

*Head south on Palafox Street one block to Main Street. Head west and turn left onto Barrancas Avenue **(SR 292)**. Follow this for 3 miles (5km) and turn left on Navy Boulevard/Duncan Road **(SR 295)** to cross the Bayou Grande. Follow Duncan Road to Hovey Road, 7 miles (11km).*

3 National Museum Of Naval Aviation

This outstanding museum is home to one of the country's largest and finest historic collections of Navy, Marine Corps and Coast Guard aircraft, plus the very latest high-tech supersonic jets and space vehicles. The stunning seven-story glass-and-steel entrance atrium features four A-4 Skyhawks, belonging to the famous Blue Angels precision flying team, which is based at the adjacent US Naval Air Station. Other exhibits range from the NC-4 Flying Boat, which in

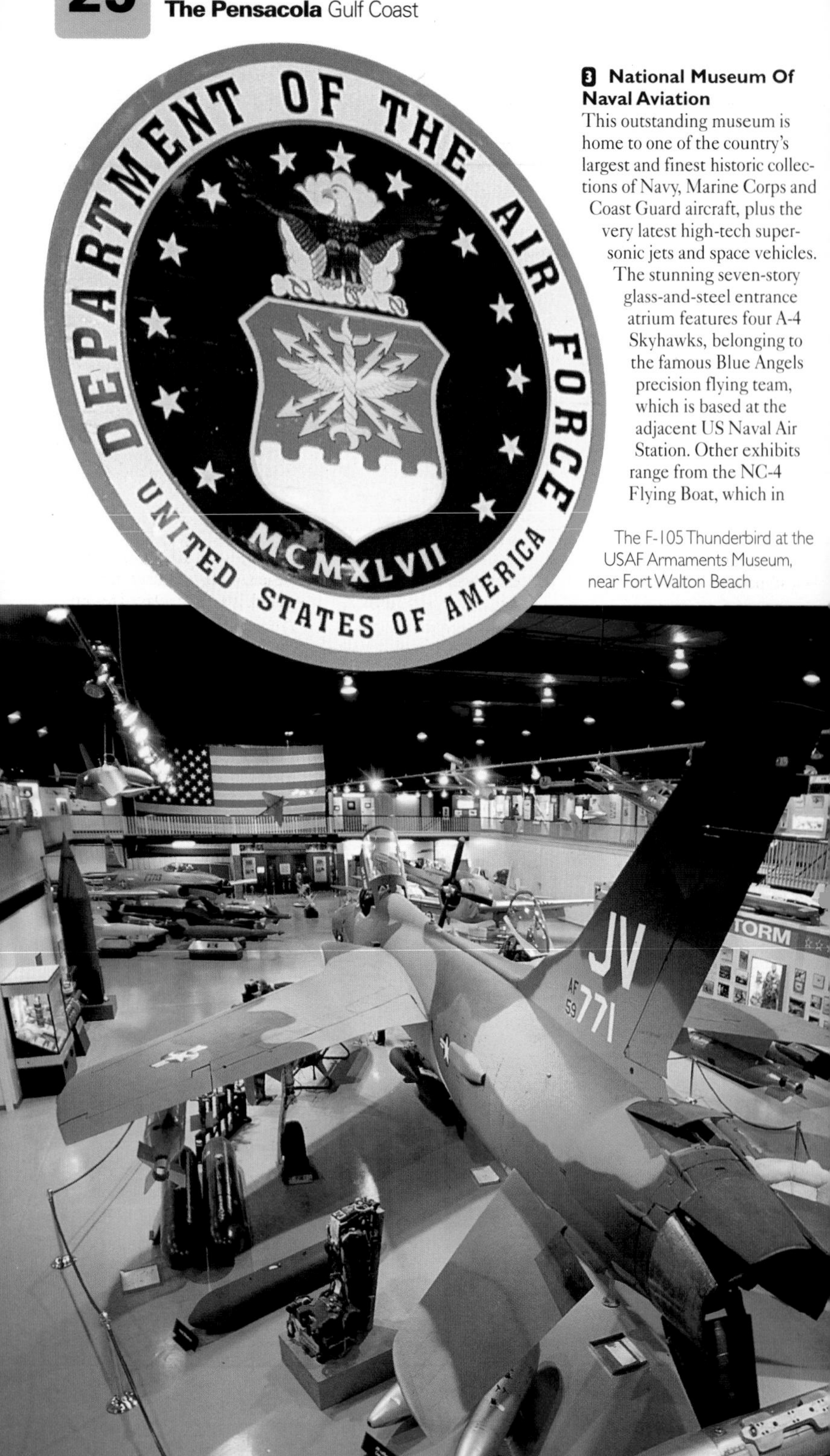

The F-105 Thunderbird at the USAF Armaments Museum, near Fort Walton Beach

1919 became the first seaplane to fly the Atlantic, to a replica of the Skylab Command Module. Budding 'top guns' can strap themselves into the cockpit simulator of a modern jet fighter.

▶ *Return by the same route via Main Street onto the Bayfront Parkway and cross the Pensacola Bay Bridge **(US 98)** to Gulf Breeze. Follow the Gulf Breeze Parkway **(US 98)** east for a further 8 miles (13km).*

4 Gulf Breeze Zoo and Botanical Gardens

There are over 500 animals here including lions, tigers, giraffes and Colossus, the world's largest captive gorilla, all in naturally landscaped environments.

BACK TO NATURE

The major conservation feature of this area is the Gulf Islands National Seashore, which protects 150 square miles (338sq km) of barrier islands. The information center is located east of Gulf Breeze on US 98 but for the best overview visit the observation tower at Big Lagoon State Recreation Area (SR 292A, 10 miles/16km southwest of Pensacola). In the grounds of the University of West Florida in Pensacola is the Edward Ball Nature Trail, a 2½-mile (4km) boardwalk over a wetlands area.

Exotic birds and other creatures entertain daily during the summer, and there is a children's petting zoo and animal nursery room.

▶ *Continue east on **US 98,** then, just after Navarre, turn right onto **SR 87** and cross the Intracoastal Waterway, 12 miles (19km).*

5 Santa Rosa Island

This long skinny barrier island, part of the Gulf Islands National Seashore, boasts miles of beautiful white quartz sand. To the west are the busy, unattractive resort of Pensacola Beach and the quiet historical site of Fort Pickens. Navarre Beach, in the center of the island, is a small relaxed resort; immediately east is a sand-duned wilderness.

FOR HISTORY BUFFS

If you are not worn out after walking around Pensacola's historic districts, visit Fort Pickens on the western tip of Santa Rosa Island. Built as protection for the Pensacola naval shipyard in 1829, its huge guns, which saw little action, are still in place. The famous Apache chieftain Geronimo was held here from 1886 to 1888, and was joined by three of this wives and his children. You can see the tiny cell where he was kept prisoner.

SCENIC ROUTES

On a sunny day the white sands and emerald waters edged by SR 339 between Navarre Beach and Pensacola Beach make beautiful roadside scenery. To the north of Choctawhatchee Bay, SR 20 will show you the old north Florida of pinewoods and fishing shacks, free of tourism developments and heavy traffic. As you turn south on SR 331 and cross the bay, you will enjoy the sight of river barges and yachts cruising to and from the Intracoastal Waterway.

▶ *Return to the mainland and head east for 16 miles (26km).*

6 Fort Walton Beach

The atmosphere in this medium-sized resort town lies somwhere between the brashness of Panama City and the calm of Pensacola. Historical associations include the Indian Temple Mound Museum (on US 98) which traces 10,000 years of local Native American life, including a 3,500-year-old temple. Fort Walton is most strongly associated with Eglin Air Force Base, which takes up a massive 700 square miles (1,813sq km) northeast of town; you can visit the base at certain times of the year. Adjacent (open all year round) is the impressive US Air Force Armament Museum. Here you can see the enormous F-105 Thunderchief, the SR-71 Blackbird Spy Plane and a whole arsenal of flying weaponry.

i Greater Fort Walton Beach Chamber of Commerce, 34 Miracle Strip Parkway

FOR CHILDREN

Take the children along to the Discovery Gallery at the T T Wentworth Museum, where they can enjoy some hands-on fun. Older children will love the aviation hardware at both Pensacola and Fort Walton Beach air museums, while the amusement parks at Pensacola Beach and Destin are perennial family favorites.

▶ *Take **SR 85** north to Valparaiso and turn right onto **SR 20**. Continue east for 23 miles (37km) to Freeport, turn right onto **US 331** and head south for 10 miles (16km). Turn left onto **US 98** and head east for 3 miles (5km). Turn left on **SR 395**.*

7 Eden State Gardens

The highlight of these isolated gardens is the fine late 19th-century Wesley Mansion. Variously described as anything from antebellum to Greek Revival, it is a mix of styles, with antiques and furnishings dating as far back as the 17th century. The best time to visit the lovely grounds is during March, when the azaleas and dogwood are in full bloom.

▶ *Return on **SR 395,** crossing **US 98,** 2 miles (3km) south to Seagrove Beach. Turn right onto **SR 30A** and head east.*

8 Seaside

This summer village of pastel-colored, traditionally styled wooden houses, straight out of Cape Cod, was actually created in 1985. The Victorian-style fretwork and white picket fences set off the pretty colors perfectly. Though contrived, this is a pleasant place to visit; just don't expect too much atmosphere and you won't be disappointed. Ironically, adjacent to Seaside is Grayton Beach, one of the oldest townships on Florida's Gulf Coast. There is a state recreation area here offering hiking, swimming, surf fishing and boating.

▶ *Follow **SR 30A** northwest to the village of Santa Rosa Beach and continue west on **US 98** for Destin.*

9 Destin

Before you reach Destin, the road divides: the Beach Highway leads to the Museum of the Sea and Indian. Destin has been renowned for its fishing since its foundation in the

Gruesome exhibit at Destin's Museum of the Sea and Indian

The 'nouveau Victorian' architecture in the summer village of Seaside

1830s and is one of Florida's major sport fishing resorts. The most abundant trophy is billfish (such as spearfish, sailfish and marlin). It is perhaps no surprise, therefore, to find out that there is a Fishing Museum in town and that the restaurants here are highly regarded for their seafood. The most pleasant stretch of sand is Crystal Beach Wayside Park, 5 miles (8km) east of Destin. Visit the Old Post Office Museum for a look at local history.

[i] *Destin Chamber of Commerce, US 98 East*

▶ *Continue west for 7 miles (11km).*

10 Okaloosa Island Beaches

At the eastern tip of Santa Rosa Island lies the beach playground for Fort Walton. The main attraction is Gulfarium. Dolphins and sea lions delight the crowds with their performances and there is a fine aquarium with many exotic deep-sea species.

▶ *Cross the Intracoastal Waterway on **US 98** to the center of Fort Walton Beach and return to Pensacola via Gulf Breeze, 43 miles (69km).*

RECOMMENDED WALKS

The walking tour outlined on the previous pages for the historic Pensacola districts covers only the main points of interests. If you would like a comprehensive self-guided walking tour of this fascinating area, ask for a brochure at the Pensacola Chamber of Commerce. For beachside strolls and hikes try the pine flatwoods and scrub of Grayton Beach State Recreation Area or Gulf Islands National Seashore (ask at the information center for details of trails).

Art Deco on Ocean Drive, Miami

FLORIDA CALENDAR OF EVENTS

January

• Three Kings Parade, Miami. A bacchanalian parade winding through Calle Ocho from 4th Avenue to 27th Avenue, with horse-drawn carriages, native costumes, marching bands. Call 305/447–1140 for the exact date during the first week of January.

• Art Deco Weekend, South Beach, Miami. Held along the beach between 5th and 15th streets, this festival, with bands, food stands, antiques vendors, tours, and other festivities, celebrates the whimsical architecture that has made South Beach one of America's most unique neighborhoods. Call 305/672–2014 for details. Usually held on Martin Luther King Weekend.

• Walt Disney World Marathon, Orlando. This 26.2-mile marathon winding through the resort and theme park areas is open to all, including the physically challenged. The $50 entry fee is included in room price with some Disney resort packages. Pre-registration is required. Call 407/824–4321 for details.

• Taste of the Grove Food and Music Festival, Miami. This fund-raiser in the Grove's Peacock Park is an excellent chance for visitors to sample menu items from some of the city's top restaurants and sounds from international and local performers. Call 305/444–7270 for details. Mid-January.

February

• Edison Pageant of Light, Fort Myers. The spectacular Parade of Lights tops off arts-and-crafts shows, pageants, and a 5km race. Call 941/334–2550 or 800/237– 6444. First two weeks in February.

• Speedweeks, Daytona. Nineteen days of events with a series of races that draw the top names in NASCAR stock-car racing, all culminating in the Daytona 500. All events take place at the Daytona International Speedway. Especially for the Daytona 500 tickets must be purchased even a year in advance. They go on sale January 1 of the prior year. Call 904/253–7223 for ticket information. First three weeks of February.

• Coconut Grove Art Festival. The state's largest art festival and the favorite annual event of many locals. More than 300 artists are selected from thousands of entries to show their works at this prestigious and bacchanalian fare. Almost every medium is represented in the outside festival, including the culinary arts. Call 305/447–0401 for details. President's Day Weekend.

• Miami International Boat Show draws almost a quarter of a million boat enthusiasts to the Miami Beach Convention Center to see the mega-yachts, sailboats, dinghies, and accessories. It's the biggest anywhere. Call 305/531–8410 for more information and ticket prices. Mid-February.

• Silver Spurs Rodeo, Kissimmee. The rodeo featuring real cowboys in contests of calf roping, bull and bronco riding, barrel racing, and more is a celebration of the area's rural, pre-Disney roots. It's held at the Silver Spurs Arena, 1875 E. Irlo Bronson Memorial Highway. (U.S. 192) in Kissimmee, on the third weekend in February. Call 407/847–5000 for details.

• Medieval Fair, Sarasota. Knights in shining armor and fair maidens in flowing gowns on the grounds of the Ringling Museum. For information, call 941/355–5101. Late February to early March.

March

• Renaissance Festival, Largo. Knights jousting for honor, arts and crafts, entertainment, rides, plus medieval food and drink. Call 813/586–5423. Weekends March to mid-April.

• Sanibel Shell Fair, Sanibel and Captiva Islands. A show of shells from around the world and the sale of unusual shell art. Call 941/472–2155. Begins first Thursday in March.

• Bike Week/Camel Motorcycle Week, Daytona. An international gathering of motorcycle enthusiasts draws a crowd of more than 200,000. In addition to major races held at Daytona International Speedway (featuring the world's best road racers, motocrossers, and dirt trackers), there are motorcycle shows, beach parties, and the Annual Motorcycle Parade, with thousands of riders. Call 904/255–0981 for details. Late February to early March.

• Calle Ocho Festival, Miami. A salsa-filled blowout that marks the end of a 10-day extravaganza called Carnival Miami. One of the world's biggest block parties held along 23 blocks of Little Havana's SW 8th Street between 4th and 27th avenues. Call 305/644–8888 for more information. Early to mid-March.

April

• Springtime Tallahassee, Tallahassee. One of the South's largest celebrations welcomes abundant blossoms. Call 904/224–1373. Runs 4 weeks from late March.

• Fringe Festival, Orlando. Over 100 diverse acts from around the world participate in this eclectic event, held for 10 days at various stages in downtown Orlando. Everything from sword swallowers to actors doing a seven-minute version of Hamlet perform on outdoor stages available to Fringe goers for free after they purchase a festival button for under $5. Ticket prices vary, but individual performances are generally under $12.

• Easter Sunday is celebrated in Walt Disney World with an old-fashioned Easter Parade and early opening/late closing throughout the season. Call 407/824-4321 for details.

May

• Epcot International Flower and Garden Festival, Orlando. A month-long event with theme gardens, topiary characters, special floral displays, speakers, and seminars.

• Sunfest, West Palm Beach. A huge party on Flagler Drive in the downtown area with five stages of continuous music, a craft marketplace, a juried art show, a youth park, and fireworks. Call 561/659–5992 for details. Late April to early May.

• Shell Air and Sea Show, Fort Lauderdale. A spectacular display of aeronautics featuring the Blue Angels and aquatic demonstrations by the navy guaranteed to evoke oohs and aahs. Call 954/527–5600 for details. Mid-May.

June

• Fiesta of Five Flags, Pensacola. Extravaganza commemorates the Spanish conquistador Tristan de Luna's arrival in 1559. Call 904/433–6512 for information. First week in June.

• Billy Bowlegs Festival, Fort Walton Beach. A fleet of modern-day pirates captures the Emerald Coast in a rollicking, week-long bash honoring notorious buccaneer William Augustus Bowles. Treasure hunt, parade, and carnival, too. Call 800/322–3319. First week of June.

• Walt Disney World Wine Festival, Orlando. More than 60 wineries from all over the United States participate. Events include wine tastings, seminars, food, and celebrity-chef cooking demonstrations at Disney's Yacht and Beach Club Convention Center. Call 407/827–7200 or 407/824–4321 for details.

• Coconut Grove Goombay Festival, Miami. Bahamian bacchanalia with dancing in the streets of Coconut Grove and music from the Royal Bahamian Police marching band. This bash is one of the country's largest black-heritage festivals. The food and music draw thousands to an all-day celebration of Miami's Caribbean connection. It's lots of fun if the weather isn't scorching. Call 305/372–9966 for festival details. Early June.

• Spanish Night Watch Ceremony, St Augustine. Actors in period dress lead a torchlight procession through historic St Augustine and reenact the closing of the city gates with music and pageantry. Call

904/824–9550 for details. Third Saturday in June.

July

• Independence Day, Orlando. Walt Disney World's Star-Spangled Spectacular brings bands, singers, dancers, and unbelievable fireworks displays to all the Disney parks, which stay open late. Call 407/824–4321 for details. Sea World also features a dazzling laser/fireworks spectacular; call 407/351–3600 for details.

• The Silver Spurs Rodeo, Kissimmee. This event returns to Kissimmee every year over the July 4th weekend (see "February," above for more information).

• Miccosukee Everglades Music and Crafts Festival, Miami. Native American rock, Razz (reservation jazz), and folk bands perform down south while visitors gorge themselves on exotic treats like pumpkin bread and fritters. Watch the hulking old gators wrestle with Native Americans. Call 305/223–8380 for prices and details. Late July.

• Lower Keys Underwater Music Fest, Looe Key. At this outrageous celebration, boaters go out to the underwater reef of Looe Key Marine Sanctuary off Big Pine Key, drop speakers into the water, and pipe in music. It's entertainment for the fish and swimmers alike! A snorkeling Elvis can usually be spotted. Call 305/872–2411 for details. Second Saturday of July.

• Blue Angels Air Show, Pensacola. World-famous Navy pilots do their aerial acrobatics just 100 yards off the beach. Call 800/874–1234 for schedule.

August

• Boca Festival Days, Boca Raton. A month of events for the summer-weary, from baby contests to swim meets. One of the best is the food and wine tasting thrown by the Hospice-by-the-sea. Dozens of Palm Beach county's best chefs turn out succulent dishes for the black-tie optional affair. Add to that a silent auction and booth upon booth of the world's most renowned vintners serving sips of fine wine, and this could be one of the year's finest, and most accessible, benefits. Call 561/395– 5031 for details.

• Miami Reggae Festival, Miami. Jamaica's best dancehall and reggae artists turn out for this two-day festival. Burning Spear, Steel Pulse, Spragga Benz, and Jigsy King participated recently. Call Jamaica Awareness at 305/891–2944 for more details. Early August.

September

• Festival Miami. A four-week program of performing arts featuring local and invited musical guests. Centered in the University of Miami School of Music and Maurice Gusman Concert Hall. For a schedule of events call 305/284–4940. Mid-September to mid-October.

• Columbus Day Regatta, Miami. Find anything that can float, from an inner-tube to a 100-foot yacht, and you'll fit right in. Yes, there actually is a race, but who can keep track when you're partying with a bunch of semi-naked psychos in the middle of Biscayne Bay? It's free and it's wild. Rent a boat, jet ski, or sailboard to get up close. Be sure to secure a vessel early though everyone wants to be there. Around Columbus Day.

October

• Destin Seafood Festival, Destin. The "World's Luckiest Fishing Village" cooks its bountiful catch in every style of cuisine imaginable. Also arts, crafts, and music. Call 904/837–6241. First full weekend in October.

• Magic Basketball, Orlando. Penny Hardaway and his teammates continue to perform Magic long after Shaquille O'Neal opted to go Hollywood with the Los Angeles Lakers. The Magic does battle against visiting teams between October and April at the Orlando Arena, 600 W. Amelia Street. Ticket prices range from about $13 to $50. There are usually a few tickets, usually single seats, available the day before games involving lesser known NBA challengers. Call 407/896–2442 for details, 407/839–3900 for tickets.

• Walt Disney World Oldsmobile Golf Classic. Top PGA tour players compete for a total purse of $1 million at WDW golf courses in October's major golf event. Transplanted local golf phenom Tiger Woods is usually among the players. Daily ticket prices range from $8 to $15. The event is preceded by the world's largest golf tournament, the admission-free Oldsmobile Scramble. Call 407/824–4321 for details.

• Oktoberfest, Miami. They close the streets for this German beer and food festival thrown by the Mozart Stub Restaurant in Coral Gables. You'll find loads of great music and dancing at this wild party. Call Harald Neuweg. Call 305/446–1600) to find out where and when.

• Fantasy Fest, Key West. It might feel like the rest of the world is joining you if you're in Key West for this inane, world-famous Halloween festival, Florida's version of Mardi Gras. Crazy costumes, wild parades, and even more colorful revelers gather for an opportunity to do things mom said not to do. Call 305/296–1817. Last week of October.

• SunBank Sunday Jazz Brunch at Riverwalk, Fort Lauderdale. This six-month-long music and food gig kicks off on the banks of the historic New River, promising leisurely afternoons of great live jazz and tasty food in the company of fellow music lovers. Call 954/761–5363 for details. First Sunday of every month from October to March.

• Clearwater Jazz Holiday, Clearwater. Top jazz musicians play for four days and nights at Coachman Park. For information, call 813/461–0011. Mid-October.

• Halloween Horror Nights, Orlando. Universal Studios Florida transforms its studios and attractions for several weeks before and after Halloween, with haunted attractions, live bands, a psychopath's maze, special shows, and hundreds of ghouls and goblins roaming the studio streets. The studio essentially closes at dusk, reopening in a new macabre form a few hours later. Special admission is charged. Call 407/363–8000 for details.

• John's Pass Seafood Festival, Madeira Beach. Tons of fish, shrimp, crab, and other seafood go down the hatch at one of Florida's largest seafood festivals. Call 813/391–7373. End of October, first of November.

November

• Florida Seafood Festival, Apalachicola. Book a room at the Gibson five years in advance of this huge chow-down in Florida's oystering capital. Call 904/653–9419 for details. First Saturday in November.

• Mum Festival, Cypress Gardens. November's month-long flower festival at Cypress Gardens features millions of mums, their colorful flowers displayed in beds, "blooming" gazebos, poodle baskets, and bonsais. Call 941/324–2111 for details.

• The Walt Disney World Festival of the Masters, Orlando. One of the largest art shows in the South takes place at Disney's Village Marketplace for three days, including the second weekend in November. The exhibition features top artists, photographers, and craftspeople, winners of juried shows throughout the country. Free admission. Call 407/824–4321 for details.

• Jacksonville Jazz Festival. This free week-long, nonstop music event in Metropolitan Park features major artists. Call 904/353–7770 for details. Early November.

• Daytona Beach Fall Speedway Spectacular. Featuring the Annual Turkey Rod Run, this is the Southeast's largest combined car show and swap meet, with thousands of street rods and classic vehicles on display and for sale. It takes place at the International Speedway. Call 904/255–7355 for details. Thanksgiving weekend.

• Poinsettia Festival, Cypress Gardens. A spectacular floral showcase of more than 40,000 red, white, and pink poinsettia blooms (including topiary reindeer) highlight this flower festival from late November to mid-January at delightful Cypress Gardens. This is actually one of the best ways to view the park. Call 941/324–2111 for details.

December

• Edison/Ford Winter Homes Holiday House, Fort Myers. Thousands of lights and Christmas music hail the holiday season. At the same time, candles create a spectacular Luminary Trail along the full length of Sanibel Island's Periwinkle Way. Call 941/334–3614 for information. First week of December.

• Winterfest Celebration's Continental Airlines Boat Parade, Fort Lauderdale. A hundred boats decorated with lights cruise up the Intracoastal Waterway from Port Everglades to Lake Santa Barbara. There's no better way to get into the Christmas spirit. Call 954/767–0686 for details. Second weekend in December.

• X/S Music Fest, Fort Lauderdale. The largest one-night music fest in the state of Florida. More than 100 local bands play jazz, blues, and rock at different nightclubs throughout Fort Lauderdale. Call 954/356–4943 for details. Second Friday in December.

• Christmas Festivities, St Augustine. The entire city is lit by thousands of lights from mid-November to New Year's. Activities include caroling, an 18th-century bazaar, a performance of Handel's *Messiah*, a Christmas parade, and more. Call 800/OLD–CITY for details.

• Walt Disney World New Year's Eve Celebration, Orlando. For one night the Magic Kingdom is open until 2am for a massive fireworks exhibition. Other New Year's festivities in the WDW parks include a big bash at Pleasure Island featuring music headliners, a special Hoop-Dee-Doo Musical Revue show, and guest performances by well-known musical groups at Disney-MGM Studios and Epcot. Call 407/824–4321 for details.

• The Citrus Bowl Parade, Orlando. On an annually selected date in late December, the parade features lavish floats and high school bands for a nationally televised parade. Reserved seats in the bleachers are $12. Call 407/423–2476 for details.

• King Orange Jamboree Parade, Miami. The world's largest nighttime parade is followed by a long night of festivities leading up to the Orange Bowl football game (see January listing). Runs along Biscayne Boulevard. For information and tickets (which cost $7.50 to $13), contact the Greater Miami Convention and Visitors Bureau at 305/539–3063. Usually December 31.

DRIVING TIPS

Accidents

If you are involved in a traffic accident, it must be reported to the local police station, County Sheriff's Office, or Florida Highway Patrol at once. Exchange names, addresses and insurance details.

Breakdowns

The AAA (American Automobile Association) operates a nationwide road service number: call 800/222–7764 and you will be given information for obtaining emergency assistance. Should you break down on a highway, lift up the hood of your car and remain in the vehicle until the Highway Patrol arrives. Do not open your doors or windows to anyone else.

Safety Belts

It is compulsory for children under five to be seated in a special child seat or restraint – your car-rental firm should be able to supply one for a small additional charge. Front seatbelts are compulsory for all passengers.

Speed Limits

The speed limit on Florida highways is 55–65mph (88–105km/h). In cities and congested areas, though, it is generally 20–40mph (32–64km/h) and 15mph (24km/h) in school zones.

GETTING AROUND

Having a car is the best and easiest way to see Florida's sights, or just to get to and from the beach. Public transportation is available only in the larger metropolitan areas, and even there it may provide infrequent or even inadequate service. When it comes to getting from one city or another, cars and planes are the ways to go.

By Rental Car

If you decide to rent a car, shop around and ask a lot of questions; the rental firms certainly aren't going to tell you how to save money. You may have to try different dates, different pickup and drop-off points, and different discount offers yourself to find the best deal. It changes constantly. Also, if you're a member of any organization (the AARP or AAA, for example), check to see if you're entitled to discounts.

Every major rental company is represented in Florida, including Alamo (tel: 800/327–9633), Avis (tel: 800/331–1212), Budget (tel: 800/527–0700), Dollar (tel: 800/800–4000), Enterprise (tel: 800/325–8007), Hertz (tel: 800/654–3131), National (tel: 800/227–7368), Thrifty (tel: 800/367–2277), and Value (tel: 800/GO–VALUE).

Most of them pad their profits by selling Loss-Damage Waiver (LDW) insurance. You may already be covered by your insurance carrier and credit- or charge-card companies, so check with them before succumbing to the hard-sell. Also, the rental companies' will offer to refill your gas tank at "competitive" prices when you return, but fuel usually is less expensive in town.

Most also require a minimum age, ranging from 19 to 25, and some also set maximum ages. Others deny cars to anyone with a bad driving record. Ask about rental requirements and restrictions when you book to avoid problems later. You must have a valid credit card to rent a vehicle.

Many packages are available that include airfare, accommodations, and a rental car with unlimited mileage. Compare these prices with the cost of booking airline tickets and renting a car separately to see if these offers are good deals.

By Plane

Most major Florida cities are connected by both the major commuter airlines and smaller intrastate airlines such as Gulf Stream International (tel: 800/992–8532), which has an extensive in-state network, and Cape Air (tel: 800/352–0714), which flies between Key West, Fort Myers, and Naples. Fares for these short hops tend to be reasonable.

By Train

You'll find that train travel from destination to destination isn't terribly feasible in Florida, and it's not a great deal less expensive than flying.

HEALTH

Florida doesn't present any unusual health hazards for most people. Folks with certain medical conditions such as liver disease, diabetes, and stomach ailments, however, should avoid eating raw oysters, which can carry a natural bacteria linked to severe diarrhea, vomiting, and even fatal blood poisoning. Cooking kills the bacteria, so if in doubt, order your oysters steamed, broiled, or fried.

Florida has millions of mosquitoes and invisible biting sand flies (known as "no-see-ums"), especially in the coastal and marshy areas. Fortunately, neither insect carries malaria or other diseases. Keep these pests at bay with a good insect repellent. It's especially important to protect yourself against sunburn. Don't underestimate the strength of the sun's rays down here, even in the middle of winter. Limit the amount of time you spend in the sun, especially during the first couple of days of your trip and always from 11am to 2pm. Use a sunscreen with a high protection factor and apply it liberally. And children need more protection from the sun than adults do.

Pack any prescription medications you need to take in your carry-on luggage. Also bring along copies of your prescriptions in case you lose your pills or run out.

If you have a serious condition or allergy, consider wearing a Medic Alert identification bracelet; contact the Medic Alert Foundation, P.O. Box 1009, Turlock, CA 95381–1009 (tel: 800/432–5378). If you have dental problems, a nationwide referral service known as 1–800–DENTIST (tel: 800/336–8478) will give you the name of a nearby dentist or clinic.

HOLIDAYS

1 January – New Year's Day;
Third Monday in January – Martin Luther King Day;
Third weekend in February – Washington's Birthday;
Last Monday in May – Memorial Day;
4 July – Independence Day;
First Monday in September – Labor Day;
Second Monday in October – Columbus Day;
11 November – Veterans' Day;
Last Thursday in November – Thanksgiving Day;
25 December – Christmas Day.

INSURANCE

Many travelers buy insurance policies providing health and accident, trip-cancellation, and lost-luggage protection. The coverage you should consider will depend on how you're getting to Florida and how much protection is already contained in your existing health insurance or other policies. Some credit- and charge-card companies may insure you against travel accidents if you buy plane, train, or bus tickets with their cards. Before purchasing additional insurance, read your policies and agreements over carefully. Call your insurers or credit/charge-card companies if you have any questions.

Here are some American firms offering travel insurance:

Travel Assistance International (TAI) (tel: 202/347–2025 or 800/821–2828); Travel Guard International (tel: 715/345–0505 or 800/782–5151); Access America (tel: 804/285–3300, or 800/284–8300); or Mutual of Omaha (tel: 800/228–9792). The Divers Alert Network (DAN) (tel: 919/6–2948 or 800/446–2671) insures scuba divers.

LIQUOR LAWS

You must be 21 to purchase or consume alcohol in Florida. This law is strictly enforced, so if you look young, carry some photo identification that gives your date of birth. Minors can usually enter bars where food is served.

NEWSPAPERS/ MAGAZINES

Most cities of any size have a local daily paper, but the well-respected *Miami Herald* is generally available all over the state, with regional editions available in many areas.

SAFETY

Whenever you're traveling in an unfamiliar city, stay alert. Be aware of your immediate surroundings. Always lock your car doors and the trunk when your vehicle is unattended, and don't leave any valuables in sight.

TAXES

The Florida state sales tax is 6 percent. In addition, most municipalities levy a special tax on hotel and restaurant bills, and some add 1 percent or more to the general sales tax.

TRAVELERS WITH SPECIAL NEEDS

Travelers with Disabilities

Walt Disney World does everything possible to accommodate disabled guests. Its many services are detailed in the "Guidebook for Guests with Disabilities." To obtain a free copy, contact Guest Letters, P.O. Box 10,040, Lake Buena Vista, FL 32830-0040 (tel: 407/824–4321).

Some nationwide resources include Mobility International USA (tel: 503/343–1284), which offers its members travel-accessibility information and has many interesting travel programs for the disabled; the Travel Information Service (tel: 215/456–9600); and the Society for the Advancement of Travel for the Handicapped (tel: 212/447–7284). In addition, Twin Peaks Press, P.O. Box 129, Vancouver, WA 98666 (tel: 360/694–2462), specializes in travel-related books for people with disabilities.

Companies offering tours for those with physical or mental disabilities include Accessible Journeys (tel: 610/521–0339 or 800/TINGLES); Flying Wheels Travel (tel: 507/451– 5005 or 800/535–6790); The Guided Tour, Inc. (tel: 215/782–1370); and Wilderness Inquiry (tel: 612/379–3858 or 800/728–0719).

In addition, both Amtrak (tel: 800/USA-RAIL) and Greyhound (tel: 800/752–4841) offer special fares and services for the disabled. Call at least a week in advance of your trip for details.

For Seniors

With one of the largest retired populations of any state, Florida offers a wide array of activities and benefits for senior citizens. Don't be shy about asking for discounts, but always carry some kind of identification, such as a driver's license, that shows your date of birth. Also, mention the fact that you're a senior citizen when you first make your travel reservations. For example, Amtrak (tel: 800/USA–RAIL) offers discounted senior fares. And don't forget that many hotels and motels offer discounts to seniors. For example, in 1996 the Econo Lodge chain instituted a 30 percent break for anyone 50 or older.

Members of the American Association of Retired Persons (AARP), 601 E St. NW, Washington, DC 22049 (tel: 202/434–2277 or 800/424–3410), get discounts not only on hotels but on airfares and car rentals, too.

Other helpful organizations include the nonprofit National Council of Senior Citizens, 1331 F St. NW, Washington, DC 20004 (tel: 202/347–8800), part of whose magazine is devoted to travel tips. Mature Outlook, 6001 N. Clark St., Chicago, IL 60660 (tel: 800/336–6330), offers discounts at ITC-member hotels and savings on selected auto rentals and restaurants. Golden Companions, P.O. Box 5249, Reno, NV 89513 (tel: 702/324–2227), helps travelers 45-plus find compatible companions through a personal voicebox mail service. Contact them for more information.

Companies specializing in seniors travel include Grand Circle Travel, 347 Congress St., Suite 3A, Boston, MA 02210 (tel: 617/350–7500 or 800/221–2610); and SAGA International Holidays, 222 Berkeley St., Boston, MA 02115 (tel: 800/343–0273).

For Families

Florida is a great family destination, with most of its hotels and restaurants willing and eager to cater to families traveling with children. Many hotels and motels let children 17 and under stay free in their parents' room (be sure to ask when you reserve).

At the beaches, it's the rule rather than the exception for a resort to have a children's activities program (some will even mind the youngsters while the parents enjoy a night off!). Even if they don't have a children's program of their own, most will arrange babysitting services.

If you call ahead before dining out, you'll see that most restaurants have some facilities for children, such as booster chairs and low-priced kids' menus. Also enquire about children's meals.

For Students

It's worth your while to bring along your valid high school or college identification. Presenting it can open the door to discounted admission to museums and other attractions. And remember, alcoholic beverages cannot be sold in Florida to anyone who is under the age of 21, so if you intend to imbibe, bring your driver's license or another valid photo identification showing your date of birth.

VISITOR INFORMATION

For information about the state in general, contact the Florida Tourism Industry Marketing Corp. (FTIMC), P.O. Box 1100, Tallahassee, FL 32399–1100 (tel: 904/487–1462; fax: 904/224–2938), which will send you its *Florida Vacation Guide* and an official state highway map.

The FTIMC also has welcome centers on I–10 west of Pensacola, I–75 north of Jennings, I–95 north of Yulee, and U.S. 231 at Campbellton. There's also a walk-in information office in the west foyer of the New Capitol Building in Tallahassee.

Once you've chosen a specific destination in Florida, you can get more detailed information from the local visitor information offices or chambers of commerce.

For information about Walt Disney World, contact Walt Disney World Company, P.O. Box 10000, Lake Buena Vista, FL 32830–1000 (tel: 407/824–4321).

Inn Route, P.O. Box 6187, Palm Harbor, FL 34684–0787 (tel: 813/786–9792), publishes the *Inns of Florida*, which lists inns and bed-and-breakfasts throughout the state. Inn Route inspects each property, insuring quality and cleanliness of its members.

At the inexpensive end, Hostelling International/American Youth Hostels, 733 15th St. NW, Suite 840, Washington, DC 20005 (tel: 202/783–6161 or 800/444–6111), offers low-cost accommodations in Miami Beach, Key West, Fort Lauderdale, and Orlando.

The Florida Department of Natural Resources, Division of Recreation and Parks, Mail Station 535, 3900 Commonwealth Boulevard, Tallahassee, FL 32399–3000 (tel: 904/488–9872), publishes an annual guide of tent and RV sites in Florida's state parks and recreation areas.

The Florida Association of RV Parks & Campgrounds, 1340 Vickers Drive, Tallahassee, FL 32303 (tel: 904/562–7151), publishes an annual *Florida Camping Directory* with locator maps and details about its member establishments throughout the state.

The Florida Sports Foundation, 107 W. Gaines Street, Tallahassee, FL 32399 (tel: 904/ 488–8347), publishes free brochures, calendars, schedules, and guides to outdoor pursuits and spectator sports. Golfers should request a copy of *Fairways in the Sunshine*, which describes all the state's golf courses.

WHEN TO GO

To a large extent, the timing of your visit will determine how much you'll spend and how much company you'll have once you get here. That's because room rates can more than double during the high seasons, when countless visitors migrate to Florida.

High season in the southern

half of the state is during the winter, from mid-December to mid-April. You'll be rewarded with incredible bargains if you're willing to brave the heat and humidity of a South Florida summer between June and early September. In northern Florida, the reverse is true: Tourists flock here during the summer, from Memorial Day to Labor Day.

Presidents' Day weekend in February, Easter Week, Memorial Day weekend, the Fourth of July, Labor Day weekend, Thanksgiving, Christmas, and New Year's are busy throughout the state.

Both northern and southern Florida share the same "shoulder seasons" (April and May and from September to November). The weather is pleasant throughout Florida during these months, and hotel rates are considerably less than during the high seasons. If price is a consideration, then these months of pleasant temperatures and fewer tourists are the best times to visit, but be aware that August through November is also hurricane season.

If you want to time your visit to Walt Disney World to avoid crowds, keep in mind that Orlando area attractions are packed during any holiday (especially Christmas) and when school is not in session during the summer.

Climate

Florida's climate is subtropical, not tropical, so the state sees more extremes of temperatures than, say, the Caribbean islands.

Spring sees warm temperatures throughout Florida, but it also brings tropical showers, and May contributes the first waves of humidity.

Summer runs from May to September in Florida, when it's hot and very humid throughout the state. If you're in an inland city during these months, you may not want to do anything too taxing when the sun is at its peak. Coastal areas, however, reap the benefits of sea breezes. Severe afternoon thunderstorms are prevalent during the summer heat (there aren't professional sports teams here named Lightening and Thunder for nothing), so schedule your activities for earlier in the day, and take precautions to avoid being hit by lightening during the storms.

Fall is a great time to visit; the really hottest days are behind you and the crowds have thinned out a bit. August through November, however, is hurricane season; you may remember Hurricanes Andrew and Opal in 1992 and 1995, respectively, which caused billions of dollars' worth of damage to South Florida and to the Panhandle. Fortunately, the National Weather Service closely tracks hurricanes and gives ample warning if there's any need to evacuate coastal areas.

Winter can get a bit nippy throughout the state, and sometimes downright cold in northern Florida. Although snow is pretty rare, a flake or two has been known to fall as far south as Miami. The "cold snaps" usually last only a few days in the southern half of the state, however, and daytime temperatures quickly return to the 70s.

A glorious sunset over the pier at Key West

INDEX

The Automobile Association

wishes to thank the following libraries and photographers for their assistance in the preparation of this book.
BASS MUSEUM 14; S BATES 93; BRUCE COLEMAN COLLECTION 32a, 33, 151; INTERNATIONAL SPEEDWAY CORP 92/3, 111/12; MIAMI C & VB 22; IMAGES COLOUR LIBRARY 142/3; ORLANDO C & VB 88; SPECTRUM COLOUR LIBRARY Back cover (a), 34, 56, 73, 74, 85, 87a; SPLENDID CHINA 121; TONY STONE IMAGES Front cover main and top; WET 'N' WILD 16; ZEFA PICTURES LTD 10, 47, 55, 57b, 59, 83, 89, 90/1, 127a; WORLD PICTURES 136/7, 144, 149, 151.

The remaining photographs are held in the Association's own library (AA PHOTO LIBRARY) with contributions from: Jon Davison 7b, 13, 27, 29, 38, 40/1, 49, 57a, 152, 154a, 154b, 157; David Lyons 9, 14/15, 18/19, 19, 24/5, 26, 79, 80; Paul Murphy 20a, 51, 52/3, 54, 70, 81, 84, 109, 110, 114, 115, 120, 126, 127b, 128, 129a, 129b, 131, 138/9; Lanny Provo 6, 24, 31, 35, 36, 37, 39, 43, 45, 50, 62, 64, 65, 66, 67, 78, 158; Tony Souter Back cover (b), 48, 58, 82, 92, 94, 95, 98, 102, 103, 104, 105a, 105b, 123, 125. The remaining images were taken by Pete Bennett.
Th author would like to thank: Holiday Inn, Hamlin's Landing, Indian Rocks; Langford Resort Hotel, Winter Park; Summerfield Suites Hotel, Orlando; Orlando Convention & Visitors Bureau in London and Orlando; St Petersburg & Clearwater Convention & Visitors Bureau in London and Orlando; and Holiday Autos (UK) for their assistance.

Contributors
Copy editor: Audrey Horne **Indexer:** Marie Lorimer